24 Dec 98

To My Little Kid Brother
Robert John

You are always in my prayers
and in my heart.
Thanks for this past year
of friendship. God Bless you

Love
Ricardo Antonio
Bravo
Brother #2

D0819725

JEEP

★ THE UNSTOPPABLE LEGEND ★

**BY ARCH BROWN
AND THE AUTO EDITORS OF CONSUMER GUIDE®**

Publications International, Ltd.

Copyright © 1997 Publications International, Ltd. All
rights reserved. This book may not be reproduced or
quoted in whole or in part by mimeograph or any other
printed or electronic means, or for presentation on radio,
television, videotape, or film without written permission
from:

Louis Weber, C.E.O.
Publications International, Ltd.
7373 North Cicero Avenue
Lincolnwood, Illinois 60646

Permission is never granted for commercial purposes.

Manufactured in U.S.A.

8 7 6 5 4 3 2

ISBN: 0-7853-0870-9

Library of Congress Catalog Card Number: 94-66811

CREDITS

Photography:
The editors gratefully acknowledge the cooperation of the following people who have supplied photography to help make this book possible:

A.H. Axelrad; Joe Bohovic; Jim Frenak; Thomas Glatch; Dave Gooley; Dan Lyons; Vince Manocchi; Michael Maxey; Mike Mueller; Gary D. Smith; Richard Spiegelman; Nicky Wright

Special Thanks to:
Jim Arnold, Jeepers Jamboree, Georgetown, CA; Peggy Dusman, American Automobile Manufacturer's Association; Dan R. Erickson, Ford Photographic Services; Marti Gansz, George C. Marshall Foundation, Lexington, VA; Ita Golzman, Irene Ackerman, King Features Syndicate; Ron Grantz, Jerry Cook, National Automotive History Collection, Detroit Public Library; Molly Jean, *Automobile Magazine*; Klaus Parr, Porsche Archives, Stuttgart, Germany; Rich Ray; Brandt Rosenbush, Chrysler Historical; Jeepin' Jeff Schwarz of The Jeep Registry, Oakland, NJ; David Shirley, Mitchell Corp. of Owosso, MI; Katie Talbot, Patton Museum, Ft. Knox, KY; Carolyn Wright, U.S. Army Transportation Museum, Fort Eustis, VA; Carl F. Walck's Four Wheel Drive, Bowmanstown, PA; The Willys Club, Bowmanstown, PA

Artists:
Mitch Frumkin; David Hogan; Mark Neeper; Tom Piagari

Owners:
Special thanks to the owners of the cars featured in this book for their enthusiastic cooperation.

A.H. Axelrad; Dale P. Aylward; D. Clinton Bailey; Charles Barnett; James E. Dinehart; Frank Donnelly; Arthur D. Gloss; Tom Haberkamp; Ronald Hattner; Forrest D. Howell; Andrew Magyer; David Marshall; Roland Olm; B.C. Pyle; Mike Scholer; H. Robert & Katheryn Stamp; Dick Tait; Richard Talanca (Talanca Military Vehicle Restorations)

CONTENTS:

The All-American Wonder

I t is safe to say that no other motor vehicle has ever inspired the kind of respect and affection accorded the World War II jeep[1]. Perhaps Henry Ford's Model T, the ubiquitous flivver of the Teens and Twenties, came closest. Yet the "Tin Lizzie's" idiosyncrasies made it a constant target of ridicule; and its owners' feelings toward their cars tended sometimes to be ambivalent. Besides, the Ford and its driver rarely shared the terrors and the deprivations of battle, as the jeep and the GI so often did.

The jeep, at least in wartime, was quite a different matter. The bond between the soldier and his mechanized steed became akin to the relationship between the old-time cavalryman and his horse. In perhaps the most famous of all his wartime cartoons, Bill Mauldin portrayed a burly top sergeant covering his eyes as he aimed a .45-caliber at his mortally wounded jeep.

Ernie Pyle, easily the most beloved of America's war correspondents, described the little car as "the greatest discovery of World War II." He added, "I don't see how we could continue this war without the jeep!" (How ironic that during an April 1945 battle on the island of Ie Shima a sniper's bullet cost Pyle his life while he was using a jeep for cover.)

It wasn't just sentimentality that accorded the jeep more mention in dispatches than any other instrument of war. General George C. Marshall, later described by President Harry S Truman as "the greatest living American," considered the jeep to be "America's greatest contribution to modern warfare." For here was a machine that could go almost anywhere—and do almost anything when it got there. Designed initially for reconnaissance work, the jeep's maneuverability and its versatility quickly turned it into a "jack of all trades."

Lyman M. Nash, writing in *The American Legion Magazine*, recalled that "The jeep laid smoke screens and furnished hot water for shaving. It served as a mobile command post, front line ambulance, field telephone station, fire engine, and snow plow. It delivered fresh socks and C rations, towed artillery and airplanes. Its broad, flat hood became a map table, dining table, or an altar for religious services. The jeep also revolutionized land warfare, permitting troops to reach the front without being overburdened by supplies and ammunition."

A. Wade Wells, in his 1946 book, *Hail to the Jeep*, notes that "the great majority of officers concerned with the equipment of the Army attribute the development and existence of the jeep directly to military needs. They realized that if America should again be forced to wage war, it would have to be a completely mechanized and motorized war." The need for a jeep in the army was motivated by two factors: military efficiency and the safety and comfort of fighting men—the primary concern of any good officer.

[1]Jeep is described by *Merriam Webster's Tenth Edition* as a small general purpose motor vehicle with 80-inch wheelbase, ¼-ton capacity, and four-wheel drive used by the U.S. Army in World War II. Later, after the Kaiser purchase, a successful attempt was made to trademark the word Jeep. This trademarked Jeep has become the make for a line of two- and four-wheel drive utility vehicles and is currently owned by Chrysler Motors.

Though Willys did not invent the jeep, they did perfect the design, provide the powerplant, and build the majority of jeeps used in World War II. Even before the United States entered the war in December 1941, the Willys model MB (and its Ford counterpart, the GPW) had earned a tough and rugged reputation in armies across the globe (right, top). Soldiers and civilians alike revered the qualities of the jeep, and stories of heroic acts in jeeps soon filled the newspapers. Today, the Jeep Corporation has endured four ownership changes, weathered an untold number of financial crises, and seen 11 U.S. Presidents come and go. The familiar profile is carried on by the new Wrangler (right, middle right) and the Grand Cherokee (right, bottom right), which offer all of the off-road ability of the original jeep plus comfort and reliability a World War II veteran could have never imagined.

"There is perhaps a third, less articulated reason why Army men wanted motorized transport," Wells continues. "Deep in their hearts, they wished to save the horse from the horrors of war. It may be true that the idea of the jeep was born in the scream of a shell-torn horse. The sight of animals being wounded or killed in battle, or dying from starvation and disease, was among the war experiences soldiers found hardest to bear."

Of course, strictly from the standpoint of the efficient use of manpower, the horse was wasteful, for it required one man to hold the animal while another was doing the fighting.

There were many other advantages to the jeep. Being small and compact, it could be transported to battle areas by plane or glider, dropped by parachute, or floated across a river. The jeep could also be entertaining. The only thing more pleasing to the eyes of a war-weary soldier than the sight of a member of the Women's Army Corps or Women Accepted for Volunteer Emergency Service getting into a jeep was a WAC or a WAVE getting out of a jeep.

The jeep became as familiar to the rich and famous as it was to the ordinary Joe. Madame Chiang Kai-shek toured Cairo in a jeep, with General Claire Chennault as her chauffeur. Queen Elizabeth used a jeep in her wartime visit to Northern Ireland. President Franklin D. Roosevelt rode in a jeep as he reviewed the troops in Morocco. Prime Minister Winston Churchill sat in a jeep as he watched the historic landings at Normandy. General George S. Patton chose a jeep instead of a staff car for his trip to Fatale, Morocco, when he accepted the surrender of the French resident general there.

Of course Hollywood got into the act, and so did Tin Pan Alley. Songs—all of them eminently forgettable, unfortunately—included such gems as "A Jerk in a Jeep" and "I'll Be Jeeping Back to You." Meanwhile, on the silver screen the world was treated to *Four Jills In a Jeep*, a piece of fluff starring Kay Francis, Martha Raye, Carole Landis, and Mitzi Mayfair. The plot was loosely based upon a 1943 USO tour undertaken by the same four ladies.

It all added up to unprecedented recognition for an inanimate yet lovable object, one that has been described by Lyman Nash as "short, squat, and ugly as sin . . . an inelegant, incredible, and virtually indestructible little vehicle, not much bigger than a fair-sized doghouse." Somehow this remarkable machine garnered trust, demanded respect, and bounced its way into the hearts and souls of all who came into contact with it.

Lee Iacocca (right), who brought the Jeep corporation into the Chrysler fold, was a man with vision. What he saw was a whole new market niche for Jeep vehicles—one that was at home in bogs, sand dunes, mud flats, rocky crevices, and country clubs. Jeeps today combine their unique go-anywhere ability with refined powertrains and supple suspensions. In the past, Jeep advertisements pushed the vehicle's usefulness, utility, and economy, but today a Jeep is as respected on the road as off. Its followers tend to be alarmingly loyal. Over the years they developed their own clubs and off-road organizations— like the Jeepers Jamboree. These clubs organize off-roading events and gatherings for Jeep owners all across the world (far right, bottom).

The Forerunners: 1906-39

*I*f the jeep represented a case of "love at first sight," it was also the culmination of a long search for a go-anywhere sort of utility vehicle. A vehicle that could answer the problems of supply and maximum utility. Almost from the dawn of the twentieth century there had been efforts to develop a machine with four rather than two driving wheels. As early as 1902, in Hartford, Connecticut, Colonel Albert Pope's Electric Vehicle Company had built a huge five-ton truck. Power for this unusual machine came from four electric motors, one located behind each of its chain-driven wheels.

Then came the FWD, a product of the Four Wheel Drive Auto Company of Clintonville, Wisconsin. In 1906 a blacksmith named Otto Zachow and his partner, William Besserdich, had become sales agents for the Reo motorcar. Their first sale was to Dr. W. H. Finney, who evidently wasted little time in getting his car stuck in the mud. This motivated Zachow to develop some means of applying power to all four wheels, rather than just two. The result of the blacksmith's efforts was a practical double-Y universal joint that, encased in a ball-and-socket arrangement, allowed the driver to steer the vehicle while both the front and rear wheels received power.

Thus was born the FWD Auto Company. The organization stumbled along, one short step ahead of its creditors, until 1911, when its vehicles came to the attention of the United States Army. An FWD truck was subjected to intensive testing, with impressive results; but no orders were forthcoming—yet. Interest renewed, however, when war broke out in Europe in 1914. That fall, two FWD trucks—one of three-ton capacity, the other a five-tonner—were shipped to England for evaluation. The two machines evidently gave an excellent account of themselves, because an order for 50 additional trucks followed almost immediately. By the end of 1917, nearly 400 FWD trucks were put to use in His Majesty's Army. Closer to home, when a dustup with the infamous Pancho Villa occurred on the Mexican border, the U. S. Quartermaster Corps ordered 147 FWD trucks. Soon the little Clintonville company was delivering 175 trucks each month. Eventually, domestic and Allied demand combined to outstrip the factory's capacity; and FWD trucks were built under license by Kissel, Mitchell, and Premier. In all, nearly 18,000 of these virtually unstoppable lorries made it to Europe before the Armistice brought the conflict to a close.

Unlike FWD, the Thomas B. Jeffery Company, located in Conch, Wisconsin, some distance to the south of Clintonville, was an established builder of passenger cars and trucks. Before the turn of the century, the organization had manufactured the Rambler bicycle in substantial numbers; and commencing in 1902, the factory turned to the production of automobiles under the same brand name. Within a year, 1500 Rambler cars had been built and sold, at $750 a copy. The figure may seem modest by modern standards, but in 1902 it was enough to propel the Rambler into second place in the infant auto industry, right behind Ransom Olds's curved-dash runabout.

In time, there were trucks bearing the

In 1907 John North Willys bought the ailing Overland Company of Indianapolis. A year later he renamed it Willys-Overland, moved into the old Pope plant in Toledo, Ohio, and began rebuilding the firm's fortunes. By 1926 Willys-Overland was the third largest automaker in the United States, behind only Ford and Chevrolet. The company remained in Toledo (right) until it was purchased by AMC, and Jeep products are still being built in its plants today.

Jeffery name, and by 1913 the company was building a four-wheel-drive commercial vehicle called the Jeffery Quadruple-Drive Truck, or simply the "Quad." Designed to meet the requirements of the U.S. Army, the Quad was powered by a 36-horsepower, four-cylinder Bud engine. It had a one-and-a-half-ton capacity (plus 20 percent overload) and was capable under its own power of going anywhere that a four-mule team could haul a load.

As John Gunnell has reported, "After its test the Quartermaster's office announced the following about the Quad in an official report: 'It plowed through hub-deep mud and sand that were absolutely impassable to any rear drive truck. It lifted itself bodily over a bulk of lumber sixteen inches high. It ran up and down seemingly impossible grades with ease. It forded a stream in which only the tops of the tires showed above the water.'"

In some respects, the Jeffery Quad (known as the Nash Quad after 1916, when former General Motors President Charles W. Nash bought the company) was a remarkably advanced machine. Although the truck was large, four-wheel steering allowed a turning circle of only 45 feet. Equally unusual for the time was the Quad's use of four-wheel brakes, said to be capable of stopping the heavy rig within eight feet from a speed of 15 miles per hour. Its builders liked to boast that "it drives, steers, and brakes on all four wheels"—an impressive claim, and a valid one.

Respected by both military and civilian users, the Quad proved to be enormously popular. Production at Nash's Conch factory peaked at 11,490 units during 1918, with additional trucks built under license by Hudson, Paine, and National. Demand dropped off sharply after the Armistice, of course; but production of the civilian Nash Quad continued—albeit on a limited scale—until 1928.

The four-wheel-drive concept had proven its worth beyond any shadow of a doubt. However, for military purposes a smaller, lighter, nimbler machine was needed. For one thing, the big, ponderous FWD and Nash four-wheelers presented altogether too visible a target for enemy gunfire. In addition, these vehicles were far from fleet. Motorcycles were used as messenger vehicles in those days. But even when equipped with sidecars, their carrying capacity was very limited; and their lack of stability over rough and muddy terrain was not satisfactory.

In the years just after World War I numerous experiments were made with "Field Cars." Perhaps the best known of these was a Model T Ford, stripped to the point that it weighed no more than 1200 pounds. To facilitate its progress through sand and soft mud, fat tires were taken from wrecked airplanes, and the Ford's wheels were cut down to accommodate them. A platform body with two bucket seats was used.

The result was a fairly useful vehicle, capable of outperforming belt-tracked machines in traversing swamps and soft ground. Yet the Model T engine developed only 20 horsepower and of course lacked four-wheel drive. Clearly, further development was called for.

In 1931 Walter C. Marmon, head of the Marmon Motor Car Company, teamed up with Arthur Herrington to build four-wheel-drive trucks. Herrington had been a military transport engineer, and Marmon's company was a veteran producer of quality automobiles, among other things. Initially, Marmon-Herrington produced heavy trucks for the United States and Belgian Armies; but in 1936—by which time Marmon was long since out of the automobile business—Marmon-Herrington conversions began to appear on Ford V-8 half-ton trucks and even on Ford passenger cars. Light, fast, and flexible, these machines could plow their way through almost any type of obstacle course devised by the Quartermaster Corps. The U.S. Army bought 64 of them, and they proved to be so popular that the men referred to them as "Our Darlings."

John North Willys (right, top) was the founder of the Willys-Overland Corporation—the company that would eventually develop the WW II jeep. The Overland company was near bankruptcy in 1907, but by 1918 this salesman supreme had turned Willys-Overland around, and they garnered the second highest sales in the United States.

John North Willys:
A Salesman
for the People

There are any number of men who could, in some sense, lay claim to the title, "Father of the Jeep." There was former General Motors President William S. Knudsen, who, in his wartime role as head of the U. S. Office of Production Management, had pushed for its development. There was Karl Probst, of the American Bantam Car Company, who was largely responsible for the design of the first prototype. There was Delmar G. "Barney" Roos, who masterminded the Willys edition, the one upon which the Quartermaster Corps finally settled as the standard version of the soon-to-be ubiquitous Jeep. And no doubt there were others.

Almost universally overlooked, however, is the man who could be called the godfather of the Jeep: John North Willys. Ironically, he had been six years in his grave by the time the stout little vehicles began to roll off the assembly lines at the Willys plant. Yet John North's stamp was upon every one of them, for it was he who, a decade and a half earlier, had introduced the Whippet automobile. And it was the Whippet that had given its engine—brilliantly reworked by Barney Roos—to the Jeep.

Willys had been a bicycle dealer in his hometown of Canandaiqua, New York, back around the turn of the century. Pierce bicycles were his stock-in-trade, so when that organization took up the manufacture of automobiles in 1901, naturally John North handled them, too. He added the Rambler line in 1902 and the Overland three years later. He eventually became owner of the Overland corporation, and within five years Willys-Overland was the second-largest automobile manufacturer in the country.

Then in 1926 Willys introduced the Overland Whippet. A brand new, long-stroke, high-speed engine that churned out 30 horsepower. The advertised top speed of the new car was 55 miles per hour, but in reality it could do a good deal better than that—especially when fitted with the lightweight roadster body—and the Whippet quickly became a favorite of the hot-shoe set of that day.

Following the Whippet was a series of larger models with four- and six-cylinder engines of varying displacements. The Whippet four continued in the Willys 77. This engine was the foundation Barney Roos would use to create the "Go-Devil" engine that would power the Jeep. Sadly, John North Willys would never see this. On August 26, 1935, he died of a cerebral embolism.

In 1937 Marmon-Herrington fitted a doorless four-seater body to its half-ton, four-wheel-drive chassis; and the Command Car was born. The original prototype was based upon a Model 77 Ford. However, when the car went into production, in 1939, a Dodge chassis was used.

The Dodge Command Car and its equally sturdy companion, the Weapons Carrier, were produced in substantial numbers throughout World War II and supplied the basis for the Dodge Power Wagon of the postwar years. Still, the army believed a more nimble machine was needed.

Meanwhile, at Fort Benning, Georgia, Major Robert Howie and Master Sergeant Melvin C. Wiley were developing a new type of vehicle, a combination reconnaissance car and machine gun carrier. Working on their own time, and reportedly at Major Howie's expense, the two men pieced together a highly unusual vehicle, made largely from scrap. Designed to carry two passengers lying prone, the machine quickly became known as the Howie Belly-Flopper. Major chassis components, including the engine, came from an old American Austin. The wheelbase, like that of the Austin, was 75 inches. Front-wheel drive was employed, with the powerplant mounted at the rear. A machine gun was located forward of the riders. The Belly-Flopper's silhouette was very low, which presented obvious advantages for combat purposes; but ground clearance was insufficient for use in rough terrain. Anyway, it lacked the advantage of four-wheel drive.

The Howie rig must have provided a punishing ride, for it had no springs. Only a set of fat tires cushioned the jolts experienced by its two prone passengers. The driver operated the clutch and brake with his feet while stretched out flat on his stomach. Steering was by means of a lever. However, the Howie was highly maneuverable, and although its top speed was no more than 28 miles an hour, its lightweight construction provided a reasonably good horsepower-to-weight ratio.

The Thomas B. Jeffery company was purchased by Charles W. Nash (left) in 1918. One of the vehicles they produced was a remarkable four-wheel-drive truck, which offered four-wheel steering and four-wheel brakes. This truck, which was also built for the U.S. Army, had a turning radius of 45 feet. Nash's company went on to produce beautifully styled automobiles in the Thirties, but its four-wheel-drive truck continued and was a basis for the Army's decision to develop a light, four-wheel-drive, General Purpose vehicle.

Major Robert Howie and Master Sergeant Melvin C. Wiley developed a lightweight attack and reconnaissance vehicle, aptly named the Belly-Flopper, for the Army in 1937 (right, top). The vehicle was driven by one person while the other fired a front-mounted machine gun. However, the Belly-Flopper did not have four-wheel drive, any sort of suspension, or sufficient ground clearance for off-road travel. Right, bottom left and right: Before Willys-Overland got into jeep production they were a maker of low-priced automobiles like the 1928 Whippet Coach and the 1933 Overland.

Major Howie was convinced that his machine, despite its obvious shortcomings, could be developed into a practical vehicle for military use. The Army took the proposal seriously enough that in March 1940 representatives of the automobile industry were invited to examine it. Largely the reaction was one of laughter. Barney Roos, executive vice president and chief engineer at Willys-Overland, later commented, "That Belly Flopper looked like nothing any automobile man had ever seen before, a cross between a kid's scooter and a diving board on wheels." Yet this odd contraption evidently set several people—including Roos himself—to thinking about the possibility of a practical light reconnaissance car.

Meanwhile, Frank Fenn, president of American Bantam, caught wind of the Army's need for this light car. Bantam was a company that had been on the verge of bankruptcy ever since its incorporation in 1929 as the American Austin Car Company, and Fenn was determined to save it. With the knowledge that America was moving toward war, Fenn began to develop his company's small car to meet the Army's need for a light reconnaissance vehicle.

The car used by Fenn stemmed from a late 1920s effort to meet the demand for a "second car in every garage." Bantam had converted Britain's diminutive Austin to better meet American needs and began to sell the car on June 21, 1930. However, due to several factors the car failed miserably, and by June 1934, American Austin was bankrupt.

Reorganized as the American Bantam Car Company, by 1938 the Butler factory was producing a much improved automobile, called simply the Bantam. This, with assorted mechanical modifications, made possible the elimination of the $7-per-unit royalty paid to Austin of England.

In 1939 Bantam was building a very competent little automobile. By lengthening the stroke and increasing the compression ratio, engineers had boosted the

Following John North Willys's death in 1925, Ward M. Canaday (left) assumed the leadership of Willys-Overland in a company-wide reorganization. Canaday stayed in the background while a procession of four presidents headed up Willys-Overland. Canaday, who held the purse strings, had finally had enough when Jim Mooney resigned and took charge himself. Only when Kaiser purchased Willys-Overland in 1953 did Canaday step down.

In 1933 Willys-Overland introduced the 77 (right), powered by the same 134.2-cid four-cylinder engine that would eventually power the WW II jeep. In fact, this engine would be modified from L-head to F-head and carry on for almost 40 years in Jeep vehicles. The 77 had a 100-inch wheelbase, and the engine made 48 horsepower at 3600 rpm.

17

horsepower to 22—a 69 percent increase. A third main bearing eliminated the problem of crankshaft "whip." A belt-driven generator combined with conventional Babbitt bearings to reduce the noise level. And of course performance was greatly enhanced. Flat-out, the Bantam would do a mile a minute, and it would cruise all day at 50 mph without complaint.

Still, sales failed to materialize in significant numbers. By June 30, 1940, the factory doors had closed, though a few leftover cars were sold as 1941 models.

Bantam's only hope for survival was to get in on the war effort. In 1938 three Bantams, supplied by the manufacturer to the Pennsylvania National Guard, created a very favorable impression. In August of that year, the Quartermaster Corps recommended the establishment of a formal project to develop a suitable body for the Bantam chassis. This would facilitate testing against the three-passenger motor tricycle.

In May 1940, Bantam officials invited members of the Quartermaster Corps Ordnance Technical Committee to inspect the reconnaissance cars they had developed from the stock Bantam roadster. The Bantam had its share of shortcomings, but evidently the committee was impressed, for specifications were shortly drawn, laying down parameters that would ultimately lead to the development of the World War II jeep. From this the Army sent out a request for bids on 70 pilot models. The specifications for this vehicle were as follows:

• Four-wheel drive, not used on the stock Bantam, was specified.
• Wheelbase, width, and height were delineated.
• A crew of three was anticipated, and a .30-caliber machine gun was to be mounted on a pedestal attached to the car.
• Standards were set for engine power, cross-country performance, and grade-climbing ability.
• Cooling capacity was to be such as to allow a sustained low speed of three miles

an hour without overheating the engine.
• Minimum ground clearance was set at 6¼ inches.
• Payload was to be at least 600 pounds.
• Overall weight limitation was set at 1300 pounds, a ridiculous number.

Word went out to 135 manufacturers, inviting them to submit proposals for a quarter-ton reconnaissance vehicle based on the rough specifications set forth by the Army. This totally new machine was to be delivered in just 49 days!

Bantam's hopes of adapting its diminutive passenger car to meet the military specifications were dashed by the horsepower and four-wheel-drive requirements. To design a brand new vehicle in the allowed time appeared impossible—particularly since the beleaguered company no longer had an engineering department. The only hope for the project rested on the possibility of securing the services of a highly competent outside consultant, someone capable of bringing off a near-miracle within the allowed time.

Frank Fenn knew just the man: Karl Probst, a Detroit-based engineer who had worked for several automotive firms. Yet with no cash on hand, any work would have to be undertaken on a contingency basis. Fenn called Art Brandt, a former Bantam executive then working for the National Defense Advisory Commission; and Brandt called Probst, urging him to undertake the assignment.

Probst demurred until he received a message from his old friend William S. Knudsen, former president of General Motors and now head of the National Defense Advisory Committee. Probst later recalled, "On Tuesday, July 16, I was reading of Winston Churchill's bulldog determination: '. . . we shall fight on the beaches, we shall fight in the fields and in the streets, we shall fight in the hills. . . .'" Appealing to Probst to forget about salary (there wasn't any), Knudsen's message added, "We think you can do this job faster than the big companies."

Barney Roos:
Engineer's Engineer

It's doubtful that anyone ever called him by his given name. "Delmar" simply didn't fit the man's image, for he was tough to the core. And even his friends admitted he had a very short fuse. So throughout almost his entire life, Delmar Gene Roos was known as "Barney." The name was borrowed from his boyhood hero, the legendary racer Barney Oldfield. The handle suited him much better than the one selected by his well-meaning but obviously misinformed parents!

Roos, a native of the Bronx, was not a self-made man in the tradition of Henry Ford and Walter Chrysler. He held degrees in both mechanical and electrical engineering from Cornell University, where as an undergraduate he was a champion intercollegiate fencer. He started his professional career in 1911 with General Electric, doing research work on centrifugal compressors and steam turbines. Still, the automobile was his real love, and he soon gravitated to it.

First with Locomobile, then Marmon, then Studebaker, and finally Willys, Roos used his engineering abilities to the fullest. Willys, in those days, was building a small, economical car powered by a 134.2 cubic inch four-banger, inherited from the company's 1926 Whippet. Barney applied his magic to that aging powerplant, adding to both its power and its durability, and creating—though nobody could have foreseen it at the time—the engine that would power the ubiquitous World War II jeep.

Roos remained with Willys during the postwar years, overseeing the development of civilian Jeep Universals, Station Wagons, and Jeepsters. He masterminded the conversion of the hoary L-head "four" to the more efficient F-head configuration, and the development of a new six—first as an L-head and then in an F-head variant. Like George Romney, Barney was convinced—long before the idea achieved wide acceptance—that American motorists needed smaller, more economical automobiles. In a 1951 paper presented to the Society of Automotive Engineers, Roos declared that it was "silly" for Chevrolet to build cars of Cadillac dimensions. He was ahead of his time, but he was right—as usual!

In 1953, Willys-Overland's golden anniversary year, the company was purchased by Kaiser Industries, and the following year Barney Roos resigned to form his own consulting firm. Among his clients was Kaiser-Willys, along with American Motors, Studebaker, and Mack Truck.

On February 12, 1960, while returning by train to his Bronxville, New York, home from a business meeting in Reading, Pennsylvania, Barney Roos was stricken with a massive heart attack. He died the following day. Barney Roos was 72 years old.

If the Willys G.P. prototype had any one particular strength over its competitors, it was the "Go-Devil" engine. Delmar G. Roos (left), "Barney" to his friends, reworked the Whippet four-cylinder engine, and history was changed forever. Roos can also take credit for getting the original Willys prototype down to the Army's restrictive weight limit by redesigning every nut, bolt, and screw.

It was an appeal that Karl Probst could not refuse. He knew the weight limit was impossible, but nobody else could meet that requirement either, so he put that concern out of his mind. That night, driving his 1938 Buick coupe, he headed for Bantam headquarters, at Butler. By 1 P.M. the following day, Probst was seated at a drafting table, laying out plans for what was to become the immortal jeep. And by Friday evening—no more than 33 hours later—the design was completely roughed out. Karl Probst couldn't have known it at the time, but he had created a phenomenon—and a legend.

Saturday was spent in estimating costs and weights, making blueprints, and filling out bid forms. The estimated weight came to 1850 pounds—more than a quarter of a ton over the limit. But on Sunday, when Probst and Fenn met with Bantam's Washington representative, retired Navy Commander Charles Payne, they were told that the bid should be made on the basis of the fictional 1300 pound estimated weight, lest it be rejected on that alone.

On Monday, July 22—five days after Karl Probst first put pencil to paper—Bantam submitted its bid, complete with layouts. Willys submitted only a time and cost bid. Ford and Crosley representatives hadn't progressed even that far. The Willys bid was the lowest, but it was deemed unacceptable because the company's chief engineer, Barney Roos, could see no possibility of building 70 pilot units by the Quartermaster Corps's deadline. So the struggling American Bantam Car Company got the initial contract.

Actually there was very little of the vehicle that was of Bantam's own manufacture. Its small engine fell far short of the required horsepower; so a Hercules four was selected, later superseded by a 40-horsepower Continental. Axles were modified from units built by Spicer for the Studebaker Champion. The transfer case was also from Spicer, the transmission from Warner Gear. And so it went.

The 70 pilot cars were to be divided among the Infantry, Cavalry, and Field Artillery. Eight of these pilots would be equipped with four-wheel steering. Each was to cost no more than $2500—enough, Probst correctly figured, to allow a reasonable profit to the manufacturer. And the first car was to be delivered to the Holabird Quartermaster Depot at Baltimore, Maryland, by 5 P.M. on September 21, 1940—a ridiculously short time line.

The first hand-built prototype, officially the BRC Quarter-Ton General Purpose Vehicle, was complete and running by September 21. To a remarkable degree, it resembled the later, standardized jeep, though its grille was rounded rather than flat.

To break in the engine, Probst and plant manager Harold Christ drove the prototype to Holabird under its own power, arriving just half an hour ahead of the 5 P.M. deadline. As Karl Probst later recalled the experience, "We drove slowly at first, telling ourselves it was important to break the vehicle in. But as we wound through the hills of Pennsylvania, the five o'clock deadline we had worked toward for those seven weeks seemed to come closer. To make Holabird come closer too, we were soon pushing the car to the limit, and it really was fun."

By way of an initial demonstration, the Bantam undertook to climb a 60-percent grade, accomplishing the feat easily in second gear. Then Major Herbert J. Lawes, Holabird's purchasing and contracting officer, put the vehicle through its paces. When he brought it back he said to Probst, "I have driven every unit the services have purchased for the last twenty years. I can judge them in fifteen minutes. This vehicle is going to be absolutely outstanding. I believe this unit will make history!"

Following this declaration was a series of merciless tests, designed to show up even the slightest weakness in design and construction. The test took the Bantam over 3410 miles, only 247 miles of which were

Sales of the Willys 77 were not strong, so Willys redesigned the car for 1936 (right, top left). This car, still fitted with the 134.2-cid engine, sold better but was nowhere near as streamlined as the 77. While Willys-Overland can take full credit for the jeep's engine, most of the design work was done by forgotten American Bantam. Bantam produced smaller cars such as the American version of the diminutive British Austin. In 1938 they released their Model "60" speedster (right, top right, and bottom). The "60" line consisted of the speedster, coupe, and light delivery: retail prices started as low as $439.

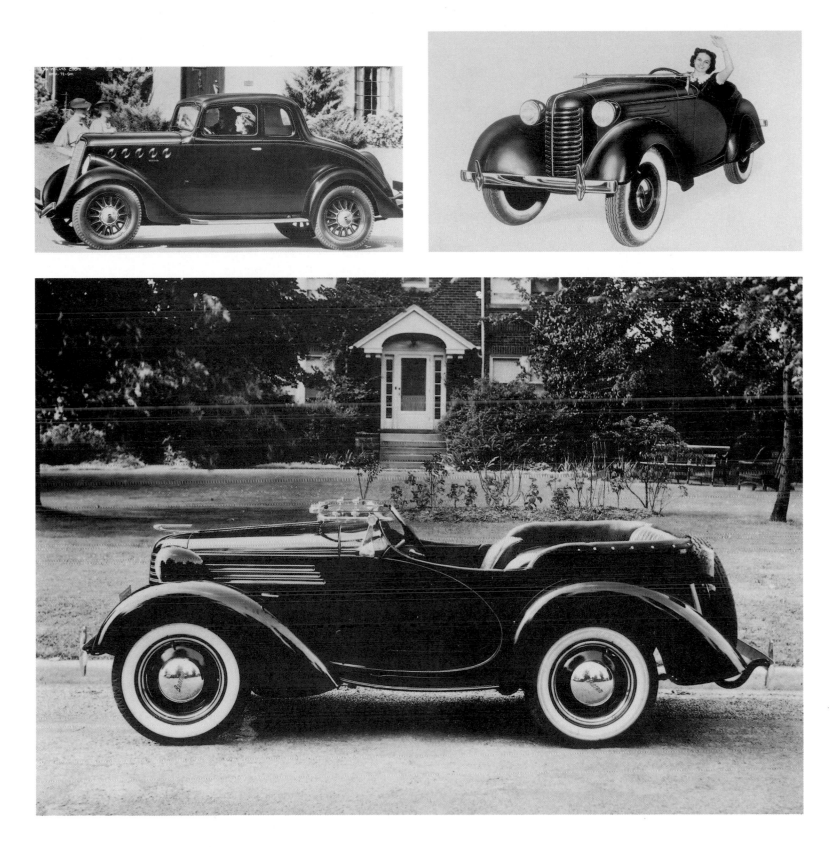

In an attempt to tailor the product to the times, in Depression-racked 1933 Willys-Overland dropped all of its full-sized lines to concentrate upon the diminutive, four-cylinder Willys 77. Priced as low as $335 for the coupe—$105 less than the four-cylinder Ford—the "77" was expected to revive the company's fortunes by making a new car available at what amounted to a used-car price. The old four-cylinder Whippet engine was dusted off for this application, providing the new model with a highly favorable power-to-weight ratio, and thus with sparkling performance.

Sales, however, failed to live up to expectations, though production for 1935 showed a 150-percent gain over 1934's low point. John North Willys died that August, and the task of reorganizing Willys-Overland fell to financier Ward M. Canaday. Canaday managed somehow to raise three million dollars, with which he bought up the company's outstanding bonds for 70 cents and claims for 25 cents on the dollar. In a year's time, he and his associates held a two-thirds common stock equity in the reborn Willys-Overland Motors, Inc. Canaday served as chairman of the board, while the presidency of the company went to Dave Wilson, whose Foundry and Machinery Company had been supplying Willys-Overland with castings.

A dramatically styled new Willys was introduced for 1937. The drivetrain was essentially unchanged, and the wheelbase remained at 100 inches. Tread was widened by five inches, both front and rear. Bodies were roomier; and the appearance of the Willys 37, though still unusual, was far more attractive than that of its predecessor. Production quadrupled, to 76,803 units for the year.

Problems, however, remained. Chief among these was the dismal (and only partly deserved) reputation of the aging Whippet engine. Thanks in no small measure to the merciless beating it had received from lead-footed owners of both the Whippet and the Willys 77, the little

logged on paved roads. Twenty separate flaws were detected, ranging from a loose grille to the failure of both frame side rails. But in their final remarks, the testers concluded, "The vehicle demonstrated ample power and all requirements of the service."

On hand to observe the Bantam's performance were representatives from both Willys and Ford. While Ford's involvement in the war was to be expected, the inclusion of Willys might seem a bit strange. However, Willys's involvement would come to play a very important role in the final development of the jeep that Bantam had pioneered.

Over the years, Willys-Overland had built some interesting products. The mainstay of the line, traditionally, was the Overland, a conventional, moderately priced four-cylinder machine. In mid-1926, Willys-Overland introduced the perky little low-priced Whippet. And it was this car that was responsible for the company's spectacular sales gain during the late 1920s.

However, the Whippet's success proved to be of short duration. By 1930 an L-head "six" bearing the Willys name was the company's mainstay, augmented by a trickle of four-cylinder Whippets and a handful of Willys-Knights.

"Cast Iron Charlie" Sorensen (left) took over as head of Willys-Overland with the 1943 "retirement" of Joe Frazer. He oversaw the release of the CJ-2A—the civilian jeep—and ran Willys operations right after the war. He also developed, along with Brooks Stevens, one of Jeep's most influential products—the Station Wagon. Sorensen picked up his nickname from his days with Ford.

four-banger had become known for excessive oil consumption, fried bearings, water pump failures, and leaking cylinder heads. Since the driving habits of American motorists were not likely to change, something would have to be done to beef up the engine if the Willys reputation was to be restored.

Ward Canaday was not an engineer. He was not really an automobile man at all, although he was responsible for introducing installment buying to the industry. (His wife used to say, "Why, Ward can't even hang a picture!" and John North Willys once alleged that Ward's mechanical ability was limited to putting a dent in someone else's fender.) But he did his homework, and in time acquired some understanding of the major engineering problems involved in automobile production.

It came to Canaday's attention that Delmar G. "Barney" Roos, formerly chief engineer at Pierce-Arrow, Locomobile, Marmon and—more recently—Studebaker, was working for the Rootes Group, in England. Roos had evidently never regarded this as anything more than a temporary assignment, and in 1938, having been out of the country for a year, he was ready to come home.

Canaday hired Roos, installing him as executive vice president and chief engineer of Willys-Overland. It was an inspired choice, for Barney, a former president of the Society of Automotive Engineers, was one of the finest engineers in the industry. And best of all, he had—despite his earlier affiliations with gargantuan automobiles like Locomobile and Pierce-Arrow—a particular interest in small cars.

Had Barney Roos been hired by an industry giant—General Motors, perhaps—or even a well-financed independent such as Packard or Nash, his obvious course of action would have been to design a new engine from scratch (something he had done several times). However, at Willys that was impossible—the company was virtually broke.

So the resourceful Roos wrought a low-cost miracle. Taking that venerable Whippet-cum-Willys 77 four-banger, he tunneled out the intake ports and increased the diameter of the intake manifold. A Carter 1¼-inch plain tube downdraft carburetor was fitted. The compression ratio was boosted from 5.70:1 to 6.48:1. Aluminum pistons replaced the old cast iron jugs. Cleveland graphite micro precision bearings and manganese valve springs were fitted. The crankshaft was strengthened and counterweighted. A quieter air cleaner and fan were devised. Taken together, these modifications raised the horsepower from 48 to 61 and resulted in much greater durability, as well.

Just to be sure he had it right, Barney directed his staff to run test engines wide open (4400 rpm) continuously for 100 hours. That kind of abuse would have destroyed the original engine in short order. In fact, a test in which one of the older jobs ran for 22 minutes at 3400 rpm resulted in scored cylinders and burned-out rod bearings. But the Roos-designed version held up admirably.

The initial application of the Roos engine (eventually dubbed the "Go-Devil") came in 1939, in a new Willys model bearing an old name: Overland. It bristled with improvements, including hydraulic brakes and a larger capacity cooling system. Beneath it all was a stout new frame, reinforced by a rugged X-member. By any measure, it was a much-improved car with a much-improved engine.

Without knowing it, Bantam and Willys had separately created what has become known as the jeep. Bantam, with its original body design, and Willys, with Barney Roos's "Go-Devil" engine, had conspired to lay the groundwork for the vehicle that would change the face of modern warfare and continue unchanged for generations to come. However, the two companies were still far from sharing their information. It would take the U.S. Army and a world war to bring them together.

The Push for Standardization: 1940-41

By late 1941, the jeep as we know it was coming together in leaps and bounds. However, Bantam was the only automaker that could meet the Army's ridiculous proposal of having a running prototype ready in 49 days. The reason for this was the singular effort of Karl Probst—who was busy readying Bantam's pilot. While all this was going on, the Army asked Bantam to build the remaining 69 cars from the original bid—including eight with four-wheel steering—without seeing the finished prototype. By confirming their order in advance, the Army did two things. First, this single act cut the silhouette of the original jeep, before Willys or Ford even had a chance to show their prototypes. More importantly, it forced Willys and Ford to get moving on their pilots lest they be left out of the process completely.

The Army Quartermaster, however, felt the need to diversify jeep production. So copies of Probst's blueprints were supplied to the rival firms despite the vehement protests of American Bantam. The Army did this on the premise that the design had become its property. Bantam's distress was understandable enough, but the urgency of the situation was such that there was simply no time for the usual niceties. Willys and Ford would soon have prototypes of their own, offering competition to the Bantam. However, the sharing of the prototype drawings cut out a great deal of leg work for Willys and Ford, and took away Bantam's advanced development advantage.

Like Karl Probst at Bantam, Willys-Overland's Barney Roos had concluded that the Army's original weight limit of 1300 pounds for its proposed new reconnaissance car was unrealistic. But unlike Probst, Roos also concluded that the specified completion date was also impossible to achieve, partly because the Spicer four-wheel drivetrain would not be easy for him to obtain. This explains why the Willys model was late coming out of the blocks.

The Willys pilot, known as the "Quad" (an echo of the four-wheel-drive truck supplied to the military by Nash Motors during the First World War) was delivered to Holabird on November 13, 1940, followed 10 days later by the Ford "Pygmy." Since both were based upon Karl Probst's design, it is hardly surprising that they looked almost exactly like the Bantam pilot whose testing had been completed the previous month. One obvious exception to this was the flat grille used by the Ford. The Willys, on the other hand, mimicked the rounded grill employed by the Bantam.

A. Wade Wells, in his 1946 book *Hail to the Jeep,* quotes Willys test driver Donald Kenower's account of the test exercise that followed the preliminary 4000-mile highway run:

"The next part of the test was what they called cross-country. This was run in a field, at the camp, which they had fixed up to simulate extremely rough country, ditches, hills, etc. Our job had light springs and rode fairly well. The result was that they drove it about twice as fast as they did other similar vehicles, as the speed was regulated by how fast it was possible to go and still stay *in* the job."

(It is only fair to caution the reader that Wells was a Willys-Overland employee, so his observations may not have been entirely objective.)

Because Willys became famous for producing the jeep, many people credit its design to them. However, this is not true. Little American Bantam came up with the first prototype (right) in August-September of 1940. Karl Probst, an automotive consultant to Bantam, can rightfully take credit for the jeep's unique design and abilities. The first Bantam car had a wheelbase of 79 inches and was 126 inches long by 54 inches wide by 51.5 inches high (with top up). The vehicle was powered by a 45-horsepower four-cylinder L-head Continental engine. Weight was 2030 pounds, which was 700 pounds over the Army's limit. (The Army would later increase its limit to 2160 pounds, allowing the Bantam in.) Because Bantam was such a small company, they had to source out all of the four-wheel-drive components. The gearbox was supplied by Warner, the transfer case by Spicer, and the rear axle was a modified Studebaker unit made by Spicer. The vehicle was tested at Camp Ripley and Camp Holabird.

Wells continues: "During the cross-country test the field became a mud lake due to continuous hard rains. At that time we found that the oil bath air cleaner was not properly mounted, and permitted dirt to get in the engine through the air inlet. Before this was discovered, the engine had been damaged, and in order to continue the test and avoid delay an engine was taken out of a Willys passenger car and installed in the pilot model, and it was again running on the course in a few hours."

Ford, meanwhile, had reservations about the project. By this time, the company was committed to larger, heavier passenger cars with much greater engine displacement than the Army specifications called for. But the Quartermaster believed that Ford's enormous productive capacity would ultimately be needed. So pressure was brought to bear, and in the end Ford entered the contest.

The Ford pilot car made use of what was by that time the company's only four-cylinder powerplant—a modified version of the Fordson tractor engine. This unit, basically half of the Mercury V-8, was roundly criticized by *Road & Track*'s John Bond for such shortcomings as "split valve guides, no adjustment for tappets, semi-steel pistons, no real concept of proper valve timing or even combustion chamber design."

Another problem Ford encountered was the fact that it did not have a suitable transmission. So, the old, non-synchro Model A gearbox was used—rugged and reliable, but hopelessly outclassed by the competition.

After the extensive testing of all three models was completed, the QMC placed an order for 1500 more of the little machines from each company. This represented a compromise, worked out on November 14, 1940, with the help of the National Defense Advisory Commission. The General Staff had wanted the original order to go entirely to Bantam, while the Quartermaster General—who took a dim view of Bantam's production prospects—preferred

to rely on other suppliers. All three manufacturers had submitted proposals that were essentially satisfactory. There were, however, some significant differences between models, and they are the following:

• Weight. The Army, in a concession to reality, had raised the limit from 1300 to 2160 pounds. At 2050 and 2150 pounds, respectively, both Bantam and Ford met that specification; but the Willys weighed in at 2450 pounds—an unacceptable figure, as far as the Army was concerned.

• Fuel mileage. Bantam, powered by a 112-cid, 40 horsepower Continental engine, won this one.

• Braking distance and steering. Here again, the nod went to Bantam.

• Driver comfort and convenience. This one was Ford's, all the way.

• Engine performance. The 61-horsepower "Go-Devil" engine put the Willys far ahead of its rivals in this respect, though both Bantam and Ford had re-rated their engines from 40 to 45 horsepower.

• Hood configuration. While the three vehicles looked very much alike, the Ford pilot had a broad, flat hood, in contrast to the rounded shape used by Bantam and Willys. The flat design was considered superior because it added usable surface to the body.

Deliveries of this new order of 1500 units from each manufacturer were to commence early in 1941. In addition, each manufacturer was to make certain modifications to correct deficiencies uncovered in the testing process. All three were to adopt the Ford's hood and grille designs, and certain requirements were laid down:

• A maximum level road speed of 55 miles per hour was specified, at an engine rpm not over the peak horsepower speed.

• A minimum level road speed of not more than three miles per hour was mandated.

• The ability to ford hard-bottom water crossings at least 18 inches in depth was required.

• Construction must permit the installa-

Willys-Overland got into the game a bit later with its Quad (right, top). It was designed under the direction of Delmar "Barney" G. Roos and made its debut on November 11, 1940, at Camp Holabird. The Quad was 300 pounds over the Army's new higher weight limit but had the advantage of the most powerful engine of the test group. Its "Go-Devil" four-cylinder, while offering just 61 horsepower, gave it a superior power-to-weight ratio. This Quad model would be further developed into the model MA, which was the successor to the WW II jeep. The Bantam model (right, bottom), despite its weak frame, was no slouch and placed second in the competition, behind the Quad. The Bantam was the lightest and most fuel efficient. However, an amalgam design was chosen using the best parts from all three prototype models. Willys and Ford were awarded the contracts, but Bantam refused to give up and actively petitioned for the right to build the improved model. Eventually they were locked out and, instead, built carts to be pulled behind jeeps and other light trucks.

tion and satisfactory use of tire chains.

Thus, though all three models differed in several ways, they were becoming increasingly similar. Willys, however, was up against a serious problem, for the Army made it known that the 2160-pound weight limit was official and final.

As Wells tells the story, "Only the decision of Under-Secretary of War Patterson broke the impasse." Colonel (later Brig. General) H. J. Lawes, the commandant of the test center at Camp Holabird, told Willys-Overland officials that there was some flexibility in the weight specification. So Patterson agreed to permit Willys to proceed with the production of their 1500 vehicles with an exemption to the weight limitation.

Not that the issue was forever settled. Ward Canaday later recalled, "We had won a first round, but we still were squarely faced with the threat of losing all future orders beyond the 1500 if we did not make the 2160 pounds weight and of losing them anyway, on a performance basis, if we abandoned our own powerful engine and rugged design in order to meet the lower weight requirement."

So it became imperative for Willys to pare 263 pounds—12 percent of the total—from the weight of an already bare-bones vehicle. And, they had to do this with no sacrifice of either strength or power.

Almost 75 pounds could have been cut by using a smaller engine—possibly the Continental unit employed by the Bantam pilot. However, Barney Roos had been told that the most impressive feature of the Willys unit had been its powerful "Go-Devil" engine. So that idea was rejected out of hand.

Roos, a patient, determined, resourceful man, disassembled the vehicle. Every bolt, every bracket was analyzed. Surplus material was cut away wherever possible. Studs, screws, even cotter pins were shortened. The sizes of clamps, nuts, and washers were reduced. The heavy carbon steel frame was replaced by one made of lighter alloy.

Lighter steel was employed for the body and fenders. Finally, the task came down to weighing the paint. It was determined that one coat would have to suffice, for a second would have meant exceeding the weight limit. The final product did meet the Army's specified figure—with just seven ounces to spare.

Roos also undertook some comparatively minor, yet important modifications to the "Go-Devil" engine. The carburetor and intake manifold were altered slightly to get even better performance on steep grades. To better cope with the mud, sand, and dust encountered in battle, special air cleaners and oil filters were used.

Praise was heaped upon Barney Roos. In a statement that appeared to completely overlook the critical work of Probst and the Bantam people, *Modern Industry* magazine noted, "When the Army handed out specifications of what it wanted, Roos went back to work and, with nothing but an engine around which to build a vehicle. He and his Willys-Overland staff designed a highly specialized job while competitors were struggling to have their existing products approved and their assembly lines kept intact."

With 4500 jeeps in service, there was ample opportunity to evaluate the respective merits of the three makes. Preference clearly went to the Willys, principally because of its more powerful engine. However, the Willys had other advantages as well, such as skid plates mounted under the motor and transmission, heavier gauge steel in the body, and durable two-piece tubular front steering rods.

On the other hand, there were complaints that the Bantam had "too many bugs." It overheated. The transmission was to be too light for the job; gears soon wore out, and the synchromesh was weak. The windshield wiper was hand-operated; and the battery hanger was too light and required constant welding.

The Ford, meanwhile, was rated a distant third. In the opinion of one of the testing

The jeep quickly proved its worth in battle. Although the United States was not yet at war, jeeps saw action in Africa, China, and Russia by means of the Lend-Lease program (right, top). President Roosevelt enacted this program so the forces "friendly to democracy" with no money or goods to trade could have the wherewithal to fight the Axis forces. Though testing continued (right, bottom), the Army ordered 1500 vehicles from each company (Willys-Overland, Ford, and Bantam) to be released in the Lend-Lease program.

officers, the Pygmy "had the most trouble with the motor, which was designed to work on a governor's speed, and there was considerable bearing trouble." As well, the non-synchro transmission did not win any friends for the Ford.

At this point, the Army had two possible solutions to the problem of achieving standardization given the existence of three types, each having its own virtues. The most satisfactory was to manufacture a vehicle combining the most desirable features in a virtually new machine. The second was to take the best vehicle of the three and graft on to it, as far as possible, the good points of the other two.

In the interest of saving time and money, the latter course was chosen. Incredibly, the Quartermaster Corps elected to give Ford, whose vehicle had placed dead last in the field tests, a negotiated contract for 16,000 units.

The Office of Production Management intervened, however, at the behest of William S. Knudsen. Though the Ford Motor Company vigorously protested, the contract was awarded to Willys-Overland. Willys, in reality, had not only supplied the best of the test vehicles but had underbid Ford by a hefty $640,000. The QMC's stated rationale for favoring Ford had been that the larger firm was considered a more dependable source of supply. However, critics called the Ford Motor Company "the country's foremost violator of the Wagner Act," citing six Labor Board decisions then outstanding against it. The potential for serious labor problems was as real as it was obvious. In any case, Knudsen, an acknowledged expert in matters concerning production, was convinced that Willys-Overland was a competent source of supply.

A conference took place at the Holabird Quartermaster Depot to consider changes in the design and specifications of the Willys unit, now designated the Model MA. As a result, several modifications were made in the forthcoming Model MB:

• An improved carburetor air cleaner was installed.

• A 40-ampere generator, known as the "QMC Standard Generator," was used with a government-standard voltage regulator.

• A 15-gallon fuel tank replaced the 11-gallon tank of the Model MA.

• Larger (five-inch) sealed beam headlamps were adopted.

• A larger, government-standard battery was used.

• The handbrake was relocated from the driver's left to the center of the car, where the passenger could reach it in case of emergency.

• The gearshift lever was moved from the steering column to the floor. The rationale here was that all Army trucks should have uniform controls, to save confusion when drivers moved from one vehicle to another.

• In order to protect the steering tie rods from damage, they were carried as high above the axle as possible.

• Suitable protection was provided for hydraulic brake hoses.

• A double bow-top replaced the single-bow type, providing increased head room without raising the jeep's silhouette.

• Spring shackles were sealed, to keep out water and dirt.

• Provision was made for the vehicle to carry a shovel and an ax.

• Standardized blackout lights, already used on other government vehicles, were adopted.

• A power take off was recommended and later utilized in operating special equipment used by the Navy and Marine Corps.

The standardized MB jeep ended up two inches longer than the MA. Its weight was 2450 pounds, a reasonable figure for so stout a vehicle. As time went along, experience with the MB led to further modifications. Larger (6.00/16) tires and heavier "combat" wheels were added. Electrically, a radio spark suppressor; an extra blackout driving light, mounted on the left front

Lieutenant General William S. Knudson: Mentor to the Jeep

William S. Knudsen (above) was the only civilian to ever be commissioned directly to the rank of Lieutenant General in the U.S. Army. His job was to speed production of wartime products.

Had it not been for the intervention of William Signius "Big Bill" Knudsen, the Ford Motor Company's prototype jeep would probably have been adopted—as recommended by the Quartermaster Corps—in lieu of the clearly superior Willys design. So although he was not directly involved in the development of this remarkable little machine, he nevertheless played a critical role in determining the type of vehicle that was eventually developed and adopted.

A huge, rugged man who, in the eyes of one contemporary, resembled "a well dressed and highly intelligent polar bear," Knudsen spoke "with a low, liquid accent."

Bill Knudsen had emigrated to the United States from his native Denmark at the age of 21 and found employment in a Bronx shipyard. In successive jobs, he repaired locomotives for the Erie Railroad, made bicycles, and then made parts for one of Henry Ford's suppliers. When Ford absorbed the firm for which Knudsen worked, Big Bill was part of the deal. He soon found himself in the role of production head for the Ford Motor Company. Between 1913 and 1915 Knudsen built an incredible 14 assembly plants for Ford. He was a master mechanic, a gifted troubleshooter, and a key figure in the development of mass production techniques.

Inevitably, the independent, individualistic Knudsen and the autocratic, paternalistic Henry Ford had a falling out. By 1921 Knudsen was fired. Early the following year, he went to work for General Motors as a staff advisor. Three weeks later he was named vice president in charge of production at the troubled Chevrolet Division, charged with the task of restoring Chevrolet to health. It was a challenge exactly suited to Knudsen's abilities, as well as an opportunity to even the score with Henry Ford. He set about overhauling Chevrolet's production methods, root and branch. By 1924 he was made president and general manager of the Chevrolet Division and a vice president of General Motors as well. The day was coming, Knudsen promised his dealers in his Danish accent, when Chevy production would match Ford's, "vun for vun."

Nineteen thirty-seven, with Chevrolet's sales supremacy firmly established, saw Knudsen appointed president of General Motors. However, war clouds began to gather. In 1940 President Franklin D. Roosevelt appointed Knudsen to the National Defense Advisory Commission. Profoundly affected by the German invasion of his native country, Big Bill resigned his General Motors post (at considerable financial sacrifice, obviously), then set about to remove the bottlenecks in the production of machine tools, aircraft engines, tanks, and other items critical to what was euphemistically called "national defense."

America's entry into the war found Knudsen commissioned a Lieutenant General in the U.S. Army, the only civilian in American history ever to be appointed directly to that rank. His job was to speed up production in plants with War Department contracts, an assignment thoroughly congenial to his talents. On a visit to the Pacific Theater of Operations at the height of the conflict he was asked, "General Knudsen, you're not a military man. Why did you come on a trip like this?" Knudsen's reply was characteristic: "I came to see how the customers liked the goods."

By war's end, Knudsen—already knighted by the King of Denmark, although he had become a United States citizen in 1914—had received many honors. As he was preparing to return to Detroit, Big Bill was told that the President wished to see him. It happened that the Distinguished Service Medal had just been awarded to him for the second time. Knudsen proudly pinned both ribbons to his chest. Discreetly informed by his executive officer that protocol demanded his wearing *one* ribbon with the Oak Leaf Cluster, Knudsen responded, "You saw [Undersecretary of War Robert] Patterson give me the medal. I got one before. I'm going to wear two!" He left the Pentagon building proudly wearing both ribbons, to say goodbye to his Commander in Chief.

This maverick general had never learned to salute. Yet, when he left the Army, as when he had left Chevrolet years earlier, he took with him the respect, admiration, and affection of everyone. He never received any recognition for his important, backstage role in the development of the military jeep. Probably he didn't want it, for Bill Knudsen was no glory-seeker. Without him, one of the most important pieces of military equipment used in the Second World War may have never come to pass, or might have been significantly less effective.

fender; and a taillight connector socket, for use when a trailer was being towed, were specified. For emergencies, a five-gallon fuel can was mounted at the back.

Just how effective a weapon of war the now-standardized jeep had become can be judged from an account given by Major J. H. Chamberlain after he had been given an obviously strenuous demonstration ride:

"Grueling tests showed that the jeep could fight as well as run," wrote the Major. "And it could go places a motorcycle couldn't. Besides, a motorcycle dispatch rider is vulnerable; a single sniper can cut him down, letting vital orders fall into enemy hands. A jeep, carrying armed men and machine guns, is a far tougher proposition. And, vital for combat strategy, the jeep is a clawing, climbing hellion in reaching good places to shoot from.

"In Mississippi I learned firsthand what it was like to ride in a jeep across pine-studded acres at 50 miles an hour. . . . [The driver] slowed down our jeep and straddled a half-burned log, front wheels tilted to the sky. I visualized a shattered crank case but was shown guard bars underneath for just such protection. Grabbing special handles on the body, we lifted the car and shoved it easily off the log.

"Army strategists especially admire the jeep's low silhouette. Only three and a third feet high, the jackrabbit-like jeep is hard to spot in brush country, still harder to line a gun on.

"At 25 miles per hour he headed for a huge live oak with gnarled branches close to the ground. I was expecting [the driver] to swerve suddenly to demonstrate the jeep's maneuverability. Soon I saw that it was not his intention to swerve at all.

"'Duck!' he yelled.

"I ducked.

"We roared under the lowest branch— the top of our car missing it by inches. Only then did I realize that I had stowed my 190 pounds in the narrow space between seat and cowl—and had lots of leg and arm room to spare.

"'Plenty o' clearance,' my driver remarked.

"We crossed a small stream, water flowing over the floor, but we had no trouble, for electric units are placed so high that the 40-inch jeep can keep going through water 18 inches deep. We clawed our way up the 30-degree bank—twice as steep as you'll ever meet in a passenger car on the highway."

In Major Chamberlain's view, and in the minds of most Americans, the jeep had come to represent the inventive imagination that had made this nation's industries the envy of the world.

By October 1941, it was apparent that the jeep's versatility and usefulness would far exceed the Army's original expectations. A second source was sought, partly to increase the supply, but apparently largely as insurance against the possibility of sabotage at the Willys plant. Bypassing Bantam, Quartermaster General E. B. Gregory sought out Edsel Ford with the unprecedented request that his company manufacture jeeps according to the Willys design— including the Barney Roos "Go-Devil" engine. All parts, Edsel was told, were to be interchangeable between the Willys vehicles and their Ford-built clones.

Edsel Ford agreed without hesitation; and on January 10, 1942, it was announced that a negotiated contract had been made, under which Ford would produce 15,000 GPW (General Purpose Willys) vehicles, to cost $14,623,900. Willys turned over to Ford its patents, specifications, and drawings—without compensation, according to one report, although another source indicates that a royalty was paid. In any case, it was an almost unparalleled example of wartime cooperation between two competing firms. Indeed, the agreement may even have been illegal, yet it was considered vital to the war effort.

Incidentally, despite its similarity to the Willys MB, the Ford-built GPW is readily distinguished by its inverted U-shaped front frame cross member. The Willys ver-

The Willys-Overland model MA was an improved and lightened version of the original Quad. Because of the Quad's serious weight problems, Barney Roos and Willys engineers redesigned the vehicle with lighter panels, supports, and even smaller nuts and bolts. Most of the 1500 MAs produced ended up in Russia. This MA model (right) was the eventual winner (with a Ford Pygmy front end graft), and went into mass production as the wartime MB. The MA differed from the Quad in several ways. It had lower, rounded door cutouts; single piece wheels; a steering-column mounted gear shift; two circular-mounted instrument clusters; and a handbrake on the left.

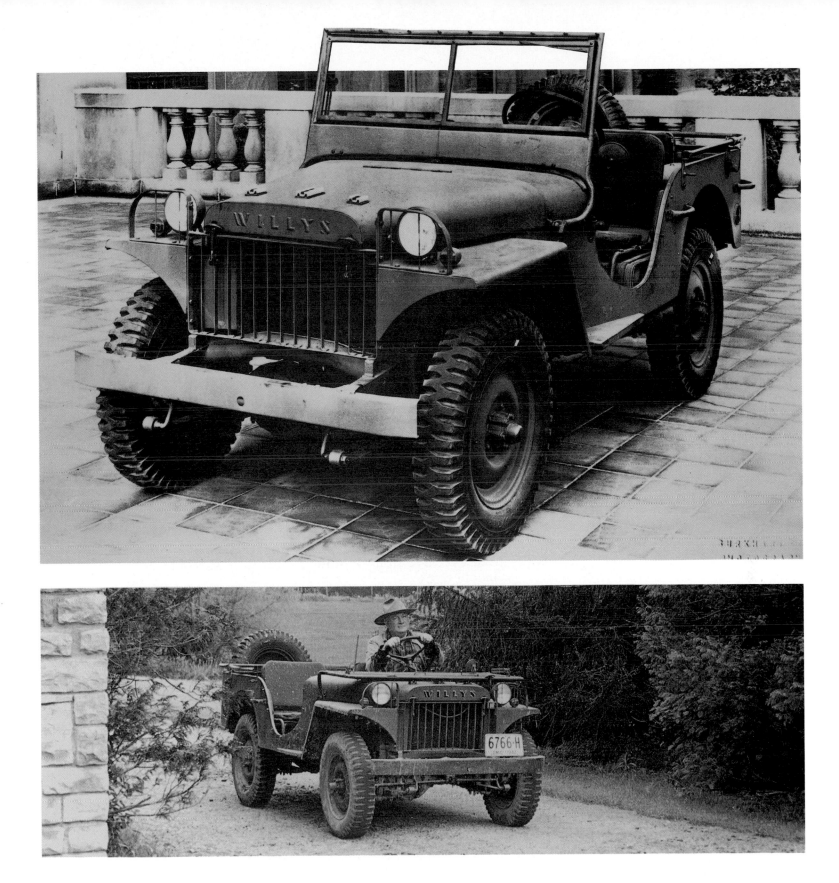

sion, in contrast, uses a tubular brace.

Over at Bantam, meanwhile, President Frank Fenn was understandably furious. In a letter dated March 23, 1942, he wrote, according to historians Denfield and Fry, that he "could not understand how Bantam had been denied a chance to bid when it had performed the major part in the jeep's development. . . ." Fenn went on to say that his company had been first to make the proposal that the standardized vehicle should be built around the best elements of the three pilot models and had wished to share in the building of the car that would result. On the financial side, he said that he had paid Spicer, in the reasonable expectation that Bantam would benefit from the work it was doing, more than $130,000 in tooling costs for axle production. He had, in effect, subsidized Ford's and Willys's production.

Despite Fenn's protests, no more jeep contracts came American Bantam's way. By the time the war ended, Willys had produced 362,841 of the little quarter-tonners, while Ford had built 281,448. Bantam, the firm responsible for starting it all, had been granted contracts for only the initial 2643 units—a proverbial "drop in the bucket."

Bantam's final, forlorn hope was that it would be asked to produce the four-wheel-steer jeep, of which eight pilot models had been submitted. But the Quartermaster Corps—despite pleas from the using arms—abandoned that proposal, evidently on the grounds that the vehicle's advantages were not sufficient to outweigh the added complexity and the potential service problems in the field.

Given the shaky condition of American Bantam and the limited capacity of its factory, the decision to go with Willys and Ford, however harsh it may seem, may not have been entirely unreasonable. Certainly the product the larger companies produced was a good one. More than that, it became one of World War II's most enduring legends.

Quartermaster General E. B. Gregory asked Edsel Ford (left) if his company would manufacture jeeps according to the Willys design—including the Barney Roos "Go-Devil" engine. Ford agreed without hesitation, and an order was placed for 15,000 units—designated G.P.W. (General Purpose Willys). This effectively bypassed Bantam and shut them out from future production. Ford and Willys-Overland would go on to produce 644,289 jeeps during World War II.

American Bantam's second model, the 40 BRC (1940 Bantam Reconnaissance Car) was shipped under the Lend-Lease Agreement to Britain to fight on the western front (right, top). A second order of Bantams went into production in 1941 and were shipped to Russia. Unit number 2675 came off the assembly line just before the attack on Pearl Harbor. Sadly, this was the last-ever Bantam car. The eventual compilation models, the MB and GPW (right, bottom), went on to create history, and the basic chassis and design would carry on for over 40 years, until the CJ-7's demise in 1986.

CHAPTER THREE

The Jeep Goes to War: 1942-44

he speed and ease with which German troops were able to sweep through the low countries—Belgium, Holland, Luxembourg—and on into northern France was a stunning blow to the Allies. Commencing on May 10, 1940, the Nazi forces moved so rapidly that within 16 days British and French troops had been driven almost into the sea. Had it not been for the remarkable evacuation at Dunkirk, thousands of Allied troops would have surely been captured. On June 14, the Germans occupied Paris; eight days later France fell. For all intents and purposes, Britain stood alone, facing the advancing Nazi war machine.

President Franklin D. Roosevelt was more acutely aware than most Americans of the gravity of the situation—especially regarding our own national security. So, on June 10, he pledged that the United States would "extend to the opponents of force the material resources of this nation." America had become, in Roosevelt's words, "The Arsenal of Democracy."

By the following March, "Lend-Lease" had been authorized by Congress, providing war materiel such as airplanes, tanks, and trucks, along with food and other supplies and services. The primary recipient was Britain, though the program was soon extended to China, and then, in September, to the Soviet Union. The legislation allowed the President to accept repayment "in kind or property or any other direct or indirect benefit that the President deems satisfactory." Of course this meant much of the total—which eventually exceeded $49 billion—was actually an outright gift;

though, the Allied nations gave U.S. troops stationed abroad some $8 million in "reverse Lend-Lease."

Of all the items of equipment supplied to the Allies under the Lend-Lease program, none was more enthusiastically received than the jeep. On September 19, 1941, American diplomat W. Averell Harriman and his British counterpart, Lord Beaverbrook, were sent to Moscow to confer with Russian dictator Josef Stalin. The purpose of their meeting was to discuss further supplies and equipment that might, under the Lend-Lease program, be placed at the disposal of the Soviet Union.

In stark contrast to the cordiality he had manifested on an earlier, similar occasion, Stalin was curt, blunt, even rude. Harriman, the quintessential diplomat, reviewed for Marshall Stalin an impressive list of goods and services that the United States and Britain were prepared to supply to the Soviets, who at the time were locked in a desperate struggle against the advancing German *Wehrmacht*.

Stalin remained unimpressed, almost hostile. Finally, running down his list, Harriman came to what was obviously the key item: 5000 jeeps.

Old Joe Stalin's eyes lit up. "Good!" he is reported to have exclaimed. "But I want more. This is a war of motors. It is impossible to have too many of them, and the side having the largest number of motors is bound to win."

Of course everybody else wanted jeeps too. For the time being, 5000 was all "Uncle Joe" got, though eventually he received several thousand more. Reportedly, Soviet propagandists were at pains to in-

Even before the Japanese attack at Pearl Harbor on December 7, 1941, jeeps had proven their worth in battle all across the globe. By calling the United States "the Arsenal of Democracy," President Roosevelt offered his "Lend-Lease" plan to the Allies. The jeep was an integral part of this policy and soon saw action in Eastern Europe, North Africa, and China (right). It served as a scout car, a command car, an altar, and everything in between. Josef Stalin called World War II a "war of motors," adding that "the side having the largest number of motors is bound to win." Replacing the mule and the cavalry horse was the job of the jeep. It did that and then some. It would go places a mule was too stubborn to, and never needed much care. In the desert and in the jungle, in the battlefields across Europe, it captured the hearts of the soldiers who drove it. This is where the legend of the jeep began.

form the home folks that these remarkable little machines were Russian-built, in a secret factory. However, the Russian soldiers evidently knew the source. In fact, the Russians became so fond of the jeep that, according to Doreen Canaday Spitzer, daughter of Willys-Overland Chairman Ward Canaday, they referred to the jeep as the "Ooeelees!" Correspondent Henry Cassidy cabled from the Russian front that "the American jeep has met the Russian mud and the situation is well in hand."

In his book, *Lend-Lease, Weapon for Victory*, Lend-Lease administrator Edward R. Stettinius Jr., later to be Franklin D. Roosevelt's secretary of state, relates the following story:

"The Russians early learned the value of our jeeps. . . . They had asked for motorcycle sidecars, but as I wrote Ambassador Litvinov late in January 1942, our own Army was using jeeps almost entirely instead of motorcycle sidecars. . . . The Russians decided to try the jeeps and soon found that our Army had good reason to rely on them. . . . They worked so well in the mire and rough going on the Russian roads that the Red Army quickly asked for more. Since then we have shipped thousands of them to Russia.

"Last year when an Associated Press correspondent visited a Soviet artillery regiment on the central front, he was driven in a jeep through deep mud and across rough fields to the regimental headquarters. Between jounces he turned to the Red Army driver and asked him how he liked the car. The driver answered with one word: "'*Zamechatelno*!' That is the Russian equivalent for 'swell!'"

Later, Britain's General Sir H. Maitland Wilson, the soldier with the longest continuous service in His Majesty's Army, sent a jeep to Yugoslavia's Marshal Josef Broz Tito. "My representative tells me that the Marshal is delighted with it," General Wilson later recalled, "and was amazed by the performance it put up during his first trip across the very bad roads of that country."

One of the greatest assets of the jeep was its utility. The basic platform was so rugged and dependable that the chassis could be converted into almost anything. Designated T14 (left), this chassis could be converted into a gun carriage, an ambulance, or a command and field reconnaissance car. During the war jeeps were modified in many ways. Some were troop transports with stretched wheelbases, and others were outfitted with treads and converted into half-tracks.

The jeep's light weight and high ground clearance allowed it to be driven directly off of a landing craft. General George C. Marshall (right, top), who oversaw the 1943 landings in North Africa, is at the center of the picture. Another useful fitting on the jeep was the .50-cal machine gun (far right, top). This enabled the jeep to become a mobile anti-aircraft unit. It could protect troops in field positions and guard airfields. Even before the United States was officially involved in the war, jeeps were sent to China to help defend mainland China from the Japanese. They garnered quite a reputation as the first vehicles to pass the treacherous Burma Road.

A 50 CALIBER ANTI-TANK GUN MOUNTED ON A JEEP

39

GIVIN' 'EM HELL AT GUADALCANAL

THEY'RE doing it in the Solomons, too. Tough, tiger-like Marines and Army men, mounted in their fast, power-packed American-built Jeeps, are showing the fanatical Japs how FREE AMERICANS fight with modern American equipment.

Jeeps driven by the Willys-designed "Go-Devil" engine carried these great fighters when they crashed the shores of Guadalcanal. And Jeeps are carrying them now—in spite of hell or

high water or anything the Japs can do—carrying them swiftly and safely where no other four-wheeled fighting vehicle in any army in the world could take them.

This swift, shifty, and amazingly durable Army Jeep of ours is an American invention—created here—built here for our own army, marines and sailor men and for our Allies. Today it is unquestionably the most spectacular automotive fighting machine on every fighting front in the world, and

in training camps in America, Britain, Australia, Alaska, Iceland and elsewhere.

Willys-Overland's civilian engineers assisted the U. S. Quartermaster Corps in designing and perfecting the Jeep adopted by the U. S. Army. The amazing world-renowned "Go-Devil" engine that drives it with such power, speed, and flexibility, is an exclusive Willys-Overland development.

WILLYS-OVERLAND MOTORS, INC.

WILLYS

MOTOR CARS   TRUCKS AND JEEPS

THE GO-DEVIL ENGINE—power-heart of WILLYS CARS and all JEEPS

COLLIER'S FEBRUARY 6, 1943

THE SUN NEVER SETS ON THE FIGHTING JEEP

On every fighting front the jeep proved its versatility. Major General Courtney H. Hodges, chief of infantry, called it "the most useful motor vehicle we've ever had." As a troop carrier it took three men easily, six in a pinch. As a reconnaissance car it could go anywhere a cycle could, and a lot more places besides. Fitted with a .30- or .50-caliber gun in the back seat, the jeep became a mobile ack-ack unit. Equipped with a two-way radio together with C-rations and some blankets, it became a mobile command post. In the island-hopping Pacific war it ran supply convoys along bulldozed tracks from coral beaches to the front line. Equipped with an improvised platform, it slipped through enemy territory in order to evacuate the wounded to forward aid stations. The jeep's low silhouette enabled it to operate closer to the front line than a regular ambulance.

The jeep was outstanding at scattering clusters of planes or hauling some of them away to revetments when an alert was sounded. It could pull a 37-mm antitank gun with comparative ease. It was excellently suited for night patrol work. At one point, there was a rumor to the effect that a jeep was about to be equipped with a 75-mm gun. Since the quarter-tonner's practical load limit was no more than 800 pounds, the idea of its carrying a 3900-pound gun was absurd. Yet, the fact that the rumor received wide circulation says something about the confidence the men placed in the stout little machine.

Children everywhere were enchanted by the jeep, identifying, perhaps, with its diminutive size. In France the youngsters called it "*le petit chariot.*"

Oftentimes the jeep's hood served as a chaplain's altar, or as a card table for the more secular-minded. Suitably equipped, it could become a portable powerplant for aircraft searchlights, floodlights, shortwave radio sets, radar equipment, even welding apparatuses. It could be used as a field telephone exchange, a food supply unit for

(continued on page 44)

Willys used the jeep in almost every one of its wartime advertisements (left). These ads, accompanied by amazingly colorful illustrations, featured the jeep in harrowing situations and in some way tried to tie the jeep to Willys automobiles. However, Willys eventually got into quite a bit of trouble for linking its pre-war Americar too closely with the jeep in advertising. While it is true both were made by the same company, the only thing they had in common was their "Go-Devil" engine.

Jeeps were the preferred mode of transportation for military brass. General Douglas MacArthur (right, top), who led American troops on an island-hopping journey toward Japan, always rode in a jeep. However, generals never rode in the back, as demonstrated by MacArthur and Lt. General Mark W. Clark (right). The reason was that the front seat had more room and offered a much better ride. Leg room at the rear was cramped, and the ride would often give backseat passengers hemorrhoids. During the war jeeps were sent overseas in wooden crates. Then they were assembled on crude lines or even in fields (far right). Jeeps in crates were packed in one of two ways. Twin Unit Packs, two jeeps in one to five crates; or Single Unit Packs, one jeep in one or two crates. Often there would be contests to see which field unit could assemble its jeep the quickest. In one of the Royal Tournament Shows in Earls Court, a jeep was assembled in 3 minutes and 31 seconds.

From Where the Name JEEP?

The conventional wisdom has it that the familiar jeep got its name from its Army designation: G.P.—General Purpose. Yet, there are other stories as to how the jeep got its name.

Some say the name jeep evolved from different variations on the word itself. John Christy, writing in *Motor Trend* (December 1973) recalled "an assistant professor of military science who absolutely insisted in 1941 that the Dodge ½-ton command car was a jeep and the quarter-tonner was a peep." Also, in the November/December issue of *Special Interest Autos,* Michael Lamm elaborated on the theme: "The controversy about who named the jeep still rages. Joe Frazer, president of Willys-Overland from 1939 till '44, says he coined the word by slurring the initials G.P."

The word jeep, though, was used as early as 1914 by Army mechanics charged with testing new vehicles. Then in 1937, tractors supplied to the Army by Minneapolis Moline were called jeeps. The forerunner of the famous B-17 was also nicknamed the jeep.

© 1994 King Features, Inc.

Despite the original designation as G.P., the jeep was called many other things as well. The more printable being Bantam, Blitz Buggy, Bub, Gnat, Quad, Pygmy, G.P., Midget, and Peep. Some believe that somewhere along the way, the name Peep gave way to jeep when soldiers and test drivers began calling it the jeep among themselves.

Yet another possible origin of the name is from a very peculiar place. "Eugene, the Jeep" was a little animal who first appeared as a character in the *Popeye* comic strip in September 1936. He was created by cartoonist E. C. Segar for King Features Syndicate, Inc.

This creature was a native of the darkest part of Africa and was supposedly a fourth-dimensional animal who lived on a diet of orchids. He had the power to go back and forth between dimensions at will. Naturally, while in the fourth dimension he was invisible to all three-dimensional persons.

With the knowledge of this comic strip creature, it is not inconceivable that test driver Red Hausmann had the personality traits of 'Eugene' in mind when he first used the name "jeep." Couldn't the midget vehicle, like the little animal, get around a lot and make itself practically invisible? To be sure, the jeep would be a lucky thing to have in time of trouble.

Whatever the origins of the name, it is clear who popularized it. Katharine Hillyer, staff writer for the Washington *Daily News,* earned this distinction. One day in February 1941, Red Hausmann took Hillyer for a demonstration ride in one of the little vehicles. Their route took them through Washington's Rock Creek Park. To the amazement of all, Hausmann began to display the amazing abilities of the jeep. He made the little vehicle claw its way up hills, wade through streams, and bounce across everything in between.

After Red had wheeled the car to a stop, somebody in the crowd asked, "What's the name of that thing, mister?"

Hausmann, with his hands still resting on the steering wheel, replied proudly, "It's a jeep."

Katharine wrote "jeep" into her story, and the photographer used the term in his picture caption. On February 19, 1941, the Washington *Daily News* ran the feature. As far as the public was concerned, the name was a *fait accompli.*

Many people attribute the name "jeep" to a character in the Popeye *comic strip. Eugene the Jeep (left) first appeared in 1936 and was a fourth-dimensional dog-like creature from the darkest part of Africa. Eugene had the ability to slip in and out of rooms unnoticed and could do almost anything—similar to the wartime jeep. Wherever the name came from we may never know for sure, but when it appeared in a caption under a picture in the* Washington Daily News, *it stuck forever.*

General George S. Patton (right, top) rode roughshod over Africa, Italy, and Europe in a jeep. He was known for his tenacity and stubborn will—two things that made the jeep famous. Pictured in Italy, General Marshall (far right, top) takes part in a liberation parade. The tall metal pole on the front of the jeep was added to prevent decapitation of the passengers; one of the tricks played by German and Japanese troops was to string a wire across the road at the appropriate height and wait for a jeep to come by. Jeeps were shipped to Africa (right, bottom) to help defeat Field Marshal Rommel's tank armies. Under the cover of darkness jeeps would speed behind enemy lines and destroy supply trucks attempting to hook up with Rommel's tanks.

front-line fighters, or a medical unit for front-line first-aid. *Popular Mechanics* reported in the November 1942 issue, "In Australia our soldiers were given the difficult task of laying an underground cable at an aerodrome without interrupting field operations. By pick and shovel it would have taken several days. But the jeep sped in, hitched to a plow, and the ditch was dug at ten miles an hour. Behind it came another jeep, towing a reel of cable, and next a third jeep pulling a roller that covered the cable and flattened the ground. The job was finished in two hours while Australians gaped."

Fitted with flanged steel wheels, jeeps were used on railroads in virtually every theater of operations. In the Philippines a little quarter-tonner pulled a 52-ton supply train for 19 miles, averaging 22 miles per hour. In France, they ran along the main rail lines, while in Australia they were used as switch engines.

Easily transported by amphibious landing craft and by air, the jeep went everywhere. It was reported that a jeep was the first motor vehicle to conquer the steep climbs and dense jungles of a new India-China route supplanting the Burma Road. At Rangoon, as the Japanese advanced, hundreds of China-bound jeeps stood on the dock, awaiting delivery to *Generalissimo* Chiang Kai-shek. To keep those jeeps from falling into enemy hands, authorities turned them over to British troops and to anyone else who would drive them north. The story is told by A. Wade Wells:

"They slogged through glue-like rice paddies on liaison missions; they yanked stalled trucks and guns out of ditches; they carried machine-gunners to front-line positions; and, peppered with sniper bullet dents, they came back for more. They carried panic-stricken women and children to points of comparative safety. In short, they made history."

Altogether, the jeep's performance bordered on the incredible, prompting one

Jeeps weren't the only transportation the military had. Dodge/Plymouth converted their Power Wagon to military use (left, top). Dodge also built a specific ½-ton Command Car for the Army. This vehicle, also four-wheel drive, was developed simultaneously with the jeep. However, it had Selective four-wheel drive. This permitted good off-road traction and sustained high-speed highway travel.

Two main figures of the British and U.S. military were Field Marshal Bernard Montgomery and four-star General Dwight D. Eisenhower. Montgomery led the British charge from Africa to Italy and across Europe to Berlin. Franklin D. Roosevelt (President of the United States from 1933 until his death in 1945), though stricken with polio, was never one to hide behind a desk. In January 1943, he met with the other leaders of Allied nations in a conference at Casablanca (right).

high Army officer to comment that the quarter-tonner could "do anything except swim or climb a greased pole." War correspondent Ernie Pyle once observed, "It does everything. It goes everywhere. It's as faithful as a dog, as strong as a mule, and as agile as a goat. It constantly carries twice what it was designed for, and still keeps on going. It doesn't even ride so badly after you get used to it."

Stories of the jeep's wartime feats have long since become a part of American folklore. There was, for instance, an incident that took place in 1944 during the Battle of the Bulge. A Belgian sentry at a checkpoint stopped a jeep carrying three men wearing U. S. Army uniforms. Speaking German, he immediately demanded their surrender. Asked afterwards how he knew they were Germans, the Belgian replied, "One, the colonel was riding in back and the aide was driving. The real American colonel drives and the aide rides next to him. Besides, the American colonel never rides in back because it gives him—how you say?—the piles!"

One of the more hair-raising jeep stories was reported by Homer Bogart, of the New York *Herald Tribune*. It took place during General Douglas MacArthur's march on Manila. A patrol consisting of one light tank, six jeeps mounting machine guns, and a half-track was driving south on the Manila Road, headed for Angeles, some 48 miles from Manila.

"I rode in the half-track," Bogart reported, "with the tank and two jeeps out in front and the other jeeps bringing up the rear. A short distance beyond Mavalacat airfield, with its heap of wrecked Japanese planes we passed the front line and sped on across a no-man's land of dried-up rice paddies and occasional clusters of grass huts.

"'O.K.' shouted Corporal Bob Lucked, of St. Louis. 'From here on it's all Nips! Shoot anything that pops out!'

". . . At the edge of Quail the road curves gently. Around the bend we saw the

Predictably, the enemy undertook to emulate the jeep. The most notable creation was the Kübelwagen (left, top) from Germany. This vehicle was basically a version of the existing Volkswagen; however, it lacked the jeep's four-wheel drive, and its engine generated only a fraction of the "Go-Devil's" power. Captured Kübelwagens paled when compared to the jeep. The Germans did have a winner with Schwimmwagen (left, middle and bottom). Model Type 128 performed as the U.S. Army hoped their aqueous version of the jeep—the seep—would. The Schwimmwagen had a capacity of four riders and could travel on land or water.

As the jeep traveled across Europe, it was put to use in many ways—as its general purpose designation indicated. Medics soon found that the jeep, with minor modification, could be converted into a field ambulance and a Red Cross unit (right, top). Jeeps were also converted into highly mobile reconnaissance and radio units (right), capable of traveling into enemy locations, reporting troop strength, and returning unnoticed. Replacing the horse-and-mule cart was another mission of the jeep, one it did particularly well, without the oats, mess, and stubbornness.

A salute to the fighting men of the United States Army Ground Forces

HEROIC OFFICERS DARE DEATH FOR MEN

(A true incident of the invasion of North Africa)

WILLYS BUILT **JEEP**

lead tank come to an abrupt halt. Its crew radioed back a message: 'Roadblock 200 feet ahead.'

"A stout red-faced second lieutenant hopped into the half-track and grabbed the radio mouthpiece. 'That block wasn't there yesterday,' he grumbled. 'Send jeep five ahead to investigate.'

". . . Then it happened. We saw the tank lurch in a cloud of black smoke and dust. Its radio went dead.

". . . Instantly, from every thicket and shed in front and on either side came the whine of snipers' bullets and the sharp explosions of grenades. A mortar shell burst 100 feet behind the half-track.

"There was a frantic moment of indecision. The red-faced lieutenant wanted to pull out and bring up mortars. Sergeant Ralph Nyquist, the radio operator, who hailed from Marquette, Michigan, was for racing up the road and saving the tank crew.

"'Well, hell,' shouted the lieutenant, 'get that No. 5 jeep up there. It's their job!'

"And he waved frantically at the three men in the jeep, who had no armor protection, urging them into the enemy fire."

Incredibly, Bogart's story has a happy ending. While the jeeps covered the action with a curtain of machine-gun fire, the half-track moved up to the stricken tank, and the entire crew was saved.

Not that the jeep didn't have its share of shortcomings. The hand brake, for instance, was all but useless. Also, Ernie Pyle's comment aside, no matter how one sat, it was impossible to stay comfortable for very long. Only two positions were at all feasible: either bolt upright or slouched down to the middle of one's spine. Either way, the ride tended to encourage the development of hemorrhoids. Army medics referred to the malady as "jeep disease."

Given the jeep's lively performance and remarkable maneuverability, there was always the temptation to push it beyond any sane limits. Mishaps were not uncommon.

(continued on page 52)

Americans received news of the war from radio, Movietone news-reels, newspapers, and wartime ads. The ads were by far the most colorful and patriotic medium (left, top). Satirical cartoonist Bill Mauldin summed up the feelings of millions of soldiers across the globe in the depiction of a sergeant putting his wounded jeep out of its misery (left, bottom). The image became famous and was carried in newspapers and magazines around the world.

Ford called its version of the jeep the GPW Many people thought GP stood for General Purpose, but this is not so. G was for Government, and P was for 80-inch wheelbase reconnaissance car (the W stood for Willys model). After development testing of the jeep was completed, the U.S. government supposedly standardized the jeep, so that all parts were interchangeable. However, the Ford and Willys versions differ in many ways and can be easily distinguished by several features; most apparent are the frame crossmembers. Willys models had round ones, and Ford's were square. Hence, the "Willys round, Ford square" saying common to army quartermasters and mechanics. The cover mounted above the dash (far right) was for a rifle. It kept the gun within easy reach of the driver but kept dirt and water off.

The Seep

It was an intriguing concept: a seagoing jeep. The Army had flirted for years with the idea of an amphibious vehicle. Then during World War II several types were actually built—among them the GP-A: General Purpose—Amphibious.

Designed by the Marmon-Herrington Company in cooperation with the boat-building firm of Sparkman and Stephens, the GP-A (nicknamed the "Seep," or seagoing jeep) was based on the GPW—Ford's version of the familiar World War II jeep. Several distinct hulls were built and tested, first in scale model form and then at full size. Somehow, while this was going on there was no jeep available for use in the experiments. All the engineers had to work from was a table of specifications, and those specs understated the jeep's weight by about 30 percent. This factor had a serious negative effect upon the performance of the end product.

When the pilot vehicle was ready, tests were run in the Huron River, at Dearborn. Ranking officers from the various branches of the service made comments, although adequate endurance and performance tests had never been made. There were those who expressed concern over this seemingly premature standardization of the design. However, it was February 1942 by this time, two months *after* the Japanese attack upon Pearl Harbor. The need for water-going jeeps was declared by field generals—General George Marshall in particular—to be urgent. Besides,

Ford was pressuring the government for a contract, even suggesting that production facilities might not be available unless the project got under way immediately.

The potential seemed enormous. *Popular Science*, describing the Seep as "essentially a specially equipped jeep with a steel hull built around it," noted, "This seagoing jeep operates on either land or water, and can pass from one medium to the other with a single minor adjustment by the driver, during which the car doesn't have to stop. Its possibilities as a reconnaissance vehicle are startling. With it an advance patrol can creep up back roads to a river, scout along the shore, cross at any point to investigate the enemy's territory. It can race back with its information about as fast as any other jeep—upwards of 60 miles an hour on good roads. Twenty of them can ferry 100 fully armed men across water to strike the enemy from the rear."

Controls were identical to those of the land-based jeeps, with the addition of two more handles, located just behind the transmission lever. One of these engaged the propeller, while the other operated the bilge pump.

A letter of intent was issued on April 11, 1942, calling for an initial production run of 5000 of the little amphibians, and the project got under way. Then, suddenly, after only 12,778 had been built, production was halted.

Why? What had gone wrong? The Germans

were apparently doing well enough with their *Schwimmwagen,* though their seriously underpowered *Kübelwagen* was a bust. Denfield and Fry, quoting from a 1971 Army Materiel Command pamphlet, explain: "Insufficient testing of early production models, inadequate inspection and supervision of production, failure to provide for a continuing development program, failure to provide adequate training, and, particularly, failure to consult the using services before production began resulted in early rejection of the project as a technical and tactical failure."

Civilians, however, appear to have seen no end of possibilities in the GP-A. Especially Ben Carlin, an Australian engineer, who made a nine-year, round-the-world trip in one of them. According to Bart H. Vanderveen, writing in *Challenge,* "Carlin first saw the vehicle when he was in the forces in India, and said, 'You know, with a bit of titivation you could go round the world in one of those things.'"

After demobilization, Carlin went to the United States, where he purchased a GP-A at an Army surplus sale. He named it, appropriately enough, *Half Safe.* After spending considerable time adapting the amphib to his purposes, Carlin, with his American wife, set out from Halifax, Nova Scotia, in July 1950. As Vanderveen recounts the story, "They crossed the Atlantic, sailing via Madeira to Cap Juby, Spanish Sahara. From there they drove and sailed by way of Gibraltar

and eight West European countries to London. There, during a two-year stay, the vehicle was extensively rebuilt and modified for the second lap—London, India, Australia, Japan, San Francisco, New York."

Meanwhile, Elinore, Carlin's wife, jumped ship in India and made her way back to the United States, where she filed for divorce. Carlin flew to his hometown of Perth, Australia, where he recruited a young yachtsman, and the voyage continued. However, Ben Carlin evidently had an irascible disposition. Upon reaching Kagoshima, Japan, in late 1956, his young helper also took his departure.

Early in 1957, accompanied this time by an American named Boye Lafayette DeMente, Carlin took to the sea once more. Four months later, *Half Safe* put in at Anchorage, Alaska. DeMente, who had quite enough of Carlin's nasty temper, flew home to Phoenix. Sometime later he learned that Ben Carlin had made it to New York, completing his globe-circling tour.

Accompanied by *Half Safe,* Carlin later took to the lecture circuit, eventually returning to Perth, where he worked at a yacht harbor until his death.

Too small and too slow to be much of a boat, yet too big and too clumsy to serve as a jeep, the GP-A appears to have represented the worst of both worlds. One wonders if it might have been more successful had normal development and testing procedures been permitted to take place.

The GP-A (left, above), or ***seep,*** *was designed by the Marmon-Herrington company to fill the U.S. military's need for a light amphibious vehicle. In April of 1942, an order for 5000 was placed, and eventually 12,778 were produced. The vehicle was not very stable in the water, however. Like the jeep, the seep was also Lend-Leased to the Russians and saw extensive action on the Eastern Front. Later, the Soviets built a similar vehicle on a GAZ-69 chassis designated the MAV (GAZ-46).*

• • In every country in the world • • • to millions of people • • • "JEEP" means WILLYS • •

VIVE LES AMERICAINS! VIVE LA FRANCE! VIVE LE JEEP!

A WORD PICTURE OF THE HOUR OF LIBERATION IN ORLEANS, 1944

Willys *Builds the Mighty* 'Jeep'

"I'll be darned! Here's one wot wuz wrecked in combat."

Bill Mauldin, in one of his priceless Willie and Joe cartoons, depicts his two GIs surveying wrecked jeeps in a junkyard. The caption reads, "I'll be darned! Here's one wot wuz wrecked in combat."

Experienced soldiers appreciated the fact that the jeep would go places that a mule would not. "Lots of times a mule will balk if he doesn't think his leader is using good judgment," one GI observed. "But a jeep will always try!"

Predictably, the enemy undertook to emulate the little general-purpose machine, most notably with the *Kübelwagen* from Germany. Yet, this militarized version of the Volkswagen lacked the jeep's four-wheel drive, and its engine generated only a fraction of the "Go-Devil's" power. So it was never much of a success.

Sometimes, military exploits involving the ubiquitous jeep seem, in retrospect, to have been downright foolhardy. There were, for instance, the lightning strikes led by a British officer, Major David Sterling. One of these attacks was directed against a German airfield in North Africa. Under Sterling's leadership, a party consisting of 18 jeeps and their crews made its way through the desert, somehow escaping detection, until the perimeter of the airfield was reached. Then, in flying wedge formation and with machine guns blazing, the jeeps roared down upon the base, catching the Germans totally unaware.

In a matter of seconds the jeeps were gone. They vanished into the desert, leaving behind them an airfield littered with the wreckage of 25 aircraft destroyed and 12 more seriously damaged.

As far as the North Africa campaign is concerned, it is to Britain's Major General (later Field Marshal) Bernard Montgomery to whom much of the credit must go for the defeat of the brilliant Field Marshal Erwin Rommel. Montgomery knew the value of the jeep and made good use of it. Once, in an effort to minimize casualties, he employed several jeeps to put Rommel's tanks out of action.

As the war drew to a close, Willys attempted to make their name synonymous with the jeep (left, top). No longer were there pictures of the pre-war Americar; now it was just Willys and the jeep. Willys would begin to sell the CJ-2A even before the war was over; it became the first civilian jeep. In another Bill Mauldin comic (left, bottom), the jeep's instability became the source of humor. This was almost unjust because the jeep often was asked to perform tasks it was never designed to do.

Some jeeps saw duty as railyard locomotives. The little ¼-tonner could pull up to 20,000 pounds when fitted with rail wheels. Brigadier General C.W. Connell is at the wheel in this shot from an air depot in Australia (right, top). Americans serving abroad were occasionally treated with visits from celebrities like Bing Crosby (far right, top) in U.S.O. shows. During the harsh winters in Europe, the rugged jeeps were often fitted with chains to help pull through and over the snow and ice. Convoys were often backed up for miles when a two-wheel-drive heavy truck became stuck (right).

"Run it up th' mountain agin, Joe. It ain't hot enough."

"Why ya lookin' so sad? I got out of it okay."

Circling wide under cover of darkness, the small fleet of jeeps made its way deep behind the German lines. Traveling by night and lying low during the daylight hours, they came to a point on a Nazi supply artery where an ambush appeared to be feasible. The target was a group of fuel tanks carrying gasoline for Rommel's tanks.

There the jeep force waited for the approaching convoy to rumble into its section of road. When the trucks reached a given point, the jeeps drove at them at high speed. Weaving in and out of the string of vehicles, the jeeps left a trail of havoc, the entire line exploding into flame as they passed. Before any effective action could be taken against the jeeps, they were gone into the night.

The following morning, the tanks arrived at their appointed station, expecting to refuel from supplies that should have arrived during the night. As the result of the hit-and-run raid by Montgomery's jeeps, fuel was in such short supply that there wasn't even enough remaining to permit their retreat, much less to check the Allied advance.

Thanks to the destruction of many aircraft and the immobilization of the tanks, Germany lost the crucial battle of El Alamein, a critical turning point in the North Africa war. Two and a half weeks after this Allied victory Montgomery was knighted by King George VI.

The jeep had proved its worth. Squat, stubby, and so ugly as to be almost cute, this remarkable product of the combined genius of Karl Probst, Barney Roos, and no telling how many others was, in Ernie Pyle's words, a "divine instrument of wartime locomotion." Lieutenant Colonel Manuel Conley summed up the record of the wartime jeep: "Versatile, reliable, and virtually indestructible, this magic motor vehicle bounced to glory as one of World War II's most enduring legends."

Little did anyone know that the successes the jeep had in war were the first of many to come.

By the end of the war the jeep had become more than a machine—it had become a companion to the soldier. Bill Mauldin tried to capture this sentiment in his cartoons (left), which originally ran in Stars and Stripes. An example of this love for jeeps could be seen at Stockton (California) High School, where students raised enough money to buy 275 jeeps for the Army. On the dash of each was a plaque that asked soldiers to report the fate of their vehicles. Eventually, one of these jeeps made its way back to Stockton and is on display there.

Many MB-model Jeeps (right, top) were fitted with .30-cal machine guns. The MBs were manufactured by Willys-Overland in Toledo, Ohio. Willys chief engineer Barney Roos's four-cylinder engine (right, top) had an F-head design and offered 60 horsepower and 105 pounds-feet of torque. This engine was used by Willys before the war and would carry on for many years in many forms. Even tiny Crosley got into the jeep act when they developed a prototype (far right) for Army testing during the war. It was turned down, but a variant appeared in 1950 as the Crosley FarmORoad.

Postwar Plans for Willys: 1945-52

ven before the Japanese attack on Pearl Harbor plunged the United States into the thick of World War II, the jeep's service with the Allied forces was making it almost legendary. This fact was not lost upon the astute Ward Canaday, Willys-Overland's chairman and principal stockholder. The fresh new image that Willys had been vainly seeking with the Americar was being handed to the company on the proverbial silver platter.

Looking ahead, Canaday began to visualize the jeep in the postwar world and to share that vision with the public. To get the ball rolling, he hired a well-known artist, I. B. Hazelton, to do a series of 24 paintings depicting the jeep in a variety of settings. In many of the pictures, the jeep was shown in the midst of battle. In other cases, the artist displayed the jeep in a number of non-combatant roles ranging from snowplow to fire-fighter to farmer's jack-of-all-trades. Advertisements based on these paintings were so effective that *Life* magazine displayed some of them in a feature article.

Another famous advertisement of the period presented the Americar as "the jeep in civvies." Willys got in a spot of trouble over that one, for in truth the only thing the Americar had in common with the jeep was its engine. But nobody could question the ad's effectiveness. Although Willys was eventually forced to pull the ads, the damage was done: Even though Willys was not the sole producer of jeeps, America began to think of them as "the jeep company."

Still, the most effective advertising the jeep received during the war years came at

no cost to its manufacturer, in the form of news releases. A human interest story from overseas, for instance, was accompanied by photographs showing some GI's with their jeep, helping an English farmer by pulling his mowing machine, rake, and loader. On the other side of the world, wide coverage was given to the jeep's role in laying underground cables linking widely separated airfields in Australia. The implications for possible postwar civilian uses of the jeep were too obvious to require editorial comment.

In December 1943, George W. Ritter, vice president and general counsel of Willys-Overland, was asked by Alabama Congressman Carter Manasco to provide advance information regarding the little quarter-tonner's possible conversion to civilian life. Ritter was only too happy to oblige. (One might logically have expected, by the way, that such a request would have come from a representative of Willys's home state of Ohio, rather than someone from the deep South. However, Congressman Manasco happened to chair the committee that was dealing with postwar pre-planning.)

In a lengthy and detailed reply, Ritter stated that although his company was highly enthusiastic about the postwar potential of the jeep, to be fully suitable for civilian use the military model would require considerable modification. Among the recommendations he outlined for the Manasco Committee were the following:

• Inclusion of a power takeoff, in order to supply power for a belt pulley attachment. Thus the jeep could be efficiently operated as a stationary power unit.

• More suitable gear ratios for both

Many people wondered what the U.S. military would do with the thousands of leftover World War II jeeps, but Willys had an even bigger question: What would they do after the wartime contract was up? Stylist Brooks Stevens circulated an idea called the Victory Car (right, top), based on the chassis and running gear of the jeep. However, chairman Ward Canaday felt that Willys's strength lay in the four-wheel-drive market. Canaday also felt that he should diversify within that market and not spend what little capital the company had on an untested small car. By 1948 the Willys stable included the first all-steel wagon, a pickup truck, a sedan delivery, and the playful Jeepster (right, bottom).

THE VICTORY CAR
A DESIGN FOR
AN ALL-WHEEL
DRIVE CIVILIAN
'JEEP'
SCALE: 2"=1'   APRIL 1942

transmission and transfer case, in order to permit both low-speed pulling of heavy loads and highway speeds as high as 60 miles per hour.

• More effective cooling, for continuous low-gear operation.

• A larger-diameter clutch, to cope with increased starting loads and other circumstances creating excessive strain.

Ritter went on to point out that an adequate network of service facilities would be required if the jeep was to be fully practicable for civilian use. Implicit here was the admission that Willys-Overland's prewar dealer organization was sparse, ill-equipped, and certainly not trained in matters pertaining to the jeep. What was needed was a brand new dealer network, with well-trained personnel and an adequate stock of spare parts.

Meanwhile, *Popular Science* magazine announced in the August 1943 issue, "Cash Prizes for your ideas on Peacetime Jobs for Jeeps." The money involved was almost ludicrous, even by the standards of the time. First prize was $100; second, $50; third, $25; and five prizes of $5 each. Even so, there were nearly 1200 entries. "So numerous and so meritorious were the ideas submitted," declared the editors, "that *Popular Science* increased the number of prizes from eight to 11 and included 11 honorable mentions."

Based on the replies they received, the editors concluded that "the jeep's reward for its part in winning the war is likely to be, for the most part, a lifetime of work down on the farm." For more than a third of the respondents, including the winner of the $100 First Prize, "thought the proper postwar place for the jeep was on the farm, where its chores would take in about everything now performed by man, beast, or machine."

Winner of the top award was R. W. Radelet, of Vancouver, British Columbia, who submitted an elaborate drawing of jeeps performing a variety of tasks in a rural setting: pulling implements such as the mower, rake,

harrow, or plow; serving as a stationary power source; acting as a light delivery vehicle or as personnel transport; and even serving as the base for an extension platform from which trees might be sprayed.

State agricultural departments and colleges and universities from coast to coast showed a keen interest in the peacetime possibilities of the versatile little machine. Washington State University even published a 20-page monograph describing various farm uses for the military version. Other experiments took place in a variety of forest, farm, government, and industrial settings. Again, it was a cost-free publicity bonanza for Willys-Overland as the company prepared for the conversion to a peacetime economy.

Hitler's suicide on April 30, 1945, was followed on May 2 by the surrender of Germany. Now the full force of the Allied war effort could be turned against Japan. Although few people were then aware of the existence of the atomic bomb (and even those few probably failed to fully appreciate its enormous destructive potential), it was obvious that the end of the war was within sight.

On July 31 the government contract with Ford ended, and the jeep reverted exclusively to Willys-Overland. Thirteen days earlier the company had dramatically announced its first peacetime model, the CJ-2A. A demonstration was held that day, for the benefit of the press. Charles Sorensen, vice chairman by then of the Willys-Overland board of directors, hosted the event at his New Hudson, Michigan, research farm.

The CJ-2A was easy enough to distinguish from the MB. Headlights were seven inches in diameter, instead of six. There was a tailgate at the rear, and the spare tire was moved to the right side. An automatic windshield wiper replaced the hand-operated number on the passenger's side. There was even a remote gas filler. (On the military model, the tank was located—like that of the Model T Ford—under the seat; and

Early design studies for the Jeepster and the Panel Delivery shared many common components with the wartime jeep (top, left and right). The most obvious was the familiar grille. However, there was a reason for this. Willys was afraid that no sheetmetal company would be able to supply them with complex-curved body panels, so special care was taken to develop a design that was very easy to stamp. Brooks Stevens handled almost all of the design work during those postwar years. His first creation was the all-steel wagon that became available in 1946 (right, middle). It was laid out in such a way as to require so little draw that even a refrigerator manufacturer could produce the stampings. The two-tone body styling and body molding gave the look of wood side trim.

the driver was forced to debark in order to take on fuel.)

Other, less obvious modifications were basically those suggested by George Ritter to the Manasco Committee, back in 1943. Gear ratios were changed in order to facilitate low-speed lugging, as well as to increase highway speed. Combustion chambers were redesigned for greater pulling power, and radiator shrouding was improved in the interest of better cooling. The frame was reinforced for greater rigidity. The clutch was strengthened, and a higher-capacity generator was used.

Several concessions were made to the driver's comfort, something Ritter had evidently overlooked: Springs were softened a bit, more effective shock absorbers were fitted, and new and more comfortable seats were installed. Though the jeep still did not offer a car-like ride, it was certainly better than the MB.

Like its Army counterpart, the civilian jeep was a bare bones vehicle; but a number of desirable options were available at very reasonable prices:

Drawbar	$6.91
Pintle hook	4.01
Rear power takeoff	90.67
Front power takeoff	24.44
Pulley and pulley drive	56.28
Radiator brush guard	4.11
Governor	27.21
Front top	51.05
Rear top	28.44
Right-hand front seat	10.51
2-passenger rear seat	12.96
Heater	17.41
Spare tire and tube	13.76

By far the most expensive "extra" was a hydraulic lift, priced at $225. Perhaps the most critical accessory was the belt-driven governor. Controlled from the instrument panel, this device permitted the regulation of engine speeds from 1000 to 2600 rpm in increments of 200 revolutions.

These improvements and additions made the jeep all the more suitable to civilian uses. According to *Popular Science*, "tests

Even before the war drew to a close, Willys unveiled the CJ-2A— the first civilian jeep. The postwar ads centered around the versitility of the jeep, now called the Universal (left). Exaggerated wartime stories had given the jeep an almost mystical aura, and Willys hoped that reputation would carry over into its civilian model.

In 1948 several changes were made to the Jeep Station Wagon. The biggest was the addition of four-wheel drive (right). Barney Roos's more powerful L-head six-cylinder engine was also put into the Wagon in 1948. Inside, the cabin was austere and functional. All of the seats, save the driver's, were removable, creating a large, flat loading area (right, bottom right). Exterior colors remained the same, though Willys added the Station Sedan with a single-tone exterior and a basket-weave trim along the sides.

with the new model indicate a sustained drawbar pull of 1200 pounds may be achieved, with reserve for grades and irregular soil conditions. On the highway the jeep will pull a trailed load of 5500 pounds with adequate reserve power for steep grades."

Power still came from Barney Roos's durable L-head "Go-Devil" engine. The wheelbase was 80 inches, and the CJ-2A was as simple to service and repair as the wartime MB had been. Best of all, for those lucky enough to be able to buy one in 1945, the jeep was a bargain at $1090—plus $46.53 federal excise tax.

The civilian edition was an unqualified success, incorporating all of the modifications outlined by George Ritter to Congressman Manasco's committee—and more. A. Wade Wells described it as "The first vehicle to combine the basic functions of the tractor, light truck, passenger conveyance, and independent power unit," adding that "the new jeep not only operated all sorts of agricultural implements but performed innumerable farm tasks in which stationary power was required. As a utility car, it sped across cow pastures, up hills and down gullies with the same effortless ease its military prototype had displayed on the battlefield. It plowed, hauled grain, pulled the disk and harrow, filled a silo, threshed wheat, and, in general, performed virtually every farm task requiring either mobility or power.

"It was no test model of the peacetime jeep which was presented in New Hudson in the demonstration before the press," Wells continued. "The vehicles which observers watched and operated represented patient and diligent research, the end product of countless experiments not only with the military jeep but with the car improved for agricultural and industrial use.

"For example, in Florida, models of the peacetime jeep had been used to harvest oranges and grapefruit. In this case, its convenient size enabled it to pass between two rows of trees with low-hanging limbs under which larger trucks could not go.

"In Arkansas, the improved jeep proved highly effective in the rice fields, taking in its stride the dikes and levees which cross the fields in irrigated lanes.

"In Washington and Oregon, forest rangers found the civilian jeep ideal for rough terrain otherwise inaccessible, and an ideal conveyance for crews of men, tools, and other supplies.

"On a New York farm, the peacetime jeep maintained equilibrium in difficult hillside plowing. Here, the 4-wheel drive with the front wheels pulling resulted in the necessary increased surface traction."

At the Doughoregan Manor farm in Maryland, a prime location for factory-sponsored tests, Wells observed a jeep attached to a three-section, heavy-duty, spring-tooth harrow. A team of two heavy draft horses would have been required to pull the implement. Yet the jeep was able to do the job, operating at a speed of four miles per hour, 10 hours a day, without overheating the engine. Indeed, the farm manager found that the ability of the jeep engine to provide high torque at low rpm's actually exceeded that of the tractor, especially in driving slow-motion machinery such as water pumps.

One of the better features of the postwar jeep was an optional governor fitted to the engine, so that sudden changes in the load, such as might result from wheel spin, could not cause the engine revolutions to go beyond an acceptable limit.

The little vehicle's usefulness was not restricted to the farm. On the golf course, it pulled gang mowers at a brisk speed, resulting in a substantial savings in man hours. Its pumping ability made it a favorite with rural firefighters. An air compressor fitted at the back made it suitable for spraying paint. Like its wartime counterpart, it could tow aircraft into position and perform other airport tasks. And an optional winch extended its usefulness even further.

By November 1945, Austria's Steyr

A Postwar Americar?

During 1946, several "teaser" ads appeared in trade journals, accompanied in some cases by photographs of a prototype Willys sedan. *Fortune* magazine, catering then, as now, to the carriage trade, carried a description of the new car, supposedly intended for 1947 introduction.

This new Willys-that-was-not-to-be promised, thanks largely to the genius of Barney Roos, to be a very interesting automobile. It wasn't particularly long on good looks. Some observers, in fact, found it downright homely, which perhaps explains why Willys was quick to note that the front-end styling of the prototype was subject to change. Company president Jim Mooney, a recent recruit from General Motors, defended the new model's conservative appearance in a statement that represented a sharp departure from the typical GM philosophy: "We'll not get out a trick or miracle car," Mooney declared in a shy, smooth voice. "It will be stylish without pretending to be fashionable. We think a car is too expensive an item to follow ever changing fashions. . . . The average family can't take it very long if you go on creating false obsolescence in their cars."

There was nothing unusual about the dimensions of the proposed new Willys. A wheelbase of 104 inches was announced—same as the prewar Americar. A standard tread was used, again like the Americar. But there was to be a brand new engine, the first six cylinder to be offered by Willys-Overland since 1932—and at 148.5 cubic inches the smallest six then available in this country. Rated at 72 horsepower, the new mill was projected to weigh only five pounds more than the 63-horsepower Willys four.

One of Barney Roos's primary objectives in the design of the stillborn postwar Willys was to endow it with comfortable seating and an easy ride. Given the technology of the time, one would not have expected to find these qualities in a light (under 2500 pound), short-wheelbase automobile. Roos, in a departure from tradition, solved the problem by designing the little car with independent suspension all around, a concept that wouldn't come into widespread use for more than a generation. Up front he employed a system similar to the "Planar" suspension he had developed for Studebaker back in the 1930s. A German-style swing axle was used at the rear.

For seating comfort, the new Willys prototype used chair-height seats (three abreast in front, two in the rear), providing ample leg room. Floors

were recessed, after the fashion of the 1948 "Step-down" Hudson, giving plenty of head room while retaining a low profile.

A two-door configuration was planned, supposedly because the 104-inch wheelbase was too short for four doors. The doors were unusually wide, and a pivot arrangement under the right-front seat made for easy entry and egress. Probably the real reason for the two-door layout had to do with minimizing tooling costs, since a coupe and even a convertible could be produced from the same stampings.

Of course, this intriguing, highly advanced little automobile was never produced. Perhaps Willys was having trouble, as Brooks Stevens has hinted, finding someone to build the bodies, given the constraints of the postwar world. Or possibly it was just that the factory was busy beyond anyone's expectations, building the Jeep and its various derivatives. Maybe the industry-wide shortage of sheet steel had something to do with the matter. Whatever the reason, the car would soon be forgotten, and several years later Willys would release the handsome Aero-Willys.

During the war, Willys president Jim Mooney pushed for a postwar model similar to the Americar. Styled by Brooks Stevens, the new car was a handsome one with very conservative lines (top). Mechanically It was to receive a 148-cid six-cylinder engine (the smallest six in production at that time) and independent suspension at all four wheels. Because of the independent suspension, the interior was roomier than expected, and a recessed floor allowed good head room and a low profile. The dash still placed the gauges at the center, but at least there was more chrome than on the Wagons.

autoplant was turning out "winterized" jeeps—military jobs fitted with a Steyr-devised enclosure to protect their occupants from the weather. Production was 25 per day.

Meanwhile, Willys-Overland was occupied pulling off what *Motor Trend* has described as "the commercial coup of the decade and perhaps the century by simply registering the [Jeep] name as a trademark of the Willys-Overland Corporation."

The CJ-2A remained in production until 1949, by which time the base price had risen to $1270—about the same as a Chevrolet half-ton pickup. But early that year the second postwar Jeep appeared: the CJ-3A. (By this time, the name "Jeep" had become a registered trademark of Willys-Overland, so henceforth the name will be capitalized.)

Virtually identical in appearance to the CJ-2A and offered at the same price, the 3A may be distinguished by its one-piece windshield. More important, however, were revisions which strengthened the transmission and transfer case. Passenger accommodations were altered slightly, providing more leg and knee room in front at the expense of the back seat passengers; and the overall height of the vehicle (windshield up) was increased from 64 to 66⅜ inches.

A sales slump occurred in 1949, and once again—as in prewar days—Willys was

losing money: $900,000, to be specific, between October 1949 and March 1950. Evidently, the primary cause of the problem was a drop in farm income, for sales of both CJs and trucks fell sharply during this period while those of the Station Wagon increased by nearly one-third.

By this time, many of the Jeeps being used by the U. S. military were showing their age, and the Army asked Willys-Overland to design a new vehicle to meet its current needs. The result, the replacement for the wartime MB, was the Model MC. Basically, it was a military version of the then-current civilian CJ-3A. Known in the Army as the M38, the MC was identical in size to the civilian unit, but it incorporated a number of changes for military purposes. Body and chassis parts were heavier, for instance, and waterproofed 24-volt electrics replaced the CJ-3A's 6-volt system. A unique vent tube arrangement connected the engine, transmission, transfer case, and fuel tank to the air cleaner, permitting these components to be vented even if the Jeep were completely submerged.

More than 60,000 MCs were built for the armed forces between 1949 and 1952. It was during this time—on June 25, 1950—that North Korean Communist forces invaded South Korea, presumably on the mistaken assumption that the United States and its allies had no particular interest in that part of the world. American reaction, however, was one of outrage. President Truman ordered General Douglas MacArthur's Eighth Army, then stationed in Japan as an occupying force, to the port of Pusan, on the southern tip of the Korean peninsula. Action was authorized by the United Nations Security Council, and once again the United States found itself at war.

Predictably, Jeeps were once again in the thick of battle. Television fans will recall that the little quarter-tonners appeared as "supporting actors" in nearly every episode of the popular series *M*A*S*H*. However,

(continued on page 68)

Because of the Station Wagon's conservative styling and lackluster engine, ads focused on the Wagon's utility and economy (left). The addition of four-wheel drive in 1948 was an additional selling point.

The CJ-2A had many civilian uses. One of the most popular was its conversion to a light fire truck (right). The four-wheel-drive CJ was ideal for rural applications. With its four-wheel drive, the CJ could go places a conventional pumper could not. A power-take-off, mounted at the front of the engine, ran the water pump (right, bottom right). The trailer at the rear could carry water or an extra hose, making the CJ fire truck a stand-alone unit.

Brooks Stevens Recalls
the JEEP Station Sedan

Nowadays, the name Brooks Stevens conjures up visions of the exotic Excalibur that he designed. But one of the cleverest of Stevens's concoctions, and certainly one of the most significant in terms of its impact upon the automobile industry, was the Jeep Station Wagon, which he developed for Willys-Overland as that firm's first postwar passenger car. Plymouth's claims notwithstanding, it was this little car that was the first all-steel wagon.

Several years ago, writer Arch Brown was privileged to interview Brooks Stevens. He asked him whose idea the Jeep Station Wagon represented.

Stevens: It was mine, entirely. This was when ["Cast-Iron Charlie"] Sorensen came to Willys-Overland from Ford, and Barney Roos was executive vice president in charge of engineering. My firm had been retained there already, from '42 on, as post-war consultants on the passenger car-to-be. In fact, we had several passenger cars up to full-size in plaster under the numerous presidents that had preceded Sorensen.

When Sorensen was to come to Willys, Barney Roos called me in Milwaukee and asked me to come to Toledo. He said, "It's all over. Tomorrow we're all going to get the pink slip. Sorensen's coming in as president. He'll bring his whole crew from Ford, and we'll all be gone."

I went over to Research and Development the day after I arrived and stayed there until midmorning or later. Finally the door opened and Sorensen came through. A marvelous-looking man. Thinking back on it, he couldn't have been very old.

Brown: What year was this?

Stevens: 1944. He had iron gray hair, a handsome fellow. Incidentally, he had come from Milwaukee originally. He ended up being one of my closest friends.

Well, he walked in with Barney and a whole group behind him; and I began to expound on the Willys 6/66, the passenger car that we were going to build. And he said, "Don't worry about that. And by the way, can you stay over?" I said I could. I walked into his office the next day with the idea that this was "it"; he would just let it down lightly, you know. But instead he asked me to sit down and talk. And he said, "I might tell you one thing that's wrong with your operation here. They don't pay you enough! So your retainer is doubled from this point on." They picked me up off the floor after that!

We went down a couple of floors to the engineering department. We all gathered around Sorensen, and he said, "We've got to do something with the fact that the only image this company's got, at the moment, is the Jeep. We just can't pass that over, because it's known all over the world. It would be silly to ignore that and come out with this Willys 6/66. It won't compete with anything!"

Sorensen asked if I could stay a couple of days. I said, "Hell, I can stay until spring if necessary!" So I sat down and took the Jeep front end. Sorensen said we had to use the front-end sheet metal and asked us to see what we could do with it.

Brown: In order for the car to be recognizable as a Jeep? Or for economy reasons?

Stevens: Well, both. Economy and identity. Most people used to think the Jeep Station Wagons were built from vehicles that were sent back from Europe, or something, and rebodied; but that was an absurdity. The wagon had to have an all-new frame, and it had no four-wheel drive, and all the rest of it.

So I went to work and produced my own sketches, which was embarrassing for me because I never used to draw my own renderings. But I had to do it while I was there. I laid out the Station Wagon as the first one. Sorensen said he couldn't get any major body builder to take it on. Murray, Briggs—they didn't want anything to do with it because Willys was known as a "failure." They couldn't see what our future would be, and they'd rather take on GM and Chrysler and all the rest. He said, "I'm going to have to go to somebody in Connersville or someplace with sheet metal equipment, where the greatest depth of draw I can give you is six inches."

So with these limitations on me, I created the slab-sided design with the recesses and indentations and so forth, which of course were to simulate the wood-slatted sides. Of course, the embossing was really there to stiffen the structure. The body was full-width; there were no rear fenders. We made it a two-door for economic reasons, and also for safety.

The color scheme, of course, was created just to simulate mahogany and birch, trying to give that illusion with the brown and cream. And that's how it was designed. Now, as I created these sketches I also cut the sides out of the upper body, and the "B" and "C" pillars. And we put screens in there and made a dog-catcher's

wagon; we left the windows blanked and made a panel truck. We truncated the cab and made a pickup, using a box on it.

Brown: Which accounts for the fact that you didn't sell more of them.

Stevens: Yes, we didn't sell too many. We built it for about three years, I think. But now they're certainly a "classic." A restored one is worth a lot of money now. I have the first one off the temporary dies, in the automotive museum.

Then I went on to Brazil and did the cars down there. We did the Station Wagon with the rear body identical, but with a new front end on it. And we created a new Jeepster there. I built a prototype in 1959-60 or thereabouts, to try to inject it in the line down there, but they didn't have enough capacity to build it. That car must exist somewhere. Ought to be worth a fortune now! It was a good-looking car.

The Jeepster is what began the dropped door and the raised rear tonneau, and of course that evolved into the Excalibur. That was really the derivation of it, in concept.

Brown: That makes sense, though it never occurred to me. But getting back to the Station Wagon, over what dates was it built?

Stevens: Oh, Lord! From '46 until some time in the early fifties. We had a whole run of those things! We kept modifying the moldings and paint jobs, and we made a pointed grille to replace the flat one. And they made a hell of a lot of them! It was a great little car. Four-cylinder, then six-cylinder. And overdrive and all the things were added to it. It was a very practical little station wagon because it was really a clean truck. You could really put something in it!

Now the Plymouth Suburban came quite a bit after that, and it was basically nothing but a sedan.

Brown: You must have been around Toledo when the Suburban came out, In June of 1949. What was the reaction at Willys when Plymouth billed the Suburban as "the first all-steel station wagon"?

Stevens: We raised hell about it! We had patents on that thing, and everything else! I can't remember exactly what the outcome was.

Brown: But there was some commotion over it?

Stevens: Oh, God, yes! The management raised hell about it, but at that time they weren't as powerful as Chrysler. But the public knew the difference! The Jeep wagon had a personality of its own. It began to show up at the country clubs; it became the "chic" thing.

Brown: What was the thinking behind the development of the Aero Willys? In retrospect, it would seem that the company might have been

better off to have stuck with building specialty vehicles.

Stevens: That may be, but you know, the management was changing so often. Sorensen, if he had stayed, would never have gone for passenger cars. The new management finally pushed it through. We worked on that as well, and another guy named Phil Wright was involved.

Brown: It was a beautiful little car!

Stevens: Yes, and of course it and the Henry J were the forerunners of what they're selling now against the Japanese. Those cars were just premature at the time. You couldn't sell the damn things, then! They weren't dreamt up, necessarily, because of worrying about a fuel shortage. They were just construed to be practical cars.

When "Cast-Iron Charlie" Sorensen came over to Willys from Ford, Brooks Stevens thought it was the end of the line for him. However, the opposite happened, and together they conceptualized the Station Wagon (above). With a passenger seated cross-wise at the rear, the Wagon offered seating for seven.

the Jeep's tactical role in Korea was not always identical to the part it played in World War II.

Though the mostly mountainous terrain of North Korea might have logically influenced the Army to minimize the use of the Jeep, this did not turn out to be the case. New support roles directly related to combat became standard requirements. In October 1950, the Jeep led the strategic withdrawal from the North when the Chinese entered the war. And once the fighting began along the 38th parallel (the line dividing North Korea and South Korea), the Jeep started to play all kinds of new combat and support roles.

Some Jeeps were equipped with communications gear that allowed them to be employed in forward positions, directing air strikes and observation airplanes. With the heavy movement of refugees from the north, the military police also began to rely more on the versatile Jeep. It could be operated on the paved streets of cities and towns or on the dirt roads of the countryside. The Jeep in Korea proved to be popular as a principal means of transportation for both officers and enlisted men.

The design created by Willys before World War II was still going strong in the postwar years. However, as WWII drew to a close, other postwar plans were being formulated at Willys-Overland. A steady and modestly profitable market had been anticipated for the Jeep Universal. Yet, it was plain to see that for the company to remain viable, the product line would have to be broadened.

With Brooks Stevens in charge of the design team, plans got under way for a postwar passenger car. Those plans were shelved when Joseph Frazer was replaced by Charles Sorensen as company president, then revived under Jim Mooney's leadership, and finally torpedoed when Ward Canaday took the helm once more.

The truth is, Willys might not have been able to produce that postwar sedan, even if Canaday and the board of directors had

wanted to. Body manufacturers in the immediate postwar years had all the contracts they could handle.

Brooks Stevens solved the problem neatly and in the process brought forth a whole new concept in automotive design: the all-steel station wagon. Laid out in such a way as to require so little "draw" that even a refrigerator manufacturer could produce the stamping, the Willys Jeep Station Wagon proved to be one of the most influential automobiles ever built.

Mounted on the same 104-inch wheelbase as the prewar Willys American, though with substantial modifications to the chassis, the Jeep wagon had none of its predecessor's pretensions to streamlining or graceful styling. Purely functional in design, it was tall and angular. Its simple, flat grille and square fenders were—by no coincidence—very nearly carbon copies of its familiar military forbear.

It had an austere look about it, and only one color scheme was offered at first: deep burgundy on the hood and fenders, with the body done in cream with reddish-brown paneling. The latter cleverly suggested, without actually imitating, the mahogany-and-birch cabinet-shop bodies typically found on the station wagons of that era.

The wagon was dreadfully underpowered. It outweighed the American by some 600 pounds; and since it was powered by the same 63-horsepower engine as the prewar sedan, performance suffered badly. Overdrive, offered initially as an option, soon became standard equipment. A good thing, for the car really needed the flexibility of four forward speeds.

But in practical terms, the Jeep Station Wagon had a lot going for it:

• Despite its modest 14½-foot length, it provided seating for seven.

• With the rear seats removed, 96 cubic feet of cargo capacity was available.

• Its inside height—nearly 50 inches—permitted the hauling of tall items.

• The all-steel construction did away

The CJ-2A (right, top) was a highly successful model; over its five-year life span, 214,202 were built. The 2A had a drop-down tailgate and a two-piece windshield. One interesting option was the engine governor ($27.21), which would keep engine rpm in a given range despite varying loads. This device was especially useful in farming applications and for use with the power-takeoff. Gauges were minimal but complete (right, bottom middle), comprising a speedometer, water temperature, oil pressure ammeter, and fuel gauges. The same "Go-Devil" engine that powered World War II jeeps was in the CJ-2A (far right, bottom). In this application, it offered 60 horsepower at 4000 rpm and 106 pounds-feet of torque at 2000 rpm.

with the persistent maintenance problems that were the bane of owners of wood-bodied station wagons.

• The Jeep wagon's price was several hundred dollars lower than that of any other station wagon on the market at the time of its introduction, unless one includes the tiny Crosley.

• Perhaps most important of all, the Jeep Station Wagon was simple, dependable, economical, and tough.

Independent front suspension was featured, a first for a Willys-Overland product. Designed by chief engineer Barney Roos, it closely resembled the "planar" suspension that Roos had developed for Studebaker in the mid-Thirties, utilizing a seven-leaf transverse spring in lieu of the more conventional coils. Willys called it "Planadyne."

A two-door configuration was used, with the seventh passenger seated sideways just inside the tailgate. All seats save that of the driver's were removable, permitting the vehicle to serve equally well as a truck or passenger car. The entire floor was flat from the driver's seat back, further enhancing the wagon's utility.

Mechanical components were conventional enough. An 8½-inch Auburn clutch and a T-96 Warner Gear transmission were used. The whooped bevel rear axle came from Spicer, the cam and twin-lever steering from Ross. Hydraulic brakes were by Bendix, and six-volt electrics were by Electric Auto-Lite.

A Willys-Overland advertisement in the *Saturday Evening Post* proclaimed, "No sedan can match a Station Wagon for all-around usefulness. And no other Station Wagon is so practical for every use as the Jeep Station Wagon—the first with an all-steel body and top for greater safety and longer service." The ad went on to declare the wagon to be "wonderfully smooth riding on country roads as well as city streets."

Initially, the Jeep Station Wagon was built only in two-wheel-drive form. It sold relatively well: 6534 units during the last half of 1946, 27,515 in 1947. It's safe to assume that Willys could have sold as many examples as they could manage to build in that postwar "seller's market." But raw materials, especially sheet steel, were in short supply, tending to hobble the aspirations of all the automakers.

Somehow, possibly because of the postwar shortages, a rumor made the rounds that the Station Wagon and other Jeep vehicles were cobbled together, using parts left over from the wartime Jeeps. Brooks Stevens, while affirming that the Jeep "look" had been retained, responded scornfully, "Anyone in their right mind knew that couldn't be. The tread was different, the wheelbase was different, everything about it was different."

A luxury version was added for 1948. Known as the Station Sedan, it was finished better than the Wagon both inside and out, though the same body shell was used. Solid body colors were featured in lieu of the Wagon two-tone paneled effect, and basket-weave trim was added along the sides. One British writer suggested that the Station Sedan "looked rather like a country hearse." However, most observers found its unique trim attractive.

Perhaps the year's best news was the introduction, in the Station Sedan, of Barney Roos's brand new six-cylinder engine. A conventionally-designed L-head, displacing 148.5 cubic inches, this powerplant was rated at 72 horsepower, an 11 percent advantage over the four-banger. Torque was similarly increased, from 105 pounds-feet in the four to 117 in the new six. Obviously, performance was enhanced considerably.

Driving one of these older Willys wagons was a unique experience. One sat up high—seats were placed a foot and a half off the floor. Visibility in all directions was excellent. Seat cushions were a little mushy in the earlier models, but zig-zag springs, introduced in 1949, overcame that problem, and the later seats gave excellent sup-

Another one of stylist Brooks Stevens's creations was the Jeepster (right), which was released on April 3, 1948. Willys management hoped to add some sportiness to the Jeep Universal lineup. Jeepster's front end was copped from the Station Wagon while the rear quarters were taken from Jeep trucks. Power for this runabout was the familiar "Go-Devil" engine. However, in response to criticism, Willys added the L-head six to the options list in 1950. Inside, the Jeepster was very similar to the Wagon, and the front seat folded forward to allow access to the rear seats (far right, bottom).

port. At the same time, the seating was rearranged for better posture and increased leg room. And the ride, though hardly equal to that of a sedan, was more comfortable than one might expect.

Even in the four-cylinder wagons, acceleration was adequate up to about 40 miles per hour; beyond that, it flattened out. The six, of course, did much better in that respect. In hilly country, the six-cylinder car acquitted itself very well, while the four-banger lagged behind.

Clutch action was smooth and light, and the remote shift linkage was better than most. Steering was quick, light, and reasonably precise. However, the Willys heeled over dreadfully in hard cornering. Yet, there was little loss of control. The little wagon was really rather fun to drive, though to deal with it daily in heavy commuter traffic would doubtless be exhausting for the average driver.

As well, crosswinds were terrifying to the driver of the Jeep Station Wagon. At times, the vehicle favored abrupt lane changes, with or without the driver's permission. In addition, the brakes—not the strongest point on the wartime jeep—were not all that competent on the wagons, either. Stopping distances were far from comfortable, and a lot of pedal pressure was required to get the job done. On the other hand, the wagon did seem to hold in a straight line, even in a panic stop; and Barney Roos's unusual front suspension acted to discourage "nosedive."

There was good news again in 1949—especially for people who had to slog their way through mud and snow. Four-wheel drive became available in the Jeep Station Wagon that July. It was reported in *Automotive Industries* that the four-wheel-drive version had first been built the previous year, on special order from the U.S. Army. Now, it was available to the general public. As with other four-wheel-drive Jeep products, it used a live front axle and longitudinal leaf springs in lieu of the Planadyne mechanism.

Power for the 4x4 wagon came from the little flathead four, which—since the six was by then available—appears in retrospect to have been a mistake in judgment. But the new model filled an important need for many people. A 4x2 six-cylinder Station Wagon was also produced, offering the power of the Station Sedan, minus some of the amenities, at a slightly lower price. Sales, which had faltered during 1948, climbed back to within reach of their 1947 level.

Meanwhile, commencing in 1947 a panel delivery was offered. Sometimes misleadingly called a "sedan delivery," it used the same body stamping as the Station Wagon but minus the windows. Doors were fitted at the rear in lieu of the wagon's tailgate, and seating was provided only for the driver.

Nineteen-fifty brought new front-end styling, the first such change of any consequence since the original Jeep Station Wagon was introduced in 1946. The front fender tips came to a peak—a potential hazard to pedestrians, but nobody thought in such terms in those days. The grille was given a modified "V" shape, and five bright metal horizontal bars were added to the nine vertical ribs. There was even a small chrome-plated ornament on the tip of the hood. Such changes were modest enough, but they added a rather attractive touch to the vehicle.

The upscale Station Sedan, never a big seller, was deleted from the 1950 line. But at midyear, the F-head four-cylinder engine became available to buyers of the four-wheel-drive wagon, supplying a welcome dose of vitamins. Sales of the various wagons were up just slightly for the year.

Given the business-like image projected by the Jeep, not to mention its sturdy construction, it was to be expected that Willys-Overland would market a light truck. Once World War II was over they did, and it was released in 1946.

The light truck market was not an unfamiliar field—the company had a long history

One of the most obvious uses for the CJ-2A was down on the farm. A rear power takeoff could be ordered from the options list for $90.87 (far right, top). This allowed the CJ to operate various farm implements. The motor for the driver's side windshield wiper was located on the top of the windshield frame. However, the passenger still had to operate their wiper manually (right, middle). Willys was still kicking around the idea of a passenger car in 1950, when Alcoa developed a variant based on the Jeepster (right, bottom). The body was constructed of aluminum. It offered a hard top and trunk, but the rear seats were removed.

of participation in the commercial vehicle market. As far back as 1910, there had been a pair of delivery trucks built on the Overland passenger car chassis. In 1912, John North Willys purchased a controlling interest in both the Gramm Motor Truck Company of Lima, Ohio, and the Garford Automobile Company of Elyria, Ohio, producer of one-ton and larger trucks. A ¾-ton utility truck bearing the Willys name appeared the following year; however, it was in reality a Gramm product.

In 1915 John Willys disposed of his interest in both the Garford and Gramm firms, though the trucks continued to be handled by Willys-Overland dealers. The manufacture by Willys-Overland of light-duty vehicles was continued, however. In 1920 the 27-horsepower Light Four series took Overland trucks into the lowest-price field, with the chassis costing only $450. Four years later, a slightly larger 30-horsepower engine was used, and the price was reduced to $395.

Nineteen twenty-seven saw the advent of the company's Whippet light trucks, powered by the 134.2 cubic inch flathead four that would ultimately become the basis for

the engine used in the World War II jeep. A six-cylinder companion was also available in both truck and passenger car lines.

The four-cylinder engine disappeared along with the Whippet nameplate in 1932, but the four-banger was resurrected the following year for use in the diminutive Willys 77. A panel delivery was offered that season in addition to the passenger car. In 1935 the line was augmented by a cab pickup. A stake truck was added in 1938, followed the next year by a walk-in panel delivery. Until World War II brought civilian production to a halt, Willys trucks continued to be available in chassis, pickup, and cab-over-engine panel delivery configurations. The commercials accounted for just over 7 percent of Willys-Overland's production in those days.

The first of the postwar Willys trucks was the half-ton panel delivery, introduced in 1946. Built on the 104-inch, 2x2 chassis of the Jeep Station Wagon, it used the wagon's body stamping. Power came from the same "Go-Devil" four-cylinder engine that had given such distinguished service during the war.

For 1947, a series of one-ton, 4x4 trucks was added. Available in pickup, platform stake, chassis and cab, or bare chassis form, these trucks used a 118-inch wheelbase and weighed as much as 3431 pounds. (For purposes of comparison, the Utility Jeep tipped the scales at just 2074 pounds, while the Panel Delivery came in at 2587. So the power-to-weight ratio of the 4x4s was not, to say the least, anything to get excited about.) By 1949, ¾-ton 4x2 trucks, using the 118-inch chassis, were added to the line.

In 1950 the trucks were restyled, again along the lines of the wagon. A pointed grille with five horizontal trim bars gave the Jeep trucks just a suggestion of style. The following year the 72-horsepower, F-head "Hurricane" engine took the place of the previous 63-horsepower flathead. Truck production for 1951 came to 22,282 units, well over a quarter of Willys-

In 1950 Willys released the 72-horsepower, F-head "Hurricane" engine (left). This powerplant offered improved performance over the four cylinder without much of a penalty in fuel efficiency.

The Jeepster could be had with an interesting two-tone paint option that added a contrasting color around the belt line onto the windshield frame (right, top). Willys's replacement for the original U.S. military jeep was the M38 (right, bottom). Though the two models were basically similar, the M38 had stiffer body and chassis parts, waterproofed 24-volt electrics, and a redesigned F-head engine that forced a taller grille and higher hoodline. The new military jeep also had an interesting vent tube arrangement that connected the engine, transmission, transfer case, fuel tank, and air cleaner. This allowed the vehicle to be driven even when the vehicle was completely submerged. M38s went on to distinguish themselves in battle during the Korean War.

Overland's total output. Available accessories included a power takeoff, pulley drive, and a speed governor for the engine.

These trucks were not particularly cheap. The 4x2 pickup, for example, cost $73 more than a ¾-ton Chevrolet. But the Jeep trucks had a lot going for them, not the least of which was their reputation for toughness. And there literally was no competition in those days for the four-wheel-drive models.

Willys began to move its trucks upscale, and by 1952 the panel had become known by the more prestigious name of Sedan Delivery. Some dress-up items, such as chromed front and rear bumpers, chromed wheel discs, and even white sidewall tires, had joined the options list.

In 1948, with the wagons, Universals, and trucks selling well, Willys hoped to capture another section of the market. This market niche was created by American GIs returning home from Europe, where they had come to love little English sports cars. The MG TA and TB (built from 1936 to 1939) were just this type of car, and when the GIs returned home they found that no American manufacturer was building a car like the MG. In fact, many soldiers who had purchased MGs during and after the war brought them home with them.

Willys hoped to play on this popularity by producing another vehicle with the flavor of a Jeep and an MG. This vehicle would be a cross between a Jeep and a sports car, and it would be called the Jeepster. True, it wasn't a genuine sports car. No American firm of any consequence was building sports cars in those days. But it was an open car—the first American phaeton in a decade—and it certainly had a sporty flair. Better yet, its squared-off styling was distinctly reminiscent of the Jeep.

Designed by Brooks Stevens, the Jeepster first appeared on April 3, 1948. The name had been coined more than five years earlier by Joe Frazer, then president of Willys-Overland. The Jeepster represented

an effort to broaden the Willys product line, tapping into a market that was more youth-oriented than that of the Station Wagon, more urbane than that of the Jeep Universal.

The phaeton was developed at remarkably little cost to its builders. The driveline came right off the Willys parts shelf: the familiar "Go-Devil" four-cylinder engine; clutch, transmission, overdrive, differential, suspension, steering, and brakes were all from the Jeep Station Wagon, though the wagon's frame was stiffened for this application by the addition of an X-member. Thus, tooling costs were minimal, as far as the chassis was concerned. With a 500-pound weight advantage, the Jeepster could be expected to perform in much more sprightly fashion than the wagon—though it obviously wasn't going to blow anybody's doors off.

Development of the body was almost equally economical. The front end of the Station Wagon was borrowed, almost in its entirety. Rear fenders came from the Jeep truck. There was no fixed glass apart from the windshield and vent wings. There were just two doors. (The first prototype, in fact, had no doors at all.) A canvas top and side curtains provided protection from the elements. Body stampings were simple, requiring very little draw. All in all, the capital investment was almost negligible.

Remarkably little fanfare accompanied the Jeepster's introduction. A product as unique as this one might have been expected to reap a publicity bonanza for Willys-Overland, but for reasons that remain obscure the company let that opportunity go.

There was, however, at least one very effective magazine advertisement. In its colorful prose—and even in its use of ellipses—the ad recalled the work, in an earlier generation, of the legendary Ned Jordan:

"Wherever there's fun, there you will find the people this car was made for . . . people with a flair for the unusual; who combine smartness, unerring good taste

In 1950 the original Jeep truck received its only styling change, when the grille added three horizontal chrome bars (right, top). Variants to the pickup were soon to follow (far right, top); a front winch was a popular option. In the late Forties and early Fifties, the U.S. Army was testing a smaller jeep-like vehicle. Designated the WAC (right, middle), this design was fitted with an air-cooled, double-opposed Harley-Davidson engine. It had a total curb weight of 1050 pounds and was constructed of steel, plywood, and canvas. The WAC's top speed was 48 mph. In 1950 Willys was already working on a replacement for the CJ-3A (right, bottom) and began building an improved version of the M38—the M38 A1—for the military. This design would later become the CJ-5.

"It was a tiny space ...but I made it"

WILLYS makes sense
—IN DESIGN —IN ECONOMY —IN USEFULNESS

Perhaps the Jeepster was a concept whose time had not yet come. In recent times, the car has become a much sought-after collector's item and is the only Willys to have been designated a Milestone car. So of course the question remains: Why was it not more successful in its own time? Several reasons:

• There was the question of its identity. The Jeepster clearly wasn't a sports car; yet it wasn't really a family car, either. Thus it may simply have fallen between two stools.

• The day of the open car was long gone by the time the Jeepster was introduced. The American love affair with the ragtop was still intense, but people wanted the comfort of roll-up windows.

• After 1948, the Jeepster's modestly successful first season, the postwar "seller's market" waned rapidly. Competition returned to the marketplace.

• Some people were disappointed at the company's failure to offer a four-wheel-drive version.

• And as Brooks Stevens has noted, the price was high. A four-cylinder Jeepster cost nearly a hundred dollars more than a deluxe Chevrolet club coupe. True, the Chevy wasn't a convertible. But then, neither was the Jeepster.

During this time, Willys had been enjoying a period of considerable prosperity. *Business Week* reported that production for 1948 came to 138,000 units, compared to a wartime top of 107,000 during 1944. However, the company's cash reserves were slim. At the time the United States entered the war in December 1941, Willys-Overland's working capital had amounted to less than $2 million. And even at war's end, only $20 million had been available for retooling and expansion.

Then as the Korean War turned the postwar economic boom to bust, Willys was in no position to endure harsh economic times. Yet, with several highly saleable models, a good export market, and a sound dealer network, they were a highly attractive proposition for a larger corporation.

and a sharp sense of value."

Not as many people found the Jeepster as appealing as Willys-Overland had hoped. For a car with sporting pretensions, the Jeepster's performance left something to be desired. In response to criticism, in January 1949 the 72-horsepower F-head four was substituted for the original flathead engine, providing an 11 percent horsepower increase. The following July, Barney Roos's new "Lightning Six" became available, as well. A new, slightly vee'd grille with five bright horizontal bars was featured for 1950, and later that year performance was further enhanced when the six-cylinder engine was bored to 161 cid, raising the horsepower from 70 to 75.

But sales of the Jeepster, somewhat disappointing from the outset, faltered badly in 1949 and made only a partial recovery the following year. Jeepsters were catalogued for the 1951 model year, but these were actually leftover 1950 cars. Production of the little phaeton had already been halted; only 19,132 had been built over a period of less than three years.

Willys ads continued to stress usefulness and economy in 1950 (left). They had to because Detroit was coming out with new iron every two years, and the basic Willys models had been around since 1946.

At the Willys plant in Toledo, Ohio, military M38s were built alongside Wagons and other models (right, top). Between 1949 and 1952, Willys built over 60,000 M38s for the U.S. Army. The Wagons received the same front-end facelift as the trucks in 1950 (right, bottom). Available in either two- or four-wheel drive, the wagons could be fitted with either the four- or six-cylinder engine. Production from 1949 to 1951 was well over 35,000 per year, but the Korean War and recession forced sales down to only 12,069 in 1952.

Kaiser and the Jeep: 1953-55

In 1952 Willys-Overland re-entered the passenger car market with its innovative Aero-Willys. The car was a lightweight, unibody compact weighing just 2600 pounds and riding a 108-inch wheelbase. It was well engineered and drew rave reviews. However, the Aero-Willys sold for $150 more than a Chevrolet Bel Air hardtop. Dealers were hard-pressed to sell the 31,000 they managed to move that first year.

At the same time the auto industry as a whole had hit a sales slump, and the Korean War was forcing new rationing policies for steel and rubber. Despite all of this, Willys managed to increase sales to 42,000 units for 1953. Yet, it was too little too

late. The combined effects of costly new tooling for the new model and the recession had put Willys in deep financial trouble again. There was no miracle salesman like John North Willys around this time, and the company was put on the block.

In April of 1953, the Kaiser-Frazer Corporation purchased Willys-Overland for approximately $60 million. Ward Canaday had turned the reigns over to Henry J. Kaiser and his son, Edgar.

Though the prospect of new ownership brought hope, there were two major problems with the Kaiser buyout. First, Kaiser was in no position to spend any money. The company had lost almost $10 million the year before and over $34 million in its five-year history. Also, the Aero-Willys wasn't much larger than the Henry J, the low-price leader at Kaiser-Frazer. Despite this, Kaiser knew that the Jeep was where the fortune would be made.

If there had been one persistent complaint about the CJ-2A and CJ-3A Jeeps—as well as the military MCs—it had to do with their perceived lack of power. The same shortcoming had been true of other Willys models, including the Jeepster and the Station Wagon. Barney Roos and his engineering staff had undertaken to increase the horsepower of the little four-banger by converting it to the F-head configuration. (For those readers who may be unfamiliar with this type of layout, the F-head engine's intake valves are in the head, while the exhaust ports remain in the block. Larger valves can thus be used, and greater power results from the improved breathing.)

So, on January 28, 1953, the Jeep CJ-3B appeared. The hood line was raised in

Though Willys was now a part of the Kaiser Industries empire, advertising did not change. The utility and practicality of the Station Wagon (left) made it a perfect Family Car—according to the ads.

The early Fifties were strange times in the U.S. automobile industry. The Korean War imposed new rationing policies and brought on a mild recession. But at the same time Willys produced over 50,000 MCs and MDs a year for the military. Production of the 1953 Station Wagon (right) climbed over six thousand units from the previous year to 18,811. There were no major changes to the 1952 model, as for most years of the Wagon, but there were new taillights and a modified licence plate bracket that allowed the plate to remain in view with the gate either up or down. Jeep began selling other products to the U.S. government during this time, like the 1953 Postal Delivery (right, bottom right).

order to accommodate the taller engine. Proportions were thus altered, making the CJ-3B a rather odd-looking machine, wearing what might be termed a "perpetually startled expression" with its high-riding headlamps. The same was true of the corresponding military unit, the M606.

The difference in performance, however, was substantial. Horsepower—listed in the CJ-3A as 60 at 4000 rpm—was raised at the same engine speed to 75, a 25-percent increase. Torque was boosted as well, from 106 to 114 pounds-feet. This increase was particularly useful at the lower engine speeds so critical in many applications.

Another improvement in the CJ-3B was a new transfer case, said to offer longer life and quieter operation. All in all, the CJ-3A was three pounds heavier than CJ-3B and was $25 more costly. Little enough to pay for 25 percent more horsepower and 9 percent more torque.

By 1955 there was another new civilian Jeep, the famous CJ-5. This model, based on the MD-MB38 A1 military jeep, was announced on October 11, 1954. However, there were some major changes made in converting the CJ-5 to civilian use.

Headlights received a chrome surround and extended slightly from the grille. The military-spec, black-out lights were replaced by conventional parking lights. Also, the military's 24-volt electrical system was replaced by a 6-volt system.

The most visible difference between the CJ-5 and the CJ-3B was the curve of the new front fenders. The frame was fully boxed and a cross member was added to increase the strength, rigidity, and carrying capacity of the CJ-5. Sheet metal was fully flanged and overlapped all around, also to increase strength. In addition, the ride was slightly altered by an increase of one inch in wheelbase (up to 81 inches) and softer front springs in conjunction with stiffer rear springs.

At 135.5 inches, overall length was up almost six inches from the CJ-3B. The new

(continued on page 86)

The Hurricane four-cylinder continued to be the only engine offered in Jeep products until 1954 (left, top). In 1952 Jeep introduced its Deluxe Station Wagon (left, bottom). This model had woven side panel inserts and vinyl plastic seats.

The M-38 A1, also known as the MD, was the military precursor of the CJ-5. This model (right) was produced for the U.S. military from 1952 through 1968 and was superseded by the M151. The MD went back to a two-piece windshield and was powered by a 72-horsepower four-cylinder engine. Ford of Canada also built this vehicle under license. Willys developed a military version of the CJ-6 as well; called the M170, it was usually converted into an ambulance or troop carrier.

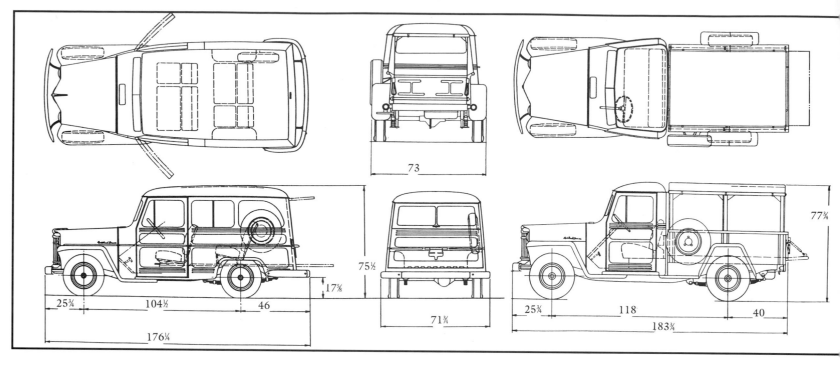

Who's in Charge Here?

For a time, it seemed that nobody remained as president of Willys-Overland long enough to take his hat off. Following Ward Canaday's reorganization of the company in 1936—the year after John North Willys died—Dave Wilson was installed in that position. Wilson, a rough-hewn type, headed the Wilson Foundry Company of Pontiac, Michigan, which for some years had supplied castings to Willys. There is little doubt that Dave Wilson's combination of shrewdness and guts did much to help keep the company alive during those dark days. But it is also evident that he was less than happy, working under the direction of Chairman Canaday and what must have seemed to him an oppressive white-collar hierarchy. Finally, in 1939—according to *Fortune* magazine—"after a spectacular Board meeting during which Wilson's formidable finger emphasized a point with such vigor that the Board Chairman was reportedly precipitated into a nearby wastebasket, old-timer Wilson went back to retirement in Pontiac."

Next up was Joseph Frazer, formerly of Chrysler (and later of Kaiser-Frazer fame). Frazer was considered one of the industry's crack sales executives, and certainly the Willys-Overland sales organization needed all the help it could get. One could speculate endlessly about what might have happened had the war not intervened. However, by 1942 Joe Frazer had nothing to sell—at least, not to the civilian market. The following year he exercised his option on 75,000 shares of Willys-Overland stock, pocketed a net of some $200,000 and locked the door on his way out.

Maybe the Frazer/Willys-Overland relationship wouldn't have worked in any case. Joe Frazer's ideas concerning postwar plans for the company were not entirely compatible with those of Ward Canaday, and Canaday held all the aces. In any event, after an interim period during which Canaday himself held the presidency, "Cast Iron Charlie" Sorensen was persuaded to take over. Sorensen, for many years the Ford Motor Company's resident production genius—that is, until he had a falling out with crusty old Henry Ford—had no patience with Frazer's rather grand ideas concerning Willys-Overland's place in the postwar scheme of things. He focused his attention primarily upon the company's utility vehicles—jeeps and trucks—seeing no future for Willys in the highly competitive passenger-car market.

It seemed as though the company was on track under Sorensen's guidance, so it came as a great surprise when, in January 1946, Chairman Canaday announced that Willys-Overland had yet another new president. This was James David "Jim" Mooney, recently released from active duty in the U.S. Naval Reserve, with the

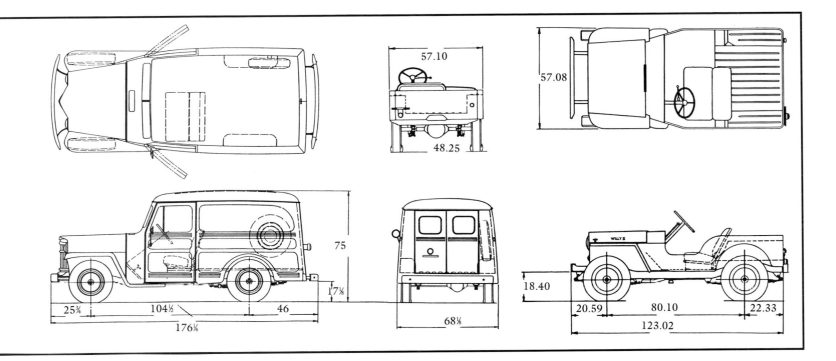

Above: *Line drawings of Willys vehicles in the late Fifties. All measurements are in inches.*

rank of captain. Mooney, in fact, was appointed as both president and chairman. Perhaps he hoped that the dual office would eliminate the conflict with Ward Canaday that had evidently been the bane of his predecessors.

In the reshuffle, Canaday was elected to the newly created post of chairman of the Finance Committee. Sorensen, whose contract guaranteed him a thousand dollars a week for 10 years whether he lived or died, was given the more or less nominal title of vice chairman.

Mooney, described by *Motor* as a "graduate engineer, production expert and two-fisted salesman," had worked for such diverse firms as Westinghouse, B. F. Goodrich, and Hyatt Roller Bearing before joining the Rein Electric Company. When Rein was absorbed by General Motors, Mooney began his ascent of the corporate ladder until, in 1935, he became a member of the Executive Committee. By the time the Navy called him up for active service, three weeks after Pearl Harbor, GM had put him in full charge of all negotiations involving national defense equipment.

Given such a background, it may be assumed that Jim Mooney came to Willys-Overland with high hopes and big ideas, one of which obviously had to do with the revival of the passenger car program that Charlie Sorensen had sidelined. Whether Ward Canaday was in sympathy with

Mooney's aspirations is, at the least, open to question. *Business Week*, speculating in 1951 on the frequent changes in top management at Willys, ventured to guess that "nearly everyone except Canaday had ideas too grandiose for the specialized Willys market. They wanted to buck the standard cars, instead of sticking to a special, utility field."

The complexity of Willys-Overland's administrative and financial structure is beyond the scope of this volume. Suffice it for our purposes to say that complete control of the corporation was vested in an organization known as Empire Securities. Empire's president and principal stockholder was—as the reader may have surmised—Ward Canaday. So although Jim Mooney was both president and chairman of the company, the real power still lay in Canaday's hands. Canaday was, above all, one to keep his eye on the bottom line.

In the end, Mooney's proposed passenger car died, and when red ink began to appear on Willys-Overland's ledgers in 1949, Ward Canaday once again took the title of chairman—and later that of president, as well. That's the way matters remained until April 28, 1953, when, in exchange for $62,381,175, Willys-Overland became a building block in the formidable Kaiser Industries empire.

This time, Ward Canaday really did step aside.

FROM THE MAKERS OF THE BELOVED JEEP KNOWN AND RESPECTED AROUND THE WORLD

The Common-sense Car that Leads a Double Life

AS A BUSINESS OR WORK CAR, more than 100 cubic feet of usable space is available for tools or bulky packages. Seats lift out easily. Interior can be cleaned almost as easily as a kitchen sink!

AS A FAMILY CAR, the Willys DeLuxe Station Wagon is amazingly compatible with the needs of most American families. With easily cleaned seats, sides and floors it is a good companion to children and pets. Carries "problem" items (such as bicycles and lawnmowers) without removing seats. Comfort for 6 adults, with huge luggage space behind rear seats. And its powerful *Hurricane* engine is so economical to run. Why not let your Willys dealer fit one of these into your life today?

Why not start this motoring season with the car that gives you *double utility; low first cost; low operating costs; high trade-in value?* At your Willys dealer now. Willys Motors, Inc., Toledo.

Willys
STATION WAGON
• With 6-Cylinder HURRICANE Engine, 2-Wheel Drive
• With 4-Cylinder HURRICANE Engine, 4-Wheel Drive

THE NEW WILLYS
4-WHEEL DRIVE **1-TON**
TRUCK

6,000 Pounds Gross Vehicle Weight
New 6 Cyl—115 H.P. Super Hurricane Engine

THE WORLD'S
MOST USEFUL TRUCK:

With famous Willys 4-wheel drive it goes where other trucks can't go— never idle because of road or weather conditions. Has more horsepower per pound than any other 4-wheel drive truck.

MORE THAN A MATCH FOR THE TOUGHEST JOB!

HAULING personnel or cargo over all kinds of terrain.

PUSHING vehicles or other heavy objects, grading and plowing snow.

PULLING by traction — towing vehicles, dragging logs, pulling implements, etc.

PULLING by winch — providing power to a winch for skidding and placing machinery, raising walls, pulling out stumps, trees or posts, or pulling itself or other vehicles out of difficult situations.

LIFTING — by means of a crane mounted on the steel bed.

FURNISHING POWER to operate other machinery — through any of three types of power take-offs.

CHAPTER FIVE

CJ-5, at 71.75 inches, was also three inches wider than the CJ-3B, although weight was up only modestly at 2274 pounds. The one-piece windshield of the CJ-5 was nearly 100 square inches larger than the CJ-3B, and the driver's-side mirror was mounted to the windshield support base.

Inside, the front seat occupants were given added leg and hip room, while the driver looked at a new back-lighted instrument cluster. A passenger car-type handbrake was added, and the glove compartment could be had with a cover. The seats themselves were new and softer, due to new coil springs; also, the driver's seat had three fore and aft adjustments. A rear bench seat could now accommodate two people comfortably, increasing seating capacity to a realistic four.

Kaiser-Willys also took pains to improve the loose-fitting "All-Weather" top of the CJ-3B. On the CJ-5, more fittings were added, and the top was manufactured to closer tolerances. One thing that did not change from the CJ-3B to the CJ-5 was the engine. It was still the same 134.2-cid F-head in-line four rated at 70 bhp and 114 pounds-feet of torque.

Production of the CJ-3B was over 35,000 for 1954, but with the introduction of the CJ-5 that figure tailed off to just over 12,000 for 1955. CJ-5 production started out with a slow build of just under 4000 units for 1954 and then took off to 23,595 for 1955. It was obvious the new CJ-5 was a much-improved version of the Jeep Universal, and it would continue with only minor modifications for almost 30 years.

The Station Wagon and panel delivery were mostly carryovers between 1953 and 1955. However, one significant option was added to the four-wheel-drive versions of both in 1954: the 115-bhp six cylinder engine. That year also brought minor revisions to the front end, including a grille that now had three, instead of five, horizontal slats.

In a September, 1954, report *Motor*

The "Common-sense" car crept up in price in 1954 to $2134 for the Deluxe. Amazingly that was only one dollar more than a Chevy DeLuxe Handyman wagon. For that extra dollar, the Willys offered four-wheel drive and an extra seat at the rear. Jeep trucks (left) were not garnering much attention but sales were always in the high teens in the early Fifties.

The CJ-5 (right, top) made its debut in 1955, two years after the military model M38 A1 was released. It offered rounded fenders, a one-inch longer wheelbase, and a three-inch wider body. Some early CJ-5s were shipped with two-piece windshields, like their military counterparts, but eventually all CJ-5s were fitted with a one piece pane. In 1953, Willys attempted to create a lightweight vehicle from existing parts. It was called the BC or Bobcat (right, bottom left) and weighed only 1475 pounds. This was 10 pounds less than the MBL (lightweight) designed 10 years earlier. The BC's top speed was a respectable 63 miles per hour, but the vehicle did not go into production. The CJ-3A (right, bottom right) had reached the end of its life after only six years and was replaced by the CJ-3B.

Trend tested a wagon with the flathead six. This engine was essentially the same one used by the Kaiser automobile, then nearing the end of its career in the United States.

Oddly enough, the term "Jeep" was being downplayed by this time, though the Willys name was still prominently featured. There was no mention of the Jeep, per se, in literature dealing with the Station Wagon. But the four-wheel-drive version still performed like a typical Jeep. According to the *Motor Trend* reviewer's report, the Station Wagon "bounded over the worst ruts we could find (we couldn't take the other cars through the same 'tank traps') and settled down quickly. One dust-covered driver got out of the Jeep complaining that he couldn't get it stuck! The way it goes through soft earth or sand, through the brush, and up and down hills is a wonder to behold: The wheels fling themselves around some, but the car just keeps digging in. On a rain-drenched, muddy incline, the Willys never faltered. In fact, its driver eagerly expected that he'd have to pull some of the other back-sliding, spinning cars out of a ditch before the slippery hill was conquered."

In summarizing their reaction to the four-wheel-drive Jeep wagon—rather a different breed than the typical *Motor Trend* subject—the test drivers commented:

• "The greatest invention since feet, for moving from point A to point B, regardless of what's in between."

• "Not in the running as a comfortable, quiet, and economical family car, but I like it for its ruggedness and fantastic pulling power."

• "If you like to head for the backwoods, or have a home in the mountains or desert (or anyplace where there are or *aren't* any roads), this is the car. It's not for city or highway use, nor is it meant to be."

• "I got a big bang (in more ways than one) out of being bounced around as if the car didn't give a hang whether I was comfortable or not. The Jeep has its shortcom-

Willys was always pushing for additional uses for its Jeep trucks and CJ models. One common conversion for both was to a light-duty fire truck (left). The four-wheel-drive capabilities of the Jeeps made them a clear choice for some rural departments.

The DJ-3A (right, top) was the first in a long line of two-wheel-drive Universal models. The rear wheels were the driven wheels, and there was a solid front axle. Production commenced in 1955; the DJ-3A quickly proved to be very popular with government agencies. One of the few changes that occurred during the early Kaiser years was the introduction of the "Hurricane" six-cylinder engine (right, middle right) in 1954. The powerplant had been standard in Kaiser automobiles since the car's inception in 1947. For the Jeep application, the engine pumped out 115 horsepower and 190 pounds-feet of torque. The CJ-5's optional hardtop (right, bottom) included steel doors with roll-up windows.

passenger car market and designated the wagon as part of the company's commercial line. Available in either 4x2 or 4x4 guise, it was designated the "Utility Wagon." The extra seat for the seventh passenger was deleted, as was the standard overdrive that had been featured with the four-cylinder models. A live axle replaced Barney Roos's Planadyne suspension. Prices were moderated accordingly, and production figures were lumped with those of the trucks. Warn hubs were optional on the four-wheel-drive units, making it possible for drivers to disconnect the front-wheel-drive mechanism by simply turning the hubs with their fingers.

Performance, thanks to the 115-horsepower engine, was considerably enhanced, compared to the early Jeep wagons. A reviewer for *Auto Age* reported an easy cruising speed of 60 miles per hour in the two-wheel mode, with 80 miles per hour within easy reach. Then with the front wheels reconnected he "rode through a marsh, across a two-foot-deep stream and climbed a 60-degree bank on the other side. . . .

"If it were possible to cover up some of the hair on the Willys chest and add some powder and paint and a bustle," *Auto Age*'s chauvinistic staffer added, tongue-in-cheek, "maybe the style-conscious females who determine America's car market would give it more of a tumble."

Willys's trucks featured the same changes and updates as the wagon line. A 4x4 sedan delivery was added in 1953, priced $451 higher than the 4x2 version. The four-wheel-drive unit appeared to have had only a limited market, and usefulness was limited.

The six-cylinder, F-head Willys passenger car engine was made available to 4x2 sedan delivery buyers in 1954, and the 115 horsepower, 226 cid Kaiser L-head six became the standard powerplant for the 4x4 trucks, supplying both with badly needed additional power. Despite all this shuffling, the big news on the Jeep truck front was still a year away—Forward Control.

ings, but I'll bet it has more fortitude than a lot of drivers when the going gets rough."

• "An austere, truck-like interior denotes its purpose. It's not a comfortable car by any standard, but I look at it as a good compromise between a non-deluxe family car and a pickup truck."

During 1955, Willys withdrew from the

Jeep trucks (left, top) were used extensively in extremely remote areas. They were highly reliable and very easy to maintain; in fact, many are still in service today. Peak production for the first-generation truck was in 1951, when 38,407 were built. Willys continued to push the CJ to farmers, citing its many applications (left, bottom).

By 1955 the Station Wagon (right, top, and bottom left) could be had with the 115-horsepower Kaiser six. The interior was still quite Spartan, but this was, after all, a utility vehicle. Willys-Overland had originally forged its reputation by building wartime jeeps; 10 years later they were at it again, associating their civilian products with the models they produced for the government (right, bottom right).

CHAPTER SIX

Forward Control to the Forefront: 1956-62

n November 27, 1956, Kaiser-Jeep announced a new ¾-ton pickup truck. This design was a completely new idea for the light truck market. It placed the driver directly over the front wheels in a forward control position. The *Commercial Car Journal*, in December 1956, stated the mission of the Forward Control Jeep trucks. "Aimed at providing maximum cargo space in relation to wheelbase," the announcement declared, "the new FC-150 has the cab situated well forward of the engine to provide more than six feet of

cargo bed length despite the 81-inch wheelbase."

Overall length was 147.5 inches, two inches shorter than the diminutive Nash Metropolitan and 38 inches shorter than a Chevrolet half-ton pickup. Classified as a ¾-ton unit, though the chassis was basically that of a CJ-5 Jeep, the FC-150 was powered by the four-cylinder F-head "Hurricane" engine producing 75 horsepower and 114 pounds-feet of torque. A three-speed manual transmission was standard, while a four-speed was optional. Four-wheel drive was featured, and the transfer case could be shifted without stopping the vehicle—a major innovation in those days. The price for the pickup was $2320, just $64 more than the conventional 4x4 Jeep truck.

The Jeep advertising program stressed the FC-150's superior visibility, claiming it to be 200 percent greater than that of a conventional vehicle. The deluxe model, in fact, provided a glass area of 2747 square inches. However, *Motor Trend* noted that "T-Birds, Corvettes, Hawks and other short-stature iron which may pass on your right are difficult to see from the driver's seat." The magazine referred to the FC's "helicopter look," observing that "your first impression, as you climb into the cab of this little workhorse, may very well be that you have ensconced yourself under the bubble canopy of a whirlybird."

Like the other four-wheel-drive Jeep vehicles, the forward control models would climb almost any kind of grade. Bob Scala, reporting for *Motor Trend*, recalled, "For our initial test hop, we pushed the transfer

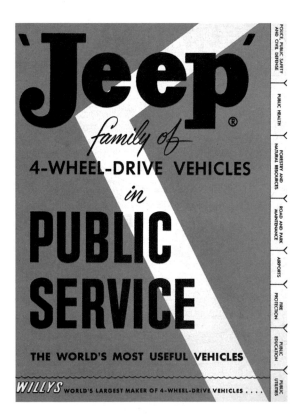

(continued on page 96)

Kaiser-Jeep's advertising maintained its familiar look in 1956 with a bright orange pamphlet on Jeep products in "Public Service" (left). Inside were black and white photos (some heavily retouched) of Jeeps powering chain saws, pulling DC-3s, and digging six-foot-deep trenches.

Though the Station Wagons (right, top left) were largely unchanged during the Fifties, they did receive several special paint and trim options. In 1957 Jeep developed the Mechanical Mule (right, top right). It weighed only 750 pounds and had a four-cylinder engine. By the end of production in 1965 Jeep had built 4618 units. A stretched version of the CJ-5, called the CJ-6, came on line in 1956. The CJ-6 (right, middle left) had a wheelbase that was 20 inches longer than the CJ-5. By far the biggest news from Jeep in a decade was the release of the Forward Control truck (right, middle right) in 1957. However, of more lasting importance was the lowly Dispatcher (right, bottom), which was released in 1955. This two-wheel-drive model was available as either a convertible or hardtop and would become familiar to postal workers throughout the United States.

Jeep FORWARD CONTROL FC-150
The all NEW 4-Wheel Drive Truck

TURNPIKE PERFORMANCE Plus OFF-ROAD TRACTION

THE FORWARD CONTROL Jeep FC-150
GVW...5000 lbs.

4-WHEEL DRIVE

WILLYS...WORLD'S LARGEST MANUFACTURER OF 4-WHEEL-DRIVE VEHICLES

FC-150 STAKE MODEL

FC-170 DUAL WHEEL STAKE MODEL

FC-150

FC-170

In 1957 the FC-150 (left, top) was a fresh idea in light truck design and marketing. Jeep engineers placed the cab directly over the front wheels, allowing a vehicle with a wheelbase of only 81 inches to offer a cargo bay that was 74 inches long. Later in that same year the FC-170 Jeep (left, bottom right) was introduced. This model had a 103.5-inch wheelbase and came standard with the L-head six-cylinder engine.

The number of different applications for the Jeep trucks by 1957 was mind numbing. A few of the custom bodies that Jeep offered were "Dump-O-Matic," Cargo Personnel carrier, Commando Fire truck, and two ambulance versions. Engine choices remained the same, and there were still two- and four-wheel-drive versions of the stake, pickup, and chassis and cab models. (right, top and middle). The base engine on the two-wheel-drive models was still the 72-horsepower "Go-Devil" (right, bottom right), and the "Super Hurricane" six (right, bottom left) offered 115 horsepower and 190 pounds-feet of torque.

WILLYS News

WILLYS...
the company on the move!

Published by the Merchandising Department for Willys Dealers and Salesmen

Vol. 2, No. 4   Willys Motors, Inc.   APRIL, 1956

NEW TWO-TONE 'JEEP' TRUCK ANNOUNCED

Striking Color Array Adds Buyer Appeal To 4-WD, Willys Line

A handsome new array of two-tone color combinations has been made available in production models of the Willys 4-WD Truck line according to an announcement by Hickman Price, Jr., Vice President, Willys Motors, Inc.

"Twelve striking combinations," Mr. Price said, "are being offered to Willys customers in keeping with the continuing program of product development at the factory."

The new paint combinations give the Willys Truck a longer lower look and add to the basic rugged appearance which characterizes the 'Jeep' family line. The following color combinations are now available in order from the factory: Juleg Green Top and Lower and Pine Tint Center, President Red Top and Lower and Glacier White Center, Glacier White Top and Lower

(Continued on page 5)

Willys Ad Features Farmer's Daughter

The fable of the traveling salesman and the farmer's daughter has been converted into a modern sales message in the first of a series of advertisements launched by Willys Motors, Inc.

Semi-institutional in nature, the new series will relate Jeep and Jeep truck success stories originating at home and in the free countries of the world where the versatile 4-wheel drive vehicles are at work.

In using the salesman-farmer's daughter bromide, Willys has the comely miss pull the salesman's mired automobile onto the highway with her Jeep, thus again changing the never standard ending. The message points out that there are probably more Jeeps doing more jobs on American farms than there are traveling salesmen on the highways.

New eye appeal of the Willys 4WD Pickup Truck blends into the rugged functional lines characteristic of 'Jeep' and 'Jeep'-family vehicles. Twelve new two-tone color combinations are currently in production at the factory and are being offered to Willys dealers throughout the United States.

Willys Salesmen Compete In Big 'Jeep' Sales-Safari

An exciting new 'Jeep' Sales-Safari, designed exclusively for Willys retail salesmen has been announced by C. A. Watson, General Sales Manager.

"The new contest," Mr. Watson says, "is the salesman's counterpart of Operation TV, the sales contest which is currently being staged for Willys dealers throughout the United States.

"It affords every salesman an opportunity to win handsome prizes regardless what other salesmen in other parts of the country are doing," he said.

Every Willys salesman who is entered in the contest will receive a credit of 2,000 points for each Jeep family vehicle that he sells during the eleven week period between March 26 and May 31, 1956. The

(Continued on page 3)

"Operation T-V" Contest Leaders Named

Sixty Group Winners Receive March Awards

Three national leaders have been named, and nearly sixty group and area winners were announced at the conclusion of the first month of the new Willys 'Operation T-V' Sales Contest.

Final tabulation of dealer retail delivery reports during March shows that Setaro Motors, Inc., New Haven, Connecticut, and R. H. Williams Motors, East St. Louis, Illinois, have taken an impressive lead in group-three and group-two respectively. Group-one leader, LeSage Sales and Service, Hubbell, Michigan was hard pressed in a close battle for top honors in that group classification.

Setaro Motors with a base of three, sold fifteen units during March for a contest score of twelve; R. H. Williams Motors posted a score of fourteen

with the sale of sixteen vehicles against a base of two; and LeSage Sales and Service sold eight units with a base of one for a total score of seven.

Two other dealers in the closely matched group-one sold five vehicles over base for the month, while several scored three and four units over base in this group classification.

Movie Camera Prizes

Willys dealers whose retail deliveries exceeded all other dealers in their area in their group classification during March will receive an Eastman Brownie Turret 8mm Movie Camera.

These dealers in group-one are: Ponder Motors, Jackson Mississippi; Emmes Service Station, Peterborough, New Hampshire; Olean Willys Sales and Service, Olean, New York; Parkersburg Willys Sales, Parkersburg, West Virginia; Herring Willys-'Jeep,'

(Continued on page 3)

Three Top Willys Dealers In National Contest

R. H. WILLIAMS — Group Two Leader

ROBERT A. LeSAGE — Leader in Group One

ROBERT J. SETARO — Group Three Leader

An All-Weather, All-Terrain Vehicle... With the Features to Prove It!

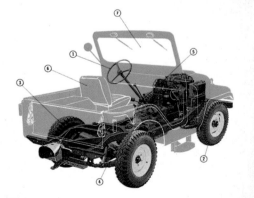

1. **STEERING.** Quick 'Jeep' cam and lever steering and the Universal's low curb weight make maneuvering in traffic and around off-road obstacles easy. 2. **TIRES.** The Universal has up to three times the optional tire sizes of competitive vehicles, offering tire types and sizes for all terrains. 3. **FRAME.** Five crossmembers (plus a rear "K" member with 4WD models) and extra-thick side members provide the 'Jeep' Universal with a strong, protective frame. 4. **SUSPENSION.** Since rugged axles and suspension are standard equipment, you won't normally have to pay extra for heavy-duty components—even if you want a winch installed! 5. **BRAKES.** Servo brakes with bonded linings are standard with Dauntless-powered 4WD Universals. Other models have non-servo brakes. A transmission brake (practically a "must" for off-road vehicles) is also standard with 4WD models. 6. **SEATS.** New bucket seats are constructed of deep molded foam rubber and firm bolsters. They provide great new comfort and inches more headroom! Standard driver's seat is adjustable. Variety of seat combinations—and tops—also available. 7. **WINDSHIELD.** High penetration-resistant windshield glass provides added safety. Windshield can be folded against hood or quickly removed.

---

control into the low-speed, four-wheel-drive position and pointed the stub nose of this heap of Jeep up a motorcycle hill climb course. This course was a narrow, deeply rutted, and bumpy trail, and while we decline to estimate the percent grade, we would never dream of attempting to negotiate it in a conventional truck or passenger car. The Jeep had no difficulty whatever with this and climbed steadily and surely to the top. We turned around, experienced the sensation of leaping from a ski jump, and allowed the engine compression to lower us safely to the bottom. We are keeping our eyes open for a hill which might stop the Jeep, but we'll bet it will have to be close to vertical."

Transfer controls on this model were reduced to a single lever, in lieu of the two-lever operation typical of other Jeeps. Steering was light and easy, though somewhat slow (a ratio of 32.0:1 gave five-and-a-half turns, lock-to-lock). Clutch and brake pedals were of the pendulum type, just then coming into widespread use. For convenience the brake fluid reservoir cover was placed on the dashboard. Access to the engine was through an easily removable cover, and heavy fiberglass insulation deadened engine noise. The payload bed stood just 24 inches above ground level, for convenient loading. However, the strange configuration of the bed somewhat limited its carrying capacity. To link the FC to other Kaiser-Jeep products, the company gave it a familiar seven-slot twin-headlight grille of contrasting body color.

Later in 1957, a second forward-control truck was introduced. The FC-170, built on a 103.5-inch chassis and available in either 4x4 or 4x2 form, had a gross vehicle weight of 7000 pounds. In several instances the FC-170 chassis became the basis for fire trucks and other specialty vehicles. In pickup form the FC-170 featured a nine-foot box, though in total length the FC measured only 180.5 inches—seven-and-a-half inches shorter than a 1960 Falcon Ranchero.

Sales for Willys products in 1955, '56, and '57 hovered just over 64,000 units, led by the CJs (left, bottom) and the Wagons. It appeared that the Jeeps had finally carved a niche for themselves in the marketplace. However, sales dropped over 20,000 units the next year.

For 1959 the Utility Wagon (right) returned with only minor changes. Base power was still the "Go-Devil" engine, and the optional L-head six was downrated to 105 horsepower. The base model was just that, though many options were on the list. Front bumper guards, two-tone paint, directional signals, heater and defroster, back-up light, radio, governor, and power takeoffs were among the many available. The tailgate (right, bottom) was a two-piece affair, with the top section opening up and the lower half opening down.

Despite the innovation, sales were never great: 9738 in its first and most popular year. Still, FC units were put to use in all sorts of situations. Their narrow stance and four-wheel-drive pulling power made them ideal for farm uses such as field sprayers and tank trucks. By far their most popular use was by gas station owners who could use the vehicle for towing, light hauling, and snow plowing.

Ironically, the most appealing of all the Jeep Forward Control vehicles never made it past the design stage. A smartly styled van was designed by Brooks Stevens and built on the FC-150 chassis by Reutter, of Stuttgart, West Germany. Stevens intended this first-ever four-wheel-drive van to be used as a commuter vehicle, providing six doors for easy access to its nine-passenger interior. Regrettably, only three prototypes were built. Brooks Stevens himself later observed, "We were probably too early with this, but we might have started the van fad with the youth of the nation at that time."

There wasn't much new on the Wagon during the Fifties, so Jeep compensated by offering trim and equipment packages. Most consisted merely of bodyside striping (left, top and middle) and comfort and convenience features. One specialty package offered by the factory was the Airport Wagon conversion (left, bottom). This stretched the wheelbase considerably, added several rows of seats, and added four more doors.

During the Fifties, the U.S. Army tested several applications for the Mechanical Mule—developed and produced by Jeep. A canvas top and support rods could be fitted to provide some protection from the elements (right, top). The cowl and windshield could be removed (right, bottom left) leaving a four-wheel-drive vehicle that was 100 inches long, 46 inches wide, and barely three feet high. The CJ-6 was another new vehicle at Jeep. Its extended bed and increased carrying capacity allowed the CJ-6 (right, bottom right) to perform a variety of tasks; however, sales in the United States never quite caught on.

On the more conventional Jeep truck front, a new option for 1957 was a "Dump-O-Matic" hydraulic hoist that converted the pickup into a mini dump truck. One could also order a four-wheel-drive ambulance, fire truck, or 12-person "Cargo-Personnel" carrier.

For 1959 the conventionally styled one-ton Jeep truck was mostly a carryover, but the 226-cid ex-Kaiser engine was re-rated at only 105 horsepower. However, the line was expanding. Counting the CJ-series Utility Jeeps, the company was producing an array of 24 commercial vehicles. According to *Automotive Industries*, Jeeps were being manufactured or assembled in no fewer than 19 foreign countries.

In July 1960, the company was awarded the first in what would become a series of contracts to build walk-in "Fleetvans" for the U.S. Postal Service. Twenty-eight different Jeep commercial vehicles were offered by that time, and production for the year came to 122,446—slightly over half of these being CJ-series Universal Jeeps.

Even more variations were added for 1961, bringing the total to 31. One of the newcomers was a Fleetvan, similar to the vehicle being built for the Postal Service. Powered by the F-head four, the Fleetvan provided 170 cubic feet of cargo area, thus making remarkably good use of its 81-inch wheelbase. Overall length was just 154 inches. The Fleetvan listed at $2380, $166 less than the comparable Chevrolet Walk-In Delivery.

The Kaiser-Jeep corporation had already developed a working relationship with the Postal Service in developing the Fleetvan and was soon to become forever linked with the service with the introduction of a new CJ variant. Known as the DJ-3A Dispatcher, this CJ variation appeared in 1956. A bare-bones, two-wheel-drive vehicle powered by the old fathead four, it came in three models: Basic, Canvas Top, and Hardtop. Prices began at $1205, $410 lower than the CJ-3B, the cheapest of the four-wheel-drive Jeeps. The hardtop model,

It didn't take Brooks Stevens long to turn the innovative Forward Control trucks into something completely different. In an early clay rendering (left, top) he designed a six-door van. This design made it to the prototype stage and was dubbed the Commuter (left, middle). Later, the photos of the Commuter were retouched to create a slab-sided pickup body (left, bottom) on the Forward Control chassis.

Brooks Stevens also did some design variations on the new Dispatcher model. One was called the Sportif (right, top), which rode on a shorter wheelbase and was fitted with a "continental" spare tire. Another design study was the 100 Dispatcher. It came in three variations and made it all the way to the prototype stage. There was a three-door steel top, a two-door hardtop, and a two-door convertible with a back seat.

equipped with a fiberglass roof and sliding doors, was the forerunner of the familiar Postal Jeeps.

In another of the endless variations of the Jeep Universal, a number of upscale, open-bodied DJ's were sold for resort use. Best known of this group was the Gala, equipped with a fringed surrey top and painted in bright colors. A fleet of Galas, featuring pink- and white-striped canvas

tops, was purchased by the Las Breezeways Hotel, in Acapulco. As automotive journalist John Gunnell has observed, these vehicles marked the beginning of the Jeep's transition.

Another new Jeep CJ model was released for 1956, the CJ-6. Based on the CJ-5, the CJ-6 had a 20-inch longer wheelbase, which added to passenger and cargo room.

(continued on page 106)

One interesting option Jeep added to their FC-170 was dual rear wheels (left, top). Though the dualie setup accounted for few sales, the heavy-duty suspension and additional rear tires increased the GVW rating of the Platform State to 9000 pounds. The price of the base FC-170 Pickup (left, bottom) had risen to $2858 by 1960. During the early 1960s, FC-150 (right, top left) production was decreasing while that of the 170 was increasing. But the numbers, as a whole, were but a drop in the light truck market bucket. By the time the CJ-5 was being produced, there were many after-market plowing and accessory packages for the CJs (right, top right). They became a workhorse at the local service station and down on the farm. In late 1959 Brooks Stevens (right, bottom left) came up with a trim and interior package for the Utility Wagon called the Harlequin.

New, high performance, professional

MEYER SNOW PLOWS

The rugged, heavy-duty HUSKYS are here! 'Jeep' owners can now have a 6½ or 7½ foot snow plow designed to meet the professional's need for brawn and speed . . . the HUSKYS will move more snow, faster than any other plow in the world.

Built to withstand the most demanding use, the HUSKY Snow Plows have higher, more heavily reinforced mold-boards with larger sectors, heavy-duty A-Frames and added trip springs for greater load capacities. The combination of these features provides 'Jeep' vehicle owners with the greatest snow clearing capacity ever.

The HUSKY line of Meyer Snow Plows has proved its ruggedness and dependability in extensive product performance tests conducted in Michigan and upper New York State.

For maximum performance in big job snow clearing—make sure your next Meyer Snow Plow is a **HUSKY!**

No doubt inspired by the success of the 1959 Gala Model, Willys came up with this Surrey design (left, top and middle) in 1960. It was based on the CJ chassis but had a wheelbase of 90 inches. It had unusual "I" shaped seating and five doors. An earlier proposal, called the Resorter (left, bottom), lacked the rear bench seat and offered twin doors on the sides. The Resorter also had a very interesting, though no doubt unsafe, single rear roof pillar.

Willys Motors hoped to cash in on the success of its Station Wagons with a similar model based on the CJ-5 (right, top). This proposal was drawn up in 1960 and carried several styling features found on the larger Wagons. The roof was given similar indentations, the rear wheel wells had the same flares, and the C-pillar had the same reverse slant. Although Willys hoped to restyle the full-sized Wagon (right, middle), any money for the restyle was probably diverted toward the upcoming Wagoneer. Despite the constant lack of working capital at Willys, Brooks Stevens was still hard at work. He devised a new cab for the Forward Control trucks (right, bottom), which in 1960 had been around unchanged since late 1956.

Other than the wheelbase the CJ-6 was identical to the CJ-5 and used all of the same running gear (although rear springs were softer). However, the CJ-6 never caught on in America, and most were sold for export. Some of the export models were fitted with Perkins diesel engines, although apparently you could get the diesel on any Universal model. Of the few that remained in the United States, some were converted into fire engines and farm wagons. CJ-6 production peaked in 1966 at 3521.

The CJ-3B and CJ-5 continued unchanged until 1961. That year a near-luxury version called the Tuxedo Park was offered. It was essentially a dressed up CJ-5 that included a chromed hood, mirror supports, and bumpers; turbine wheels, whitewall tires, and a spare tire cover. The Tuxedo Park remained an option until 1964, when it was given its own model designation.

Jeep's venerable wagons and trucks returned unchanged over most of this period. The four-cylinder Utility Wagon disappeared for 1959, only to be reintroduced the following year as the 4x2 "Maverick Special." (The name had a link to Kaiser's

(continued on page 110)

The I.V.I (International Vehicle Investigation) program was the pet project of Henry Kaiser, head of Kaiser-Jeep. This project was funded, in part, by the government in an effort to develop a low-cost vehicle that could be produced in third-world countries. There were several body styles including a troop carrier (top left) and a pick-up panel (bottom left).

Jeep Wagons and trucks continued to soldier on through the late Fifties and early Sixties with only minimal changes (right, top). However, one big change was the switch from a two-piece windshield to a single-pane unit in 1960. As usual, Willys continually modified side trim and paint schemes of the aging vehicles, adding some semblance of vitality. The CJ-5 (right, middle and bottom left) moved into the Sixties with no major changes, but sales continued to climb reaching 19,753 in 1960. Kaiser Industries was very active in South America building both Willys and Kaiser cars in Brazil. The model JA-2PA/B (right, bottom right) was built during the early Sixties in Argentina. Based on the CJ-5, the JA-2PA/B had a different, two-piece windshield.

- EXCITINGLY ORIGINAL, DIFFERENT, PRACTICAL
- THE 'SURREY' WITH THE FRINGE ON TOP
- CREATED FOR CAREFREE BUSINESS-PLEASURE TRANSPORTATION
- PERFECT FOR ECONOMICAL DELIVERY SERVICE
- LOWEST INITIAL COST, LOWEST OPERATING COST

Jeep 'SURREY'
MODEL DJ3A

Jeep 4-CYLINDER, L-HEAD ENGINE

World-famous 'Jeep' L-Head engine has powered 'Jeep' vehicles on nearly every continent — now improved and perfected brings 4-cylinder economy and unequalled efficiency to the 'Jeep' 'Surrey.' Positive exhaust valve rotation and aluminum alloy pistons mean longer engine life, more maintenance-free operation per mile.

60 H. P. @ 4000 R.P.M., 105 lbs. ft. Torque @ 2000 R.P.M., Displacement 134.2 cu. in.

WE HAVE A 'JEEP' VEHICLE FOR YOUR TOUGHEST JOB!

WILLYS MOTORS, INC.
TOLEDO, OHIO

GO·FOR·DIGGER TRENCHING MACHINE

back hoe

MOBILE — Travels from one job site to another without need of trailer or secondary unit.

COMPACT IN TRAVEL POSITION but quickly made ready when digging is required.

APPROVED HYDRAULIC SYSTEM — The hydraulic system used on this machine is of the latest design, giving greater vehicle body at less maintenance cost. This has been brought about by the use of a dual output pump, supplying two different volumes of oil to a dual control valve.

GO·FOR·DIGGER
AND ITS MANY EXCLUSIVE FEATURES

APPROVED Jeep EQUIPMENT

Since 1950 — 15 YEARS OF CONTINUOUS IMPROVEMENT NEWEST OF WHICH ARE:

- HEAVY DUTY RIGHT ANGLE DRIVE
- HYDRAULIC CRAWL
- FRAME REINFORCEMENT PLATES
- 5 YEAR GUARANTEE REAR AXLE

MOBILE — Travels from one job site to another without need of trailer or secondary unit.
COMPACT IN TRAVEL POSITION but quickly made ready when trenching is required.
QUICK CHANGE ANGLE DOZER BLADE — Hydraulically activated dozer affords both up and down pressure of blade. Newly designed — will not dig in. Permits only back filling of loose spoil.

digs 1500 ft. an hour forward
also digs backward

Due to the fact that the Wagon was now approaching 15 years without a major redesign, Willys began to promote variations and option packages for the original Jeep Universal. The "Back Hoe" and the "Digger" (left, bottom) were two popular options for the CJ-5, both of which required the addition of hydraulic pumps. In 1959 Jeep offered the Gala, a two- or four-wheel drive CJ-3B (above) with a pink-and-white canvas fringe top. Jeep advertised this vehicle as being "perfect for economical deliveries" and thought it was perfect "for carefree business and pleasure transportation." In 1960 Jeep changed the name to Surrey and added two new colors—Cerulean blue and Fountain green. These vehicles were mostly used by hotels and resorts. In fact, a fleet of them was purchased by Las Brisas resort in Acapulco. Some models deleted the side curtains around the upper body shell, and others came with a matching canvas spare-tire cover.

sponsorship of the popular TV western *Maverick*, starring James Garner.) Once again the F-head four-cylinder engine was employed, and the familiar Borg-Warner overdrive was available at extra cost. The price was $1995 f.o.b. Toledo, several hundred dollars less than any other full-sized American-made station wagon.

An effort was made to dress up the 1960 model. Bodyside moldings were changed,

eight two-tone paint combinations were offered, and harmonizing interiors of "breathable" vinyl-coated fabrics and Pompano carpeting were supplied as standard issue. Continuing the modernizing effort, the two-piece front windshield and rear glass were replaced by single pane units. Also standard were white sidewall "Captive Air" tires.

(continued on page 114)

During the Cold War, the U.S. military was looking for alternative vehicles to the venerable M38. A contract was awarded to Ford for just such a purpose in 1951. A little over a year later, pilot models began appearing, and testing continued until production began in 1959. What appeared was designated by the military as the M151—known by civilians as the A-1 MUTT. Testing indicated that the independent rear suspension led to rollover problems, so a revised model with a trailing-arm suspension was adopted in 1968. Compared to the M38, the M151 had superior cargo space and interior room (left, top and bottom left). The four-cylinder engine was waterproofed, and all electrics were sealed (left). Overall weight came in at 2773 pounds. The U.S. military was still using the vehicle as late as 1989. Over the years the M151 was produced by Ford, Kaiser-Jeep, and AM General.

The Brazilian Jeepster

Although few people are aware of it, there was a postscript to the original Jeepster—regrettably, it never got beyond the prototype stage. In the early 1960s, with the Aero-Willys being produced by Willys do Brazil, Brooks Stevens was employed to restyle the car. The result was the handsome Willys 2600, introduced at the Paris Salon in October 1962. (Regrettably, the 2600 was never marketed on this continent.) Regardless, this new Willys was so well received at the Paris Salon that Stevens, with the blessing of the company's South American managers, undertook to redesign the Jeepster as well.

The prototype was a beauty, and as journalist Robert Ackerson related, "Enthusiasm for this sports roadster ran high and, amidst plans for its production, its name was changed to Saci, which in South American folklore was a little, and likeable leprechaun-type of creature.

"But in the more somber world of money, labor, and capital the Saci met its match. There simply wasn't room in the Willys do Brazil assembly plant for the Saci's construction. This decision may very well have been the wrong one, for at the first international automobile show held in Sao Paulo, the Saci was a sensation."

Be that as it may, the effort was abandoned. Today, Brooks Stevens wonders if perhaps that neat little Saci prototype might still exist, somewhere.

Willys do Brasil was producing Jeepsters and Station Wagons called the Rural (left, top and bottom left) in both two- and four-wheel drive in 1960. Brooks Stevens contributed greatly to their unique front-end appearance. Advertisements, like in the States, proclaimed the Jeep a "Car for the Public" and "A Companion for any Task." At home, Kaiser was now building M151s in their Toledo, Ohio (above), plant right alongside the CJ-5.

The Maverick name was dropped for 1961, but otherwise the car was unchanged. *Motor Trend* found it "so conventional it brings back memories." By this time, for some obscure reason, the steering had been slowed drastically. Six full turns were required to swing the wheel from lock to lock—one of the slowest ratios to be found on any 1961 car or light truck. The reviewer commented, "Of course, this

makes extremely poor maneuvering potential at parking lot speeds where the road is good. It does have an advantage in the back country . . . ."

Performance of the F-head four-banger was, by that time, hopelessly out of date. Zero-to-60, in *Motor Trend*'s test, took a leisurely 26.6 seconds, which to most people was simply not acceptable. Fortunately,

(continued on page 118)

Nineteen sixty-two was the last sales year of any significance for the Willys Utility Wagon. The 4x2 "Maverick Special" (left and right) returned with new bodyside trim. Kaiser's sponsorship of the popular TV western Maverick was the original idea behind the options package. Once again the F-head, four-cylinder engine was employed, and the price was $1995. An available option late in the year was the OHC "Tornado" six which would go on to power the new-for-1963 Wagoneer.

Kissing Cousin: The Mighty Mite

Developed by the Special Products division of the Hudson Motor Car Company, the M422 Mighty Mite (above) was a lightweight version of the World War II jeep.

Cars magazine, after examining the first Mighty Mite prototype back in 1953, called it the "Successor to the Jeep." Things didn't work out that way, of course, and we'll take a look at the reasons why. But the Mighty Mite (officially designated "Truck, Utility: ¼-Ton, 4x4, Lightweight") merits a good deal more than just a passing glance.

The Mite was developed by the Special Products Division of the Hudson Motor Car Company in the years just prior to the time when Hudson merged with Nash to form American Motors. As its name suggests, the Mite was much smaller and lighter than the familiar Jeep. It was designed by Ben Gregory, of Mid-America Research Corporation, to specifications laid down by the U.S. Marine Corps. What the Marines wanted was a four-wheel-drive vehicle that would weigh at least half a ton less than the Jeep, yet would be capable of performing essentially the same functions as the heavier machine. With cargo-carrying helicopters just then coming into widespread use, the advantage of such a design, particularly in jungle warfare, was obvious.

There was more than a touch of genius in the Mighty Mite. Compared to the Jeep, wheelbase was reduced by 10 inches, yet the carrying capacity was nearly the same. The use of aluminum for the hood, cowl, front fenders, and side panels resulted in a substantial savings in weight. The lightweight engine was constructed with an aluminum block and was air-cooled. This design did away with the pound-per-pint weight of the coolant.

That first prototype was powered by a horizontally-opposed, 44-horsepower Porsche engine, evidently selected primarily for its availability. It was expected from the outset, however, that a more powerful, American-built V-4 would eventually be substituted—as indeed it was. *Popular Science*, road-testing an early Mite prototype, found that it rode and handled better than the Jeep and would climb an 87 percent grade.

Strangely enough, although prototypes were on the road by mid-1953, production didn't commence until January 1960. By that time the power source was a 55-horsepower V-4 of American Motors' own manufacture. The earlier three-speed transmission and two-speed axle had been dropped in favor of a simpler four-speed gearbox, synchronized on second, third, and fourth gears. First speed, with a ratio of 5.24:1, was a genuine "granny" gear; and limited-slip differentials, front and rear, provided excellent traction. Suspension was independent all around, and brakes were mounted inboard. Longitudinal quarter-elliptic springs were mounted in such a way as to virtually eliminate rollover.

Because the Mighty Mite was developed with jungle warfare in mind, windshield-height snorkels were provided for both carburetor intake and exhaust. Thus the driver might be up to his shoulders in the drink, but the vehicle would determinedly make its way through whatever water hazard happened to be at hand.

Early predictions notwithstanding—and despite its undisputed advantages in weight, handling, and riding comfort—the Mighty Mite was not destined to replace the Jeep. Indeed, only 3922 examples were built over the three-year period ending January 1963. No doubt its aluminum body was less durable than the stout steel hull of its competitor. But the Mighty Mite's principal drawback had to do with its price. At $5200 a copy, this impressive little machine cost the Marine Corps nearly three times as much as the familiar Jeep.

Few Mighty Mites turn up today at gatherings of off-road aficionados. Not only was the initial production very limited, but distribution was confined solely to the Marine Corps. In an undated memorandum issued by American Motors, the company declared, "At the time of development and manufacture, there was no intent that this vehicle would have a commercial application. . . .

"At the completion of manufacturing, the Marine Corps ordered what it then considered to be a lifetime repair parts order. After these parts were delivered, American Motors was directed to dispose of all special tooling then owned by the Government. This completed the company's obligation to the U. S. Government. (American Motors never has had an obligation to the public.)"

All of which meant, of course, that there was no source of spare parts, or even instruction manuals, available to anyone who might have purchased a Mighty Mite from surplus sales at the U. S. Marine Corps Supply Agency.

Predictably besieged by requests for parts and technical assistance, American Motors clearly had little patience with the matter. One company official pointed out that all Mighty Mite vehicles and spare parts were built exclusively for the U. S. Marine Corps, and all printed maintenance and service manuals were developed *by* the Marine Corps. To this he added, "We tell purchasers of surplus Mighty Mites that their only recourse is to be sure to buy two vehicles if they are concerned about parts."

How very unfortunate it is that the maintenance and restoration of these fine little machines has been made so difficult. For the Mighty Mite was—and remains—an impressive vehicle, and one of special interest to collectors of four-wheel-drive and military vehicles.

Though shorter in wheelbase by 10 inches, the Mite offered a similar carrying capacity. The motor was an AMC V-4 (above, middle) that produced 55 horsepower. A variation, model 422 A-1, had a six-inch longer wheelbase.

six-cylinder power was optionally available.

Production of the Jeep Utility Wagon (nee Station Wagon) continued as late as 1965, in both 4x4 and 4x2 form, but by 1963 production had slowed to a trickle. However, in May 1962 a new engine choice was available, Kaiser-Jeep's sophisticated new 140-horsepower overhead-cam six. Time had brought changes in a number of respects, yet the final edition of the little wagon was basically the same car that had first appeared some 17 years earlier—a remarkable record of longevity.

A new Jeep Station Wagon was about to make its debut. This one, like its predecessor, would set a new trend for the industry. In addition, it would remain in production even longer than the original.

For 1962 the CJ-5 (left and far left) *returned unchanged, though Willys offered a "Parade Blue Convertible Top Accessory Kit" ($130.20), which was Scotchguarded for the first time. In 1961 the Tuxedo Park accessory package was made available. This dress-up option added chromed hood hinges, exterior mirror supports, and bumpers, along with other appearance improvements. The M151 (below and bottom) saw continued production in Toledo and was later produced by AMC's subsidiary, AM General.*

CHAPTER SEVEN

The Origins of a Classic: 1963-69

ompare the exterior of a 1963 Jeep Wagoneer with the same model built almost 30 years later, and—apart from differences in trim—you could mistake one for the other. Finally replaced in 1993 the Wagoneer carried on for 29 years, with a body shell that had remained basically unchanged. Its design was so sound that it would define the four-wheel-drive utility market until the end of its lifetime.

The Wagoneer also represented, at its introduction, an important new concept in four-wheel-drive transportation. Jim Wright, technical editor at that time of *Motor Trend*, had this to say when the Wagoneer made its debut: "Long a builder of strictly, almost starkly functional, utility-type vehicles, Willys adds a whole new dimension to the line with the Wagoneer. Up to this time, almost all of the four-wheel-drive enthusiasts (of which there are thousands) have been faced with the problem of two cars in the garage. With the new Willys station wagon in the garage, the other car is no longer a necessity."

In contrast to the earlier Jeep Station Wagons, the Wagoneer looked more like a passenger car than a truck. Compared to its predecessor it had, as John Gunnell has noted, "more power, more luxury and ten times as much comfort." What the article failed to mention was the new Jeep had much more style and class.

Wheelbase grew to 110 inches, up from 104 in the previous Jeep wagons. Overall length was just short of 184 inches—about 10 inches longer than the earlier model. The Wagoneer was by any measure better looking and more car-like. Yet, with its familiar rectangular grille and generally squared-off appearance, the Wagoneer kept its unmistakable Jeep identity.

Space was provided in generous measure. With the tailgate open, the cargo length was 111 inches. Floor width was an ample 55 inches, and the unobstructed rear opening height was 39½ inches. Cargo volume came to 78.5 cubic feet, and space utilization was excellent.

Like the earlier Jeep Station Wagons, the Wagoneer came with either two- or four-wheel drive, though it was the latter type for which it was chiefly noted. However, the 1963 Wagoneer offered a couple of features never before supplied in a 4x4 vehicle: independent front suspension and an automatic transmission, both available at extra cost. Power, far greater than any previous Jeep product, came from a brand new six-cylinder engine, the only single overhead camshaft powerplant being produced in the United States at that time.

Two trim lines were offered, Standard and Custom, the latter commanding a premium of $194. Compared to earlier models, none of the Wagoneers came cheap, though the prices sound like bargains today. The least expensive Wagoneer—the Standard 2x2 in the two-door configuration—came to $2546 f.o.b. Toledo, $451 more than the corresponding 1962 model. And the top-of-the-line Custom 4x4 four-door cost $3526, plus options. As tested by *Motor Trend*, that model—equipped with automatic transmission, independent front suspension, power steering, power brakes, Warn hubs, electric wipers, heat, and radio—was priced at $4479, $643 more than a Buick Invicta station wagon. But

The M170, or Military CJ-6 (right) could be fitted with several different body packages. One was a light troop carrier with the capacity for six people. The engine was still the familiar "Go-Devil" four, albeit with heavy-duty waterproofing (right, bottom right). An interesting feature fitted to many Marine jeeps was a pair of parachute hooks. Mounted one on each bumper end, the hooks could be attached to a parachute so that the vehicle could be dropped out of a plane; or the hooks could be attached to a winch cable and lowered from a helicopter.

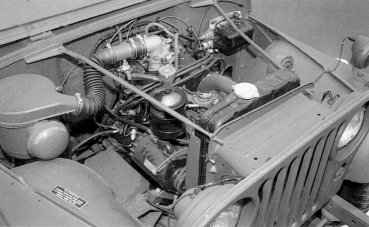

at this point all Station Wagons look alike...

but...at this point the
similarity
ENDS

CLASSIC BEAUTY,
UILT FOR DUTY!!!!!

then, a 4x4 Wagoneer could go lots of places and do lots of things that were quite beyond the Buick's reach. Almost no comparisons could be made between the new Wagoneer and stubby, top-heavy, and under-powered (if enormously practical) Willys forebear.

With commendable honesty, Willys advertised the horsepower of its overhead cam "Tornado" engine in net terms, rather than gross, a practice almost unheard of at that time. So the advertised rating of 140 horsepower was equivalent to a gross rating of 155. By way of comparison, the contemporary six-cylinder Chevrolet engine, whose 230 cubic inch displacement exactly matched that of the new Willys unit, produced only 140 gross horsepower.

This overhead-cam engine had been designed by A. C. "Sammy" Sampietro, the company's chief engineer since the retirement of Barney Roos in 1954. The name will be familiar to sports car buffs—Sampietro, an Italian expatriate, had been associated with Donald Healey in a number of enterprises. At one point, when he was helping to prepare a Nash-Healey to compete at LeMans, "Sammy" was credited with raising the horsepower of the aging Nash Ambassador Six engine from 140 to 189. Later, he played a critical role in the development of the original Austin-Healey.

Surprising as it may seem, this sophisticated powerplant was actually derived from the 226-cid flathead that powered the Kaiser and Frazer autos of 1946-55. This was the engine that was known as the L-head Continental six used by Graham in prewar times. The design was inherited by Jeep after Kaiser absorbed Willys in 1953. Before Sampietro worked his magic that engine produced only 115 horsepower. Certainly not enough for the Wagoneer.

Sampietro's solution was to adopt the old Hall-Scott idea of a chain-driven overhead camshaft with inclined overhead valves operated by single rocker arms. Combustion chambers were hemispheric, echoing a design used in earlier years by

Finally, in 1963, Kaiser Jeep had something new to advertise. That was the all-new Wagoneer (left). The advertisements were clever and inventive, stressing how similar the Wagoneer was to other full-size wagons, yet with the security of four-wheel drive. Kaiser Jeep also didn't miss a beat in advertising the SOHC six-cylinder engine and available automatic transmission.

The old Station Wagon, now called simply the Utility Wagon (right, top) carried on for two more years. One interesting change was the availability of the SOHC engine (right, bottom right). The engine was, in fact, available in the Utility Wagon in 1962, a year before it was introduced in the new Wagoneer. Sales, however, were unaffected and trailed off to next to nothing with the Wagoneer's debut.

Have twice the fun. Put your camper on a 'Jeep' Gladiator.

Just flip one simple lever into 'Jeep' 4-wheel drive.

Put the camper unit of your choice on a 'Jeep' Gladiator, and leave the crowds far behind (isn't that really why you want a camper?). Shift smoothly at any speed from 2-wheel to 4-wheel drive, and you've got twice the traction of ordinary camper trucks! Take your camper into the back country. Where ordinary camper trucks can't go. Churn through mud, sand ... go almost anywhere. On the highway, it

handles like a passenger car. Even your wife will enjoy driving it — the new 'Jeep' Gladiator with 4-wheel drive.

(Tailor your Gladiator to fit your needs: 250 hp V-8 engine or hi-Torque 6, a choice of colors, standard or custom cab and trim, full width or bucket seats, 7 or 8 foot box, power steering, power brakes, camper modifications available, 3- or 4-speed transmission with standard shift, or Turbo Hydra-Matic* (the only pick-up offering automatic transmission) with 4-wheel drive). GVW's 5000 to 7000 lbs. KAISER Jeep CORPORATION

You've got to drive it to believe it. See your 'Jeep' dealer. Check the Yellow Pages.

Chrysler. The advantage to this pattern was that larger valves could be used, resulting in superior breathing.

Rocker arms in the new engine were steel stampings, not unlike those of the Chevrolet V-8. The overhead camshaft eliminated long pushrods and potentially noisy tappets, resulting in relatively quiet operation—especially for what was, after all, a truck engine. (John Bond noted "a trace of what Wills Ste. Claire owners used to call 'cam-chatter,'" but reported that the noise was slight, and in any case it disappeared as soon as the pressure oiling system did its job.)

Because the OHC engine was designed to operate at high rpm, its crankshaft received a patented heat-treating process called "Tufftriding," in which metal components were soaked in a liquid nitriding solution. The treatment was said to impart a high surface hardness to the journals—a critical factor for use in conjunction with heavy-duty bearing inserts.

The torque numbers produced by this new engine were just as impressive as the horsepower numbers. Danny Collins, writing in *Auto Topics*, observed, "The overhead camshaft engine pulls mightily on mountain passes leaving Detroit cars with much higher advertised horsepower and less weight behind wondering what had passed them. The engine is extremely smooth and quiet. It performs with a turbine-like feel."

Despite the generally favorable reviews received by the overhead-cam mill, there was some difference of opinion as to the noise level. John Bond may have been closest to reality when he wrote, in *Car Life*, "On street or highway the engine is commendably smooth and quiet, but we must note that this is indeed a truck engine and it is not as smooth and quiet as the modern V-8 passenger car engine. In our opinion it is also not quite as smooth as any of the passenger car sixes when pulling hard or when cruising at speeds over 60 mph." To which Bond hastened to add, "Never-

The introduction of the Wagoneer was hailed by a flurry of advertising activity. As on all other Kaiser Jeep's products, the ads focused on utility, but now they were in beautifully detailed color. Camper top, hitch, and plow attachments (left) were featured in ads and postcards proclaiming the new vehicle's utility. The Wagoneer was "the comfortable ride into the backwoods."

When the original work was done on the new Wagoneer, designers took into account both two- and four-door designs (right, top) as well as a pickup. An early Sixties clay (right, bottom left) had the general front end locked in but lacked several key features. The grille badge, turning indicators, bumper design, and headlight styling would all be changed before production. Pickups were finally given a name, Gladiator (right, bottom right), and came in both two- and four-wheel drive in 120- and 126-inch wheelbases.

where Mercedes uses a pivot point several inches below the axle's longitudinal axis, Willys's pivots it right on the center line. . . . Because the Willys unit is used at the front, it naturally contains steering knuckles at each end and there are no camber changes at the wheel. So in effect, while it's basically a swing axle, the steering knuckles allow it to operate just like a full independent system."

The Wagoneer's IFS layout—another Sampietro design—utilized torsion bars as springs. Nothing tricky here; there simply wasn't adequate space for both the front-wheel-drive mechanism and the traditional coils.

Contemporary reviewers were unanimous in their praise of the Wagoneer's independent front suspension, and there was general agreement that the $135 it added to the price of the vehicle was money well spent. John Bond wrote, "We rate the ride as quite exceptional: Definitely somewhat firmer than a typical passenger car wagon and all the better for it. Certainly there's no truck-like ride here and the Wagoneer feels stable and controllable over roads that would make lesser vehicles wobble, wander and weave."

However, if the overhead cam engine and the new suspension system were the hallmarks of Sampietro's sophisticated, race-bred engineering practices, it was the combination of four-wheel drive with an automatic transmission that created the major stir with the public. Purists scoffed at it initially, regarding the slush box as out of keeping with the Jeep's macho image. However, the combination performed so well that even the critics were soon won over.

The automatic transmission was a three-speed Borg-Warner unit with a torque converter, similar to the one employed by the Rambler and Studebaker V-8s. It was hooked to a single range transfer case, providing an underdrive ratio of 2.03:1 for extra pulling power. Used with the standard transmissions as well as with the automatic, the transfer case was a silent mecha-

theless, this 'Tornado' six feels exceptionally strong and solid at all speeds and especially so at low speeds, where the torque peak at only 1750 rpm may be a factor."

Motor Trend's Jim Wright concurred. "This engine will really buckle down and pull when the going is rough and slow. Out on the highway the high horsepower peaking speed allows the Wagoneer to keep up with traffic and still have plenty left for passing." Wright speculated that "This is the only single overhead cam engine produced in America at this time and could mean that if Willys is successful with it, other manufacturers might follow suit."

"Next to the new engine," wrote Jim Wright, "the most significant engineering advancement [on the Wagoneer] was the independent front suspension layout. In a way it resembles the famous Mercedes unit. Basically, it's a single pivot swing axle, but

In sales literature the Wagoneer (left, top) was given a highly civilized, almost sophisticated look, but uses were still highly utilitarian. Though the Forward Control was at the end of its run, Kaiser Jeep still promoted unusual uses for the unorthodox vehicle.

Don't be fooled by the five vehicles in the publicity photo (right, top)—Kaiser Jeep had no less than 53 distinctly different models in their fleet for 1964. (This does not include variations and creations of outside coachbuilders.) For 1964 the Tuxedo Park option that had been available on the CJ-5 and CJ-6 was now a separate model unto itself. It included chrome trim, fully adjustable driver's seat, and a column mounted shifter for the three-speed automatic. At the Inaugural Parade on January 20, 1965, every float was pulled by a CJ. Kaiser Jeep used this opportunity for some free publicity (right, bottom right). As with all other Jeep products, the Gladiator found a strong export market. Many of the models shipped overseas were converted to right-hand drive (right, bottom left).

127

'Jeep' Universal

Now available with hot new Dauntless V-6 Engine option

down the center of the chassis rather than being off to one side. The result is that driving along in two-wheel drive is as quiet as any conventional automobile. However, if you engage the dog clutch for four-wheel drive, the same old gear whine comes back. In two-wheel drive the transfer gears merely free-wheel, in four-wheel drive they run under load."

Actually, there was nothing particularly innovative about any of this, yet the Wagoneer layout nevertheless represented two important advances. It was the first successful attempt by Willys to overcome the annoying transfer case whine, and it was the first time anyone had hooked a four-wheel-drive mechanism to an automatic transmission.

The slush box was an extra-cost option. Standard issue was a three-speed manual gearbox, with a four-speed available at additional cost. There was even an overdrive on the options list, but it was available only on the 4x2 models.

The Wagoneer's brakes were conventional hydraulics with cast iron drums. Lining area appears to have been on the skimpy side, and Jim Wright complained of excessive fading on repeated hard stops. And once the binders got hot, he noted, "they had a tendency to lock up suddenly, and this was accompanied by swerving." The vacuum booster, an option not supplied with the *Auto Topics* test car, would have been a welcome addition, according to Danny Collins. Pedal pressure was found to be excessive. With that qualification, however, Collins found the Wagoneer "very docile and easy to manage," and comfortable as well.

An interesting variant of the Wagoneer—and a prime collectible today, because of its rarity—is the Panel Delivery. Available on either the 4x4 or 4x2 chassis, it used the Wagoneer's 110-inch wheelbase. Body stampings were identical to those of the Wagoneer but with the windows eliminated. Chassis components came directly from the passenger-carrying version. These at-

nism, quite different from anything employed on previous Willys vehicles. The company's earlier practice had been to bolt the transfer case to the rear of the standard transmission, conveying all power sideways via three gears. Quoting John Bond, "The drive gear was at the engine centerline, then there was an idler gear, and finally the driven gear. This third or driven gear, being outboard far enough to clear the engine, was then used for both the front and rear propeller shafts. And anyone who has ever ridden in a Jeep knows that the gears whine whenever they are engaged.

"To obviate this," Bond continued, "the Wagoneer design drives the rear wheels directly—i.e., the rear propeller shaft runs

In late 1965 Kaiser Jeep offered the "Dauntless" V-6 in their CJ models (left). This powerplant was derived from GM's aluminum-block V-8 and displaced 225 cubic inches. Horsepower was 155 at 4400 rpm, and torque was 225 pounds-feet at a low 2400 rpm. This was the first time a six had been put into the CJ; in fact it was the first time any gasoline powerplant, other than the "Go-Devil," powered a Universal.

Jeep had trouble selling its Forward Control on the civilian market, but the U.S. military found all sorts of uses for this go-anywhere truck. A Cargo Pickup (right, top left) with four doors and an Ambulance (right, top right) were both built off of the FC-170 chassis. They had four-wheel drive, were rated at 7000 pounds, and were powered by a Cerlist diesel engine. There was also news for the Wagoneer and Gladiator in 1965, when they became the first Jeep vehicles to be offered with a V-8 engine (right, bottom right). This "Vigilante" V-8 offered 250 horsepower and 340 pounds-feet of torque. As with so many other Jeep engines, it was a refinement of the 1956 Nash Ambassador engine. Jeep was also offering an OHV V-6 (right, bottom left) to compensate for the noisy and somewhat unreliable original Sammy Sampietro SOHC unit.

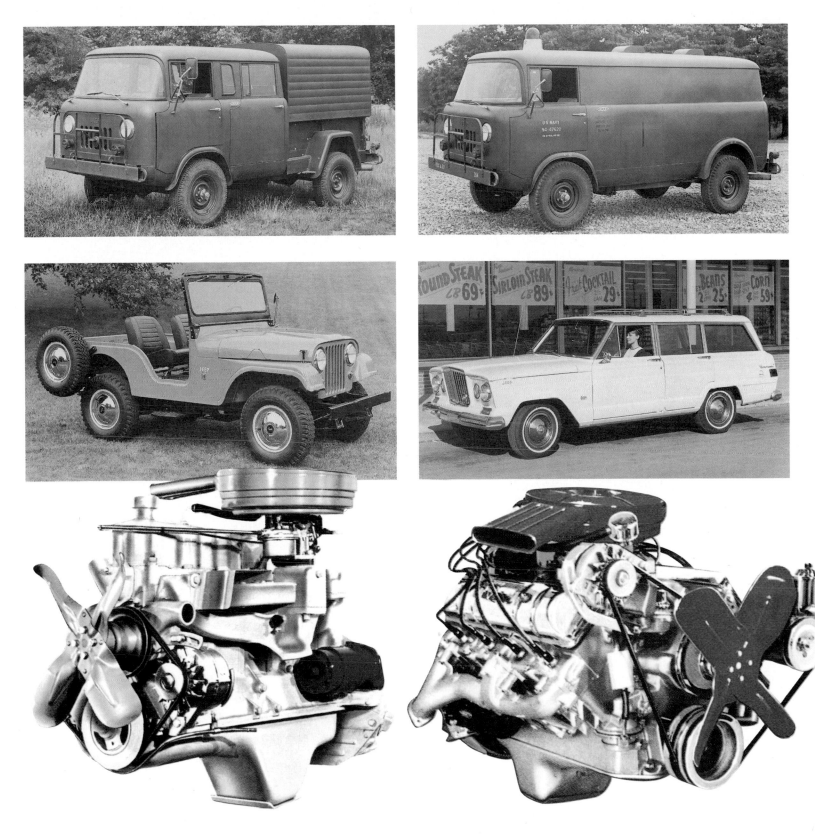

When it's steep and risky, get twice the "hold" with a 'Jeep' Wagoneer.

Just flip one simple lever into 'Jeep' 4-wheel drive.

Your 'Jeep' Wagoneer drives like any other station wagon— until you tackle a hill like this. Or some other danger spot. Then, shift smoothly into 4-wheel drive, at any speed, and you've got twice the traction. Twice the "grip" on wet, slippery pavement. Or ice. Or snow. In emergencies like these, it's the world's finest protection for your family. Very reassuring —especially with kids in the back! Yes, your 'Jeep' Wagoneer

gives you all the comfort, riding and handling ease of any fine car. Plus the incomparable safety—and fun—and adventure—of 'Jeep' 4-wheel drive!

All the features and options you'd expect in any fine car. 250 hp V-8 or Hi-Torque 6 cylinder engines. Turbo Hydra-Matic* automatic transmission. Power steering. Power brakes. Air-conditioning. 'Picture Window' visibility. 10 added safety features. Choice of colors, custom trim, accessories. Also available in 2-wheel drive. KAISER Jeep CORPORATION TOLEDO 1, OHIO

You've got to drive it to believe it. See your 'Jeep' dealer. Check the Yellow Pages.

Get twice the "grip" on slushy streets with a 'Jeep' Wagoneer.

Just flip one simple lever for the safety of 'Jeep' 4-wheel drive.

Winter driving is no fun, no matter how you look at it. It can mean slipping, sliding, spinning your wheels, skidding round corners—or worse! But a 4-wheel drive 'Jeep' Wagoneer cuts winter driving dangers with twice the traction, twice the grip of ordinary station wagons. 'Jeep' 4-wheel drive helps you keep control when roads turn to ice and the snow piles up. You get where you're going comfortably, confidently, with greater safety, greater peace of mind. When roads turn bad, it's the best automotive insurance you can own. Plus, you have

the fun of 'Jeep' 4-wheel drive. With luxurious interiors, your Wagoneer compares with any quality station wagon, inside as well as out. It has all the options you'd expect: like V-8 power, Turbo Hydra-Matic* automatic transmission, power steering, power brakes, air-conditioning. 'Picture window' visibility, complete choice of colors. No other wagon gives the combination of luxury...confidence...and sheer adventure... of the 'Jeep' Wagoneer with 4-wheel drive. Call your Jeep dealer for a test drive today!

KAISER Jeep CORPORATION

UNIQUE SAFETY PACKAGE AT NO EXTRA COST!

You've got to drive it to believe it. See your 'Jeep' dealer. Check the Yellow Pages.

tractive commercial jobs were built for several years but in very limited numbers.

The Wagoneer was a trailblazer in a number of respects, and it sold well from the start. *Motor Trend* noted, in March 1963, "Willys is selling all of this model they can produce," complained the magazine's test crew because they had been unable to keep the car as long as they might have wished. Their Wagoneer, it appears, had already been sold.

Yet for all the bouquets that the Wagoneer received, a number of shortcomings began to surface, leading as time went along to some significant changes in the original design.

The instant appeal and sustained popularity of the Jeep Wagoneer probably came as something of a surprise to its builders. One unanticipated result of this was the widespread use of even the four-wheel-drive types for highway travel. You may recall from earlier in this chapter that "Sammy" Sampietro's single overhead cam engine was basically a truck powerplant, at its best in pulling hills and lugging heavy loads at relatively moderate speeds. Owners soon found, however, that it was less than ideally suited to sustained high-speed travel on the open road. And it's a safe bet that Kaiser Industries—which of course had purchased Willys nearly a decade before the first Wagoneer appeared—was less than delighted to learn that a single overhead camshaft engine is not particularly cheap to build.

Furthermore, the Sampietro engine, despite its advanced design and mechanical sophistication, had drawn some criticism. Detonation prompted the 1964 introduction of an "economy" version in which the compression ratio was lowered from 8.5:1 to 7.5:1. Net horsepower this time was given as 133 @ 4000 rpm. But Peter Sessler probably goes to the heart of the problem with his terse comment that "although [the SOHC] six was a sound design, it did suffer from oiling problems." Nothing that Kaiser could not overcome, presumably, however. They found it more cost-effective

Kaiser Jeep advertisements continued to focus on the go-anywhere ability of the Wagoneer, but the places it was going weren't necessarily the farm or construction site. Several ads portrayed the vehicle slogging through snow-covered city streets (left), a new trend in Jeep advertising.

Nineteen sixty-five was a changeover year of sorts for the Gladiator. Two series were produced: the old J-200 and J-300 series (right, top and middle right); and the new J-2000 and J-3000 series (right, middle left). The new models had the same V-6 and V-8 engines available on the Wagoneer, plus a Safety Package consisting of a padded sun visor and dash, seatbelts, dual speed wipers with washer, side view mirror, four-way flashers, high-impact windshield, dual brake system, and self-adjusting brakes. Kaiser Jeep also added the Super Wagoneer (right, bottom) in late 1965, which Jeep claimed to be the "the most elegant four-wheeler ever crafted."

to make a switch. As a result, in 1966 AMC's unspectacular but thoroughly competent seven bearing, overhead-valve six was substituted for the overhead cam engine.

Meanwhile, for those who wanted more performance, starting in 1965 there was an attractive new option: For an extra $190.83, the Wagoneer buyer could have a 327-cid 250-horsepower V-8 known as the "Vigilante"—also supplied by American Motors. With the switch to AMC engines, Kaiser also substituted the General Motors Turbo-HydraMatic transmission for the Borg-Warner unit previously employed. It was a potent combination, for the V-8 generated a substantial 340 pounds-feet of torque, enabling the Wagoneer to scramble from zero to 60 about 11 percent faster than the SOHC-powered version. In high-speed highway travel the "Vigilante" V-8 was in its element. Even at 90 miles per hour it turned at only 3800 rpm.

For those who wanted something more and didn't mind paying for it, from 1966 through 1968 there was a model called the Super Wagoneer. Think of it as the precursor of the Grand Wagoneer. Priced at a premium of $2163 (which is to say, 57 percent) over the cost of the Custom model, the Super Wagoneer was equipped—in addition to the V-8 engine—with almost every conceivable extra. Included were air-conditioning, automatic transmission, power steering, power brakes, bucket seats (together with a sumptuously appointed interior), tilt wheel, and even a vinyl roof. Never before had off-roading been so comfortable.

In the meantime, problems had surfaced with Sampietro's highly advanced independent front suspension. Its effect upon both ride and handling was highly favorable. However, experience demonstrated that over the rough terrain for which four-wheel drive was primarily designed, the IFS lacked the durability of a live axle. Ultimately, then, it went the way of the overhead cam engine. Perhaps sophisticated en-gineering isn't always the best answer to heavy-duty, off-road use.

Motor Trend took Wagoneer for a test run in 1965; their unit had V-8 power and a live axle. Even without the independent front suspension, Technical Editor Bob McVay found that "Comfort is [the Wagoneer's] strong suit. . . . It's a big step up into the interior for ladies in tight skirts, but once inside, everyone's comfortable on long or short hauls. Bench seats are firm, give good support and plenty of room."

McVay loaded the car with five adults and a child and evidently gave it a stiff workout. His review was enthusiastic: "Our test car . . . was a comfortable family wagon on the highway, equally at home clawing its way through deep sand, up slippery hills, or smashing through the boondocks. No two-wheel-drive, six-passenger vehicle could hope to follow it once the pavement ended. . . .

"Even in the roughest going, power steering took the fight out of deep sand, dips, ruts and rugged ground. We've driven many other four-wheel-drive rigs over rough country and always came back hot, dusty, tired and sweaty—in short, we were beat. In our Wagoneer we covered nearly 100 miles of off-road, rough driving and returned to the highway as fresh as ever, thanks to air conditioning, power brakes, and the power steering. . . .

"Acceleration was more than adequate, despite the load, and the ride wasn't choppy except when the road surface was rough. . . . Body lean when cornering at above-average speeds seemed pronounced because of the car's height and lack of an anti-roll bar. But Kaiser doesn't claim it to be a road racer. . . .

"As a go-anywhere, do-anything station wagon," McVay concluded, "equally at home on a cross-country trip or plowing snow in the dead of winter, the Wagoneer is one of the most versatile automobiles available. It can be equipped to winch itself out of the mud, bulldoze earth, pull a trailer, or charge through axle-deep mud with

One interesting option available to CJ (right, top) buyers was the Perkins "Four 192" diesel. The motor had a cast iron block and head and displaced 192 cubic inches. Stroke was a very long (though not for a diesel) 5.00 inches, and the bore was 3.50 inches. Horsepower was only 62 at 3000 rpm, but torque was a stump-pulling 143 pounds-feet at an incredibly low 1350 rpm. During 1966 Jeep offered the "Prairie Gold" special on the CJ-5 chassis (right, bottom left). The package included chrome dress-up trim pieces, a special paint and top, and interior upgrades. As on the CJs, the Gladiator offered a camper top option (right, bottom right). GM's Turbo Hydra-Matic 4-speed transmission was available and standard on the J-3800. This vehicle had a full 1-ton capacity.

Your wife will be twice as safe this winter with 'Jeep' 4-wheel drive.

In a 'Jeep' Wagoneer with 4-wheel drive, she's got twice the traction of ordinary station wagons...twice the "bite" in deep snow. And she's twice as safe on slippery streets. That same extra grip will take you off the road...up onto the ski slopes, hunting, or just plain exploring. Choice of engines: 'Vigilante' V-8, or new Hi-Torque 6. Turbo Hydra-Matic* automatic transmission, other power options. Your family will be safer on the highway...on city streets...or off the road...have more fun this winter, in a 'Jeep' Wagoneer with 4-wheel drive.

NOW! THESE 10 SAFETY FEATURES ARE STANDARD:
☐ Seat belts front and rear
☐ Padded sun visors
☐ Padded dashboard
☐ High-impact windshield
☐ Outside rear-view mirror
☐ Dual brake system
☐ Self adjusting brakes
☐ 4-way warning flashers
☐ Back-up lights
☐ Windshield washer and dual-speed wipers

KAISER Jeep CORPORATION

'Jeep' Wagoneer
You've got to drive it to believe it. See your 'Jeep' dealer.

The all-weather, all-terrain, all-year **Jeep** Recreation Fleet.

equal aplomb. It does these things while pampering passengers in true family-car size and style."

A new grille and a general freshening up of the styling were featured for 1966, and for those who wanted a little performance edge a 270-horsepower, four-barrel premium fuel version of the Vigilante V-8 was

offered. *Motor Trend* recorded 0-60 and quarter-mile times of 12.8 and 18.7 seconds, respectively. Compared to the two-barrel engine, this meant that the car was one second faster in the quarter mile and nearly two seconds quicker in the zero-to-sixty run. The test car, on this occasion, was a Super Wagoneer. Its luxury was almost decadent, but its off-road capability was as strong as ever.

It was at about this time that Tom McCahill, writing in *Mechanix Illustrated*, said, "My front yard usually resembles a clearing house for a hot car ring. At present, better than $50,000 worth of autos stand there broiling in the hot Florida sun. . . of the whole kit and caboodle, my choice would be the 'Jeep' Wagoneer. . . .

"It rides like the best Detroit has to offer," McCahill continued. "But it'll go places you just wouldn't dream of going in an ordinary car. And, it looks just as much at home in the parking lot of the most posh country club as it does next to a prairie camp fire. . . .

"The Wagoneer is built like a bank vault," Uncle Tom concluded, "and, if my calculations are worth a hoot, it will experience a lot less trouble in five years than many of the fancy Dans that can crack above 130 and easily eat you out of house and home."

The Wagoneer was undergoing a gradual metamorphosis. By 1968 the Vigilante engine was no longer available except in the Super Wagoneer. In the Standard and Custom lines, Buick's brand new 350 cid V-8 was used. The change appears to have been an economy move on Kaiser's part. (Incidentally, the switch came at about the same time that Kaiser purchased from Buick the tooling for the 90-degree V-6 engine, which had been offered as an option in the CJ Jeeps since 1966.)

The Buick V-8 was a 230-horsepower unit, producing 350 pounds-feet of torque. Thus, horsepower was slightly less than that of the regular fuel AMC "327," and torque—the more critical factor in an off-

As the Sixties drew to a close, safety concerns about automobiles were on the rise. The government was enacting new laws to make cars safer for riders and the environment. Jeep reflected this safety issue in their 1967 ads (left). By virtue of its large size and four-wheel drive, the Wagoneer was already a fairly safe vehicle, but the same cannot be said for all Jeep products; some would come under close scrutiny for their safety problems.

The M151 A1, though not designed by Kaiser Jeep, exemplified the same traits that got the CJ-5 into a rollover controversy. Designed and built originally by Ford, The M151 (right) had an independent rear suspension that gave little warning of impending rollovers. This forced a design change to a solid axle. The CJ-5 had a solid axle, but the Jeep had several other design-related problems that tended to increase the possibility of a rollover crash. The vehicle had a narrow stance, a short wheelbase, and a high center of gravity. These, coupled with owner modifications, encouraged rollovers and gave the CJ its undeserved bad reputation. In fact, the U.S. government cleared the CJ-5 of any design-related flaws that could lead to rollover accidents.

Happy combo! Racy and rugged. Holy Toledo, what a car!

Leave ordinary, garden-variety driving behind...in this 'Jeepster' Convertible. The rugged rascal only Toledo could build—because that's where 'Jeep' ruggedness comes from.

Settle back in those bucket seats. Take the wheel. And go!

You'll be noticed...thanks to snazzy features like that continental spare. Now, hit the highway and open 'er up! What a smooth performer...specially if you choose that hot new V-6 with automatic transmission.

Then flip one lever...you're in 'Jeep' 4-wheel drive! You've got excitement ...and safety, too...you just won't find with ordinary sports cars. What's your idea of fun? This baby will get you there!

Or, maybe you'd rather choose from the 'Jeepster Commando' models. Roadster. Station wagon. And the sportiest pick-up ever!

The 'Jeepster' family. It's tough. Terrific! You've

got to drive it to believe it! See your 'Jeep' dealer. Check the Yellow Pages.
KAISER **Jeep** CORPORATION TOLEDO, OHIO 43601

'Jeepster'
Family of fun cars

road vehicle—was increased slightly.

Motor Trend again tested another Wagoneer. Whereas it had been necessary to read carefully between the lines in order to detect anything negative about the early Wagoneers in the magazine's previous reviews, this time columnist V. Lee Oertle was up front in his criticism. Reporting on his test of a 1969 Buick-powered Wagoneer, Oertle recalled, "The memory of my first road test in a Wagoneer left me with some pretty rough edges. I freely admit that I approached the 1969 model with a slight frown tucked between my brows. To say that the early Wagoneers 'had a few bugs' could be comparable to saying that Interstate 40 'carries a few cars.' But that was yesteryear."

There were kind words for this 1969 model, however. "It's a vehicle that grows on you. With one, a buyer enjoys the best of two worlds: extra passenger comfort in a rugged trail buster.

"I said trail buster, not tail buster! For those drivers familiar with the unyielding seats and boomerang-like springs of sporty 4x4's, the Wagoneer will be a genuine surprise. The new Wagoneers are equipped with variable-rate rear leaf springs, with double-acting shock absorbers at all four corners. The result, much modified and refined over the years, is a firm and well-controlled ride on paved streets and a rugged strength over rough terrain. There is a nice compromise here that a backroads artist should find impressive. . . ."

Not that Oertle judged the Wagoneer to be flawless. He noted, for instance, that "for all its versatility the turning circle diameter seemed annoyingly large. Considerable jockeying was required to get out of box canyons and rocky bottlenecks. . . . It seems to me that if some method of reducing that circle could be found, this vehicle would be twice as maneuverable and many times more valuable to a true off-road driver.

"But then, all things automotive are a compromise. . . ."

Another Jeep vehicle that could be con-

In 1967 a familiar name appeared in a new Jeep model. The Jeepster had returned, and Jeep advertising hailed its mission (left). It was a "Happy combo! Racy and rugged." Touted as a four-wheel-drive sports convertible, the new Jeepster was aimed at the same market as the previous Jeepster. However, the new model had an optional automatic transmission and, later, could be equipped with a V-8 engine.

The Jeepster was available in four different models: Convertible (right, top), Station Wagon (right, bottom left), pickup, (right, bottom right), and roadster. Introduced in January 1967, the second-generation Jeepster was the only four-wheel-drive convertible available with a power top. Originally, the available engines were the 134-cid F-head "Go-Devil" four and the Buick designed 225-cid OHV V-6.

sidered a compromise was the Jeepster. Four years after the Jeep became a part of Kaiser Industries and 17 years after production of the original edition had ceased, the Jeepster was resurrected. Known this time as the Jeepster Commando, it was equipped with part-time four-wheel drive and came in four body styles—roadster, sport convertible, station wagon, and pick-up—rather than just one.

Based on the 101-inch chassis of the then-current Jeep CJ-6 but clearly intended more for play than for work, the Commando borrowed the grille and front fenders of the Jeep Universal. In general, however, styling was reminiscent of the original Jeepster, though it was perhaps not quite as crisp.

As first introduced, the Jeepster Commando used the familiar F-head four as its standard engine. Most buyers, however, were happy to pay $194 extra for the "Dauntless" V-6, which raised the horsepower from 75 to a neck-snapping 160, and the torque from 114 to 235 pounds-feet. (Originally developed by GM's Buick Division, this engine had been purchased, lock, stock, and block, by Kaiser in 1966. In the fuel crisis in the 1970s, General Motors re-purchased the tooling and put the V-6 back into production.)

Unlike the first-generation Jeepster, the Commando offered a number of amenities, some standard, some optional. The Convertible, for instance, came with roll-up windows and bucket seats. The options list, in addition to the larger engine, included the Turbo-HydraMatic transmission, power brakes, air conditioner, and a power top on the convertible. Power steering joined the roster in 1969, available only on units with V-6 power.

It is said that Kaiser had intended to put the Jeepster back into production during the 1950s, only to find that Willys-Overland had destroyed the jigs and dies. However, at least Kaiser did not repeat the Willys mistake of failing to publicize the Jeepster adequately. So, due no doubt to

Kaiser Jeep had hoped to resurrect the tooling from the previous Jeepster, but that was lost, and new tooling had to be constructed. The Station Wagon (left) had a solid steel top, with a hinged rear window casing. A rear seat was also fitted as standard. The Jeepster Wagon also was offered with a Deluxe Trim group option not available on any other Jeepster. This included deluxe seats, interior trim, and carpeting, as well as chrome mirrors and bumpers, and opening rear quarter windows.

The dash of the Jeepster (right, top left), like those on all Jeep products, was purely functional, but the power top was a nice convenience feature. Also, outfitted properly, the Jeepster's exterior could display a good deal of chrome and classy character. A Continental spare tire (right) was a dealer-installed option, as were snowplow or camper conversions.

many causes, advertising among them, the Commando was far more successful than its predecessor.

Reviews were generally favorable, though the car was not altogether flawless. Off-road traction was deemed excellent. Traction in uphill reverse-gear situations, sometimes a tricky proposition with four-wheel drive, was also very good. Passenger comfort, according to *Motor Trend*'s test crew, was "way above average," and coming from the same source there was the comment, "No matter where you point it, the Jeepster displays amazing ride control."

On the other hand, shifting the transfer case into front-drive position was a hassle, steering was somewhat imprecise, the convertible top slatted and popped noisily, the level of fit and finish left something to be desired, and the inherent lope of the 90-degree V-6 could be disconcerting, particularly at idle.

Car Life described its overall performance as "excellent," and the figures from its road test are impressive. Driving a convertible powered by the V-6 engine and equipped with the automatic transmission, the magazine's test crew did the standing quarter-mile in 19.2 at 71.8 miles per hour. Zero-to-sixty took 12.6 seconds, and top speed was 87 miles per hour. Respectable figures, for a car that was set up primarily for off-road use. Braking was commendable, as well. Stopping distances were no better than average, but the magazine noted that "attempts to fade the Jeepster's brakes failed utterly."

In summary, *Car Life*'s praise was somewhat muted: "The Jeepster Sports Convertible seemed eminently roadable and off-roadable. Its performance was excellent, yet it lacked utility, particularly in cargo carrying capacity. Its seating was comfortable, yet it was uncomfortably noisy. Its outward appearance, white vinyl top against chromium trimmed fire engine red body paint, was boxy and brisk, yet somehow lacking in businesslike mein displayed by pure Jeeps. It was delightful to drive in

All-steel hardtops (left) *were a curious aftermarket option that were available from many manufacturers. (This due to the fact that the factory offered their own hardtop.) Jeep model production was up again, and the company was healthy and in the black for 1968.*

Special Jeep vehicles were built for all occasions. Fire truck modifications had become common on the Gladiator platform, but in 1967 a paramedic truck (right, top) *was added to the line of "factory available" specials. Jeep also offered a dump body. In that same year, Jeep built a number of CJ-6 ambulances for UNICEF* (right, bottom left). *In addition to the top-mounted spare and siren, the UNICEF CJ-6 received a two-piece windshield. There were other, more pleasurable applications for the two-wheel-drive DJ-5, such as golf course duty* (right, bottom right).

141

the bush, yet highly irritating with such things as interior door latch handles positioned so they hammered painfully against the knees of driver and passenger during rough going. It was a car for fun—which sometimes wasn't. . . .

"Final assessment is that the Jeepster Sports Convertible is a capable cream-puff for the non-camping, short-haul dilettante driver. . . . [It] is soft, smooth, sweet—a dude, a tenderfoot."

Not exactly a ringing endorsement, though one has to wonder just what it was that the reviewer was looking for. Surely not a dressed-up family car with off-road capability, which was what the Commando was, after all, intended to be.

In 1969 a luxury convertible, known simply as the Jeepster, was added to the line—at a premium of $532 over the price of the base convertible. In this one, most of the complaints dealing with the creature comforts were overcome.

In the Jeep Universal lineup things did not change so dramatically. Nineteen sixty-five was the last year for the CJ-3B in America, though by that time production was down to a trickle. The big news came in 1966 with the addition of the "Dauntless" V-6 and the single lever, dual-range transfer case to the CJ-5 and CJ-6 models. Both features were pulled from other Jeep models and, in addition to servo brakes and a padded driver's seat, made the Universal much easier to drive.

In 1969 the Tuxedo Park dress-up option was dropped but another interesting option became available—the camper top. The camper was attached to the Jeep by a hook that slipped into the CJ's rear body. It offered accommodations for four people and had a two-tone exterior paint treatment. Included as standard was a kitchen with running water, built-in cabinets, stove, and oven. A 10,000 BTU heater, a gas/electric refrigerator, and a second roof vent could be had as options with the camper.

The same year also featured another in-teresting option package called "462." To the base CJ-5 it added a roll bar, swing-out spare-tire carrier, Polyglas tubeless tires, electric ammeter, oil gauge, and skid plate.

Coinciding with the introduction of the Wagoneer was a new line of Jeep trucks known as the Gladiators. Sharing the styling as well as the mechanical components of the Wagoneers, the Gladiators were the largest, most useful, and most stylish trucks yet to bear the Jeep name. Ranging in capacity from half- to one-ton, the Gladiators came in both 4x4 and 4x2 form, on wheelbases of 120 and 126 inches. Pickups were built in two styles, "Thriftside" (flare fender) and "Tensed" (slab fender), the latter being by a narrow margin the costlier of the two. In all there were 46 distinct Gladiator models, in addition to three Utility Jeeps, three Dispatchers, eight Forward Control models, and 16 conventionally-styled trucks—a total of 76 Jeep models, not counting the Utility Wagons, Wagoneers, and Wagoneer-based Sedan Delivery. It was an astonishing proliferation.

It's hard to argue with success, because all those models added up to increased market share. Sales for 1962 had lagged somewhat, but with an assist from the new Wagoneer and Gladiator models, the firm racked up a 42 percent increase in dollar volume during 1963.

Like the Wagoneers, the Gladiators blazed new trails for the industry with such innovations as an automatic transmission and independent front suspension. For these features to be offered in conjunction with four-wheel drive was unique to Jeep vehicles. Development of the Gladiator generally paralleled that of the Wagoneer, including the 1965 introduction of an optional V-8 engine from American Motors and the substitution in 1966 of AM seven-bearing overhead-valve six for the sophisticated but not altogether successful overhead cam job.

The Forward Control trucks had never been particularly successful on the sales floor, and production ceased after 1966.

Not only did Kaiser Jeep build the basic Army Jeep, they produced CJ-5-based vehicles for many other governmental agencies. One such model was a light reconnaissance and radio patrol vehicle (right, top). The J-3000 carried on with the original grille, but the Wagoneer was given a freshened front in 1966—the J-3000 would not get a restyle until 1970 (right, bottom). However, in 1969 the wheelbase of the Gladiator J-3000 was stretched from 126 inches to 132.

They were unquestionably cute and practical in certain situations. However, as *Motor Trend* noted, "Getting into the cab is a long step from the ground and we suspect frequent delivery stops would be tiring to the driver." The small engine and numerically high (5.38:1) gearing limited the FE speed to no more than 50 miles per hour. There were also mechanical difficulties as well, including problems with spring mounts, front suspension, and steering. Worse, there were reports that the FC-150s were prone to tipping over.

A year before the FC trucks were dropped, the other trucks and Utility Wagons—apart from those of the Wagoneer/Gladiator family—were deleted from the roster. Even the Gladiators, in fact, appeared in diminishing numbers. By 1969—the Jeep's final year under Kaiser ownership—the model count was reduced to 20, down from 48 just three years earlier.

During the Kaiser regime, Jeep had gone through some very interesting and telling changes. For some time the Willys name had been downplayed by the company's new owners. After the 1953 purchase by Kaiser Industries, the vehicles continued to bear the "Willys Jeep" label; however, by 1957 the name "Jeep" stood alone on the side of the cowl. Then in June 1963, the name of the company itself was changed from Willys Motors Inc. to Kaiser Jeep Corporation. From then until the AMC buyout, the vehicles were known as Kaiser Jeeps.

Kaiser was known as a maker of automobiles—though their automaking days were few. Yet, the Jeep benefited from this image. Jeep's new identity, suggested by the adoption of the Kaiser name, was reinforced by the car-like Wagoneer and Gladiator. Once the FC and traditional Jeep trucks were dropped, Kaiser Jeep offered what appeared to be a cross between a rough-and-tumble four-wheel-drive vehicle and a car for the occasional huntsman and country-club set. Jeeps were now situated in an unusual market niche—one that would bear fruit in years to come.

The interior for the 1969 Wagoneer (left) was very similar to that of the original, which had been introduced seven years earlier. However, there were new foam-padded seats with simulated leather vinyl coverings. Additionally, in order to meet growing federal safety regulations, the dash and several interior surfaces were now padded. The Super Wagoneer (right, top) was no longer its own model, but it was available as an options package. Both the Jeepster/Commando and the CJ models were carried over unchanged into 1969 (right, bottom).

The Jeep Comes of Age: 1970-83

y 1968 Kaiser Jeep had become a role player in the immense Kaiser Industries Corporation empire. This empire included Kaiser Aluminum & Chemical, Kaiser Steel, Kaiser Cement & Gypsum, Kaiser Jeep, Kaiser Aerospace & Electronics, Kaiser Hawaii Kai, Kaiser Broadcasting, National Steel & Shipbuilding, and Kaiser Foundation Medical Care. All in all, over 64,000 men and women were permanently employed with Kaiser.

Edgar Kaiser, now chairman of the Kaiser organization, decided to concentrate on the corporation's other holdings, especially mining, aluminum, chemicals, and construction. One way to do this was to sell off Jeep. However, Jeep had net operating profits of $15 million on sales of $477 million in 1968 and was producing roughly half of all Kaiser Industry sales. Therefore, Edgar Kaiser wanted to maintain some control of this cash cow.

Selling to one of the "Big Three" was not feasible for two reasons. Firstly, each one had 4x4s and trucks of their own. Secondly, there would be no way for Kaiser to reap extended financial profits from the sale. In stepped American Motors Corporation.

Last of the independents, American Motors had nudged past the break-even point in 1968 for the first time in several years. They earned $11.8 million in 1968 and $7.9 million in 1969. AMC also had no truck or 4x4 line of their own.

Kaiser Industries and AMC worked out a merger whereby AMC would purchase Kaiser Jeep, and Kaiser Industries would receive cash and a large share of AMC stock in return. The merger would offer the best to both corporations. AMC would get lucrative trucks and 4x4 companions to sell alongside their line of cars without having to tie up a large sum of capital in the purchase. Kaiser, on the other hand, would receive an infusion of cash and the possibility of gaining control of AMC at a later date (if Edgar was ever again interested in building cars).

On December 2, 1969, AMC and Kaiser Industries Corporation formally signed an agreement to sell Kaiser Jeep to AMC. The agreement called for AMC to pay $10 million cash, 5.5 million AMC shares, $9.5 million in five-year AMC notes, and $500,000 in other assets to Kaiser Industries. The value of the sale was approximately $75 million. This sale effectively gave Kaiser Industries 22-percent ownership in AMC—25 times the holding of the company's largest stockholder.

However, Roy D. Chapin, Jr., chairman of AMC, stated that he had talked to Edgar Kaiser and that Kaiser had no intention of assuming control of AMC at that time. Chapin said, "I have a verbal understanding, Mr. Kaiser will not sit on the American Motors board because he does not want anyone to think that Kaiser is seeking control." As a postscript, though Kaiser Industries had a controlling interest in AMC, they did not interfere and would never again play a role in Jeep or AMC. Kaiser Industries Corporation eventually sold its holdings in AMC.

One of AMC's first actions as owner of Jeep was to separate civilian and military/government production, effectively establishing a new division. On March 21,

(continued on page 150)

As the Sixties came to a tumultuous close, the automobile industry was in a state of flux. Until only a few years earlier, car makers had free reign to build whatever they chose and sell it at any price they could. But now, the U.S. government was enacting air, noise, and safety regulations that would put new restrictions on how automobiles were produced. Also on the way were imports, by the millions, ready to wage a price and economy war against Detroit. Kaiser Industries may have seen all of this on the horizon and, in 1969, chose to sell out. The last major independent, American Motors Corporation, seized upon the opportunity to fill out their line and purchased Jeep Corporation from Kaiser for approximately $75 million. However, before Kaiser left the stage they started the Hurst/Jeepster project. AMC completed this program, and in 1971 the Hurst Jeepster (right, bottom) was released. The powertrain consisted of the "Dauntless" V-6 mated to a Hurst three-speed manual or GM-built automatic. Other modifications included a hood mounted tach (right, bottom right), racing stripes, fiberglass hood scoop, and Polyglas tires. Approximately 100 were built. Linda Vaughan (right), also known as Miss Hurst, modeled with the car. She was a great fan of Stock Car racing.

JEEP CJ Variations

Kaiser Jeep created the XJ-001 in 1969. The playful vehicle was an attempt to create an even more lively Jeep (above). The vehicle was based on the CJ-5, but neither Kaiser nor AMC had the money for tooling. Another rolling testbed was the Jeep II (top, right). AMC, as with all other automakers in the Seventies, was in a mad rush to downsize their lineup. The result was a Jeep-like vehicle "that explored new ways to reduce vehicle size while maintaining useable interior room."

For all the many Jeep spin-offs that have appeared over the years, the basic CJ and its concurrent military counterparts stayed remarkably the same. But that's not to say that Willys, Kaiser Jeep, American Motors, and most recently, Chrysler haven't tinkered with the basic concept.

For example, Willys tried grafting a downsloped hood onto a CJ-3B in 1953, with the aim of improving forward visibility. The idea never reached production, but a surviving photo from Willys Engineering suggests that it probably would have improved aerodynamics as well, even though the industry wouldn't be concerned with such things for decades. Some 15 years later, Kaiser Jeep created XJ-001, a styling exercise on the 81-inch-wheelbase CJ-5 Universal chassis. Boasting a sporty and very modern fiberglass body with an open back, door-less sides, and sculptured, car-like contours, it was designed in 1969, just before the AMC takeover. A company press release described it as "an experimental test platform for innovations in the growing recreational field." But according to AMC historian John A. Conde, Jeep's new owners "didn't know what to do with it, not having the finances to tool up for such a radical departure from the CJ.

"Fate solved the problem . . . On the way back from the Texas State Fair several years later, the truck carrying the model flipped over, caught fire, and the XJ-001 was lost forever."

Fuel economy concerns and the industry's embryonic "downsizing" movement prompted the Jeep II of 1977, one of several "Concept" vehicles AMC displayed late in that decade. Its press description was disarmingly honest: "Concept Jeep II demonstrates Jeep Corporation's exploration of new ways to reduce vehicle size while maintaining useable interior room. This scaled-down version of the CJ-5 preserves the ruggedness and fun-to-drive character of the popular CJ series. In contrast to the current-production CJ-5, the Jeep II is two feet shorter and nine inches lower, and the wheelbase, at 76 inches, is eight inches shorter." With less weight, a lower center of gravity, and more angular front end and fender styling, the Jeep II represented a return to the nimble efficiency of the wartime original.

Unfortunately, faltering AMC wouldn't have the wherewithal to rethink the basic Jeep in earnest for another three years. While the impetus likely came from "Energy Crisis II" of 1979-80, the means were unquestionably provided by Renault, which bought a controlling interest in AMC at about that time and still sells CJs in Europe. The development effort leading to the new Wrangler didn't get underway until about 1981. Although Concept Jeep II may have influenced its early phases, the notion of simply shrinking the CJ was soon discarded, and the program was ultimately coordinated with development of the XJ-series Cherokee/Wagoneer compact wagons that arrived for 1984.

Early 1971 brought a special run of 600 Jeep Renegade II (top) models, with 200 each painted Baja Yellow, Mint Green, and Riverside Orange. Early in the model run, 150 were finished in Big Bad Orange. By 1972 the Jeepster name was dropped from the Jeepster/Commando (middle, left). Also the convertible did not return, and the F-head four and V-6 were dropped. They were replaced by two six-cylinder engines and a V-8. In 1970 the Gladiator was given a new front clip—more in keeping with the Wagoneer model. The trucks could be had in either "Townside" or "Thriftside" and had an available automatic transmission and independent front suspension.

1970, AMC formed AM General to assume the function of the Defense and Government Products division of the old Kaiser Jeep Corporation. This division was producing military and postal Jeeps and expanded later into the manufacture of transit buses. Eventually AM General would go on to develop and produce the military jeep's replacement, the Hummer or High Mobility Multi-Purpose Wheeled Vehicle (HMMWV), though they would no longer be a part of AMC by this time. Thereafter, as a wholly-owned AMC subsidiary, what had once been known as Kaiser Jeep became known simply as the Jeep Corporation.

From the merger on, there were slow but sweeping changes at Jeep. The AMC engineering staff began to make improvements to the various Jeep products. On the truck front, the Gladiator name was dropped, and trucks were thereafter designated "J Series." At the same time, the handsome grille of the post-1965 Wagoneers replaced the upright Jeep-like grille on previous Gladiators. Changes to other models included the addition of power steering to the V-6 Jeepster Commando and a new grille for the Wagoneer.

Road & Track took its turn at evaluating the Wagoneer. While admitting the four-wheel driver to be outside the magazine's field, the editors evidently enjoyed the change of pace:

"One of the most appealing things about the Wagoneer is that it looks enough like a conventional station wagon to be tolerably acceptable even though the styling, basically unchanged since it was introduced in 1962, is now seriously dated. It's something a housewife could stand to drive to a PTA meeting, which most four-wheel drives aren't, it is quiet in operation and when it is equipped with power everything it's an easy machine to drive. On the city street or highway, it doesn't 'handle' in any sports car sense of the word, you understand. The power steering is numb, the

AMC began advertising the Jeeps as "2-Car Cars," meaning that you could go to the store to get the groceries and take the long way back through the mountains. Sales literature (left) also pushed the modifications AMC was making to engines and suspensions.

The Renegade package for the CJ-5 was first offered in 1972. In 1973 (right, top) it included a 304-cid V-8, styled wheels, white-wall tires, blackout hood, body-side racing stripe, transmission skid plate, fender extensions, extra gauges, dual visors, dual mirrors, vinyl interior (right, bottom left), and a rear-mounted spare. Though production was still good—9538 in 1973—it was the last year for the Commando (right, bottom middle). Under AMC, Jeep products went racing. A 1973 Wagoneer became the first American vehicle to win an international world auto rally when it captured first place in the grueling 1571-mile Michigan "Press-On-Regardless." The Jeep was equipped with the new Quadra-Trac, full-time four-wheel-drive system.

"even given its shortcomings the Wagoneer is still the most satisfactory dual-purpose four-wheel-drive machine. The best available compromise between a pure off-pavement vehicle and one that is also satisfactory for normal around-town use as well."

In 1971, customized Jeepster Commando station wagons were built by Hurst Products, in conjunction with American Motors. Custom rally stripes, wide-tread tires, styled wheel covers and a hood-mounted air scoop with a tachometer riding atop the "power bulge" were among the special features of this model. A T-handle gearshift was supplied with the manual transmission, or Hurst's Dual-Gate shifter with the automatic. It goes without saying that the Hurst/Jeepster Special is a prime collectible today.

The Wagoneer and Gladiator both received minor trim changes in 1971, but the big news was new engine choices. AMC's 258-cid six replaced the "232" as the Wagoneer's standard powerplant, and the recently introduced, in-house 360-cid V-8 was substituted for the Buick engine. In both cases, a slight performance edge was the result. Unladen, according to *Motor Trend*, the Wagoneer could now accelerate from zero to sixty in 12.6 seconds—a respectable figure by anyone's standards.

But the live axles, stiff springs and preponderance of unsprung weight—the latter resulting primarily from heavy-duty axles—gave the Wagoneer an overly harsh ride, according to *Motor Trend*'s appraisal. (The *M/T* test car was fitted with eight-ply tires. Great for climbing over jagged rocks but no help to passenger comfort.)

Although the CJ was again a carryover, there was an interesting option package—the Renegade II. It included body striping, roll bar, and tachometer. It was offered only in "Big Bad Orange" with charcoal gray striping.

The big news in 1972 centered around Jeep's slowest selling model, the Jeepster Commando. The Commando's wheelbase was stretched to 104 inches, and the

power brakes are unduly sensitive and because the center of gravity is well up in the air, it rolls considerably in any turn. It has wholly adequate acceleration with the 350-cu-in. Buick V-8 engine but it is a car that needs to be driven with considerable care. Unladen, it has a poor, jiggly ride, even with conventional street tread tires, because of the stiff springing and crude suspension system.

"Off the pavement, however, it is undoubtedly one of the very best four-wheel-drive machines. . . . The automatic transmission, contrary to what you might think, is also an excellent feature for off-pavement driving. With the automatic . . . you can make much gentler applications of power when the going is tricky. This often enables you to munch on through deep sand or mud without breaking traction where, with a conventional transmission, an increase in throttle opening is much more likely to cause the wheels to spin and dig in and letting up to shift could let you get bogged."

Road & Track's conclusion was that

The big news on the Jeep sales front was the Cherokee (left). This new model, based on the Wagoneer, was a carefully positioned entry in the low-cost sport utility field. The Wagoneer, of course, moved up the price scale. The Cherokee was immediately identifiable by its two-door body style and pickup truck grille.

The familiar Dispatcher 100 (right, top left and middle) was most commonly seen in use by the U.S. Postal Service. Although very similar to a hardtop CJ-5, the Dispatcher had only two-wheel drive, and the steering wheel was moved to the right-hand side. The CJ-5 itself received only minor improvements for the 1974 model year (right, top right). The V-8 engine was massaged to meet new evaporative and exhaust emissions standards, and the heater and brakes were improved. The Jeep Renegade was made into a regular production model for 1974. The only colors available were Renegade yellow or Renegade Plum.

Jeepster name was dropped. The reason for the wheelbase stretch was the addition of two new engines. Both the F-head engine and the Buick-derived V-6 were dropped, and AMC's excellent seven-bearing, in-line "six" became the standard powerplant. The optional engine was AMC's 304-cid V-8, which pumped out 150 horsepower and 195 pounds-feet of torque.

Outside the revised Commando there was a longer hood and a new mesh grille which incorporated directional/parking lights and single headlights. Because of the stretched wheelbase the front shocks were now located ahead of the axle rather than behind it.

The CJs received the same engine treatment for 1972. The base engine was now the 232-cid inline six offering an even 100 horsepower. One step up was the 258-cid inline six with 110 horsepower, and for the first time a V-8 was installed as a factory option on the CJ.

The same AMC 304-cid V-8 as the Commando could be had as a regular option on the CJ-5 or CJ-6, but it came standard with the Renegade package. Also included in the package were American Racing aluminum wheels, roll bar, dual exterior mirrors, fender lips, and striped seat upholstery. Mandatory options to this package were Trac-Lok rear differential, dual sun visors, heavy-duty cooling system, rear seat, fuel tank skid plate, passenger safety rail, ammeter and oil pressure gauges, and a solid black tail panel with spare tire mount. It was clear that AMC was making an attempt at civilizing the CJ while at the same time moving it upmarket.

The Wagoneer and J Series were little changed in 1972. The trucks were given larger-diameter clutches. Payload was increased through the use of Dana axles, front and rear. And suspended brake and clutch pedals were extended to these models.

Then in 1973, AMC introduced the Quadra-Trac full-time four-wheel-drive system. Manufactured by Borg-Warner, and under development for more than four

years, Quadra-Trac represented a major advance because the vehicle could be run at all times in four-wheel drive, regardless of road conditions. Prior to its introduction it had been necessary to use two-wheel drive whenever a hard road surface was encountered, then shift manually to four-wheel when marginal traction conditions prevailed.

Car and Driver explained the reason: "You can best understand AMC's Quadra-Trac by driving any four-wheeled vehicle in virgin snow. If you turn the steering to full lock and drive slowly, you'll trace four neat arcs through the white stuff, each with a different radius. This demonstrates a kind of wheel-to-wheel independence that has absolutely nothing to do with the suspension. . . .

"Four different arcs mean that each track is a different length, and all four wheels must rotate at different speeds to reach the end of the turn together. This is no problem in cars because a differential between the two driving wheels accommodates their speed discrepancies, and the non-driving wheels roll at any speed they wish.

"But what about four-wheel drive? In off-road applications, there is no problem; sufficient slippage exists to allow cornering with all four wheels locked together at the same speed. The problem arises on paved roads. If you run a conventional (not full-time) four-wheel drive *engaged* on dry pavement, you're asking for trouble. Even with two differentials underneath, front and rear axles must turn at the same speed in curves when they'd really rather not. The result is wind-up in drivetrain components, severe torsional stresses and eventually an expensive snap somewhere."

With Quadra-Trac, however, there was no such problem. *Car and Driver*, again: "The magic element is installed in the middle of the Wagoneer, firmly bolted to the output end of the transmission: the Quadra-Trac transfer case, a device capable of many varied feats. Power goes in the front end and is split internally before exiting to

The new Cherokee was offered in two models, base or S (for sport). The S model (right, top) had chrome bumpers and window moldings, fancy body-side striping, movable quarter windows, aluminum wheels, a roof rack, and an "S" medallion on the rear panel. Jeep trucks received new model designations for 1974—the second time in their design lifetime (right, middle). There was now the J-10 and J-20, on either 119- or 131-inch wheelbases. There were also improvements inside with heavier frame cross members, front disc brakes, a new front axle, and six-stud wheels. Though Jeep advertised the Commando (right, bottom) in 1974, it was already out of production.

drive the front and rear axles. The intriguing feature is an inter-axle differential. This is a third differential, and it gives the Wagoneer's front and rear axles the required independence in rotational velocity they need for dry-pavement cornering. The Quadra-Trac inter-axle differential is also spin-resistant to divide up torque according to traction instead of the lack of it. Some really tough off-road circumstances demand full lockup between the differentials, so this is available at the turn of a knob in the glove compartment. . . ."

In addition to the benefit of maximum handling on and off the road at all times, the new Quadra-Trac system was quieter, cut down on tire wear, and eliminated the need for selective drive hubs. Quadra-Trac was standard on a Wagoneer with the automatic transmission and 175-horsepower 360-cid V-8. However, the top-of-the-line 195-horsepower V-8 could also be fitted with Quadra-Trac.

There were a host of other changes in 1973; most were made to improve the quality of the Wagoneer. Both the clutch and axle propshafts were toughened, for extended life. A new instrument panel housed a three-section cluster, speedometer, warning lights, and fuel, temperature, oil, and ammeter gauges. Knobs now had a "Soft-Feel" and were marked with international symbols instead of words. Completing the interior makeover were a restyled steering wheel, new armrests, an optional clock, and locking column ignition switch. The steering column was also now energy absorbing.

The J Series carried most of the Wagoneer's changes in 1973 but also received a new taillamp assembly, and double-wall side panels were added to the pickup bed. The biggest model was now the ¾-ton J-4800, with a GVW of 8000 pounds.

CJs also received a mild freshening. "Soft-Feel" knobs were added to the dash, and gauges had green lighting with orange needles. Also a new two-speed wiper system with integral washer was made stan-

dard. Along with the Renegade package, AMC offered the Super Jeep. This was basically a 6-cylinder CJ-5 with a dress-up package.

The final edition of the Jeepster, which remained in production through 1973, was probably the best of the lot despite an unfortunate frontal appearance applied by American Motors stylists. AMC's 304-cid V-8 was listed as an available option and surely must have done great things for the Commando's performance.

The Jeepster Commando was never a match for the CJ Jeep when it came to exploring the wilderness or performing chores around the farm. It wasn't meant to be. But as a dual-purpose family car, suitable to drive to the office during the week and to the old fishing hole come Saturday, it really had no equal.

The SJ (Wagoneer) product line was expanded for 1974 to include a new model called the Jeep Cherokee. The two-door Wagoneer had been dropped after 1968, and the Cherokee—somewhat plainer in trim than the 1974 Wagoneer—became, in a sense, its replacement. But more importantly, the Cherokee was designed to compete with the popular Blazer/Jimmy twins from General Motors.

By this time the Wagoneer's base engine was the two-barrel 360-cid V-8, with the four-barrel version as well as a larger, 401-cid mill on the options list. The Cherokee, on the other hand, still used the "258" as its standard powerplant, with the V-8's available at extra cost.

There were a number of significant improvements in the 1974 models, both Wagoneer and Cherokee. They stopped better. The Wagoneer's brakes had been a sore point from the start, but now, power-assisted disc/drums were used, effectively eliminating the problem of excessive brake-fade that had plagued the earlier cars. A Dana 44 front axle cut the turning diameter by nearly six feet, though the wheelbase was reduced by only an inch; and a new Saginaw variable-ratio power steering unit

The CJ-5 (right, top) returned for 1975 with a host of improvements. They had stronger frames, a factory-installed AM radio, and a Levi's seat and interior surface package. Jeep introduced the Cherokee Chief in January 1975 (right, bottom). The package retailed for $349 more than the "S" model. This package was more than just exterior stripes: Wider axles were added, and larger front and rear wheel cutouts, with wider moldings, were incorporated to accommodate larger wheels. There were also interior upgrades to the Chief as well. This new model created a three-tiered pricing structure for the Jeep wagons. At the low end was the Cherokee, the middle model was the Chief, and the top of the line was the Wagoneer.

Jeep for '73

Introducing the Jeep CJ/5 in "Jeans"

Look what the well dressed Jeep CJ/5 is wearing! New Levi's® styled seats with matching fold-down top. Made of rugged, easy to care for vinyl fabric in absolutely authentic styling—right down to the copper rivets. Built to take plenty of rough treatment and most anything the weather can dish out. Choose Levi's® blue or

Levi's® tan—to complement vehicle color. The Levi's® interior is standard on the Jeep Renegade (shown above) and optional on the standard Jeep CJ/5.
Levi's® and Jeep Corporation—two names at home in the great outdoors—waiting for you! Jeep wrote the book on 4-wheel drive.

Jeep CJ/5

From a Subsidiary of American Motors Corporation

provided far greater "road feel" than had previously been experienced.

Suspension was still comparatively crude, and the SJ's ride tended to be harsh. But the 1974 edition represented a tremendous advance in four-wheel-drive vehicles, for all that. Just a few years earlier, the idea that a four-wheel drive could be purchased with such amenities as automatic transmission, power steering, air-conditioning, power disc brakes—and yes, full-time four-wheel drive—would have sounded almost like science fiction. *Road & Track*'s editors called the Wagoneer "the most sophisticated four-wheel drive built in this country."

The Commando was gone in 1974, but the CJ-5 and CJ-6 carried on. However, changes were very minimal. Brakes were given new linings, master cylinder, and, for the first time, proportioning valves. To meet increasing government evaporative and exhaust standards, all CJs with the V-8 were given new fuel control and management systems. Also five-mile-per-hour bumpers were now optional.

Meanwhile, the appeal of the Jeep trucks was being enhanced by a number of dress-up items including custom decor group, dual horns, courtesy lights, tan cover, two-tone paint, and wood grain trim. Starting in 1974, and carrying on till 1978, those who wanted an extra measure of performance could have it in the form of AMC's four-barrel 401-cid V-8. The cost was an extra $94 beyond the price of the 360-cid engine.

AMC focused on the CJs for the majority of the 1975 changes. What they did was make the CJ more of an all-purpose vehicle while, at the same time, making it more user friendly. The frames of the CJ-5 and CJ-6 were strengthened, and another, more cosmetic, option package was offered.

The Levi's package offered a weather-resistant vinyl seat trim. In blue or tan it covered the seat, instrument panel pad, and padded sun visors. There was also a Levi's badge above the Jeep lettering on the cowl.

Other changes to the CJ for '75 included

AMC continued to push the ultimate utility of the Jeeps in their advertising (left, top), but the products continued to appear with more comfort and convenience features. One interesting feature was the Levi's package, which covered the interior and roof in a denim material (left, bottom).

Most Jeep products received a new electronic ignition system in 1975 to better manage fuel. The truck (right, top) received minor improvements to its engine, suspension, and interior. Four Wheeler magazine reported that "the ½-ton Jeep truck may be one of the best kept secrets in the four-wheel-drive world." The Wagoneer (right, bottom left) was available with a much larger wood-grained side panel, and the grille had been updated the year before. Early in 1976, AMC released the Honcho pickup. This aggressive appearance package cost $5680 and included the wider tires, axles, and fender flares from the Cherokee Chief.

159

a factory-installed AM radio, a first for the four wheeler. It was mounted underneath the dash in a weatherproof case. A factory-installed hardtop was another first-time option. The CJs also received catalytic converters and were now forced to use unleaded fuel.

The Wagoneer and Cherokee benefited from new electronic ignition systems and new heat insulation for the engine compartment and the exhaust system. The suspension system of the SJ was slightly modified with five-leaf springs (progressive at the rear) and longer shock absorbers. Inside the Custom Wagoneer, a number of user-friendly features were added. A convenience Light Group, AM/FM radio, rear window-defogger, cruise control, and padded carpeting were standard. The Levi's package could be fitted to the SJ models also.

By 1975 the pickups could be purchased with a Pioneer trim package consisting of wood grain exterior trim, deep pile carpeting, pleated fabric seats, chromed front bumpers, bright exterior window moldings, bright wheel covers, dual horns, wood grain instrument cluster trim, and assorted other amenities. A "Camper Special" package was also available. It addition the J Series added the same mechanical improvements as the Wagoneer.

Production numbers for Jeeps were beginning to creep upward toward pre-AMC levels. In 1974 Jeep produced 93,317 vehicles, and in 1975 that number rose to 108,612. Sales in Canada were up 11 percent over the previous year, and AMC and Jeep dealers had their third-best sales year in history. In April 1975 the 400,000th Jeep vehicle built since the purchase by AMC rolled off the assembly line.

Things continued to roll in 1976 with the introduction of a new CJ model. The CJ-7 effectively replaced the CJ-6 as that model was dropped in 1976. (Though an export model, it was designated the CJ-6A and continued through 1981.) The CJ-7's wheelbase was 93.4 inches—10 inches longer than the CJ-5. The reason for the

stretch was to accommodate an automatic transmission, but it also allowed the Quadra-Trac full-time four-wheel-drive system to be offered as an option—making the Jeep a stellar off-road performer.

A new, beefier frame with stronger cross members greatly increased bending strength. Also it was clear that AMC was attempting to promote luxury in this new CJ. Evidence of this existed with the addition of an optional one-piece injection-molded structural polycarbonate removable hardtop, lockable metal doors, and roll-down windows.

All CJs received a new taillight assembly and folding windshields with interior wiper motors. The locking steering wheel now had two spokes and was mounted on an energy absorbing column with an anti-theft ignition. The CJ-5 gained interior leg room with a redesigned dash panel and new floor. Also defroster vents were improved, and the entire front-passenger seat could be moved forward for easier entry into the vehicle. The Renegade package was available in either the CJ-5 or CJ-7.

Consumer Guide® tested a CJ-7 with the soft top and 258-cid engine. They found the CJ-7 a "true on-road/off-road performer. On the road the CJ came very close to equaling a passenger car in ride and handling; a car, that is, equipped with heavy-duty shock absorbers. The six-cylinder engine was able to hold the Jeep at top highway speeds on everything but long uphill grinds, and it remained relatively quiet all the while. . . . The only limitations we could find in the CJ's performance were those imposed on it by time and our test drivers' skill. The CJ-7 is a very strong vehicle that usually is more capable of handling rough country than are the people who drive it."

In 1976 several interesting packages were added to the truck line. Included were a trailer-towing package, a "Snow Boss" plow package, winches (mechanical or twelve-volt), locking hubs, and an auxiliary fuel tank for the J-20 long-wheelbase

Nineteen seventy-six brought the first new CJ model since 1956. The CJ-7 (right, top) effectively replaced the CJ-6. Though closely related to the CJ-5, the Seven rode on a 93.4-inch wheelbase. The reason for the wheelbase increase was two-fold. One was to provide more passenger room, and the second was to allow for an automatic transmission and the Quadra-Trac four-wheel-drive system. The 1976 Wagoneer (right, bottom left) and Cherokee (right, bottom right) received stiffer frames and an improved front suspension. The suspension allowed for more up-and-down travel as well as a redesigned straight-through steering linkage. In an effort to combat body roll in turns, Wagoneers and Cherokees could now be fitted with an optional front stabilizer bar.

models. A "Honcho" package was supplied for the short-wheelbase pickups commencing in 1976. Thus equipped—at a premium of $850—the J-10 took on a flashy appearance, with wide wheels and tires, blue Levi denim interior, sport steering wheel, and gold striping on bedside, fenders, and tailgate. A choice of six colors was offered.

Complementing the Honcho package in the Cherokee line was a wide wheel, tire and fender flare package called the Cherokee Chief. Both the Wagoneer and the Cherokee were given stronger and more rigid frames. For the first time a front sway bar could be had as an option on the SJ models.

This sway bar was an interesting feature in that it was a concession to on-road drivers. For years the Wagoneer had heeled over badly in turns due to the fact that it had such a long-travel suspension and lacked sway bars. The reason for this was, of course, the tremendous off-road ability this type of set up afforded. Yet, with the addition of a sway bar, the body is more tightly tied to the movement of the wheels and, while this makes the vehicle a better on-road handler, it becomes a less stable off-road platform.

By 1977 a four-door Cherokee was offered in addition to the two-door model. Mechanically, of course, it was identical to the Wagoneer, differing only in appointments and trim. And in the fact that, unlike the Wagoneer, it came standard with six-cylinder power. Part-time four-wheel drive was standard, requiring the driver to manually connect and disconnect the front hubs as road conditions changed. However, Quadra-Trac was optionally available.

Also available on the Cherokee were two appearance groups, the "S" package and the Cherokee Chief. In addition to interior and exterior trim, the Chief package—priced at $469—included a wide-track setup consisting of wider wheels and tires, and fender lips, while the "S" package—at $599—contained, as *Car and Driver* put it, "all the stuff you thought was simply

AMC proclaimed that the new Jeep Cherokee was a "Jeep and-a-half" (left). It offered all of the off-road ability of the ried-and-true Jeep, with the comfort and convenience of your everyday car.

Jeep followed up the 1976 Honcho package with the Golden Eagle for 1977 (right, top right). This package, priced at $749, included most of the features from the Honcho, and eight-inch wheels, pickup-bed roll bar, grille guard, driving lamps, Levi's seats, and an exterior package featuring accent stripes and an eagle hood decal. Changes to the Wagoneer were extremely limited in 1977, but Jeep did drop the custom model. AMC made up for the loss with the introduction of the four-door Cherokee (right, bottom left). It was priced at $5736, positioned between the four-door Wagoneer and the two-door Cherokee.

part of the vehicle (the armrests, cigarette lighter, ash trays, dual horns, carpets, vinyl seats *et al*) that make the difference between a light reconnaissance vehicle and something you wouldn't mind driving every day."

That magazine's editors borrowed a six-cylinder Cherokee, putting it through a month-long, 4500-mile test encompassing a variety of road and weather conditions. The test car was equipped with Quadra-Trac and automatic transmission—once again the Turbo-HydraMatic from General Motors—along with the "S" package, air-conditioning, power steering, radial tires, front anti-sway bar, and a number of other amenities. So it was no bare-bones machine, even though the six-cylinder engine was intended to be an economy measure. In fact, as equipped the Cherokee had a factory price of $8010, which was about $2000 higher than the base price of a Buick Estate Wagon in 1977.

One man's poison is another man's meat. Evidently the *Car and Driver* crew liked the stiff suspension that had been so roundly criticized by other reviewers:

"The Cherokee wagon, like the Wagoneer and all other Jeep vehicles, has a suspension that would bring tears to an aged purist's eyes—very solid axles front and rear, hung from the chassis on elliptical [sic] leaf springs at all four corners. Classical! Fundamental verities! Excellent shock damping and power steering filter out most of the resulting thumps and jerks, but the ride is still best described as 'reassuringly firm.' . . . It's kind of a cobby ride, friends, but for some perverse enthusiast's reason, we liked it."

The six-cylinder engine performed admirably. "In fact," the reviewer noted, "several staff members never twigged to the fact that they were being propelled down the road by a lowly two-barrel inline six generating a mere 110 horsepower and 196 pounds-feet of torque." Top speed was 89 miles per hour, a good deal higher than one might expect. The rig ran through the

quarter mile traps in 21.2 seconds at 63.5 mph—a creditable enough time.

But it was Quadra-Trac that was most impressive to the magazine's test crew. To test its limits, they took the Cherokee on something called "The Sons of Danger Ransom E. Olds Memorial Motocross":

"At one point, the impromptu motocross circuit crossed a deep drainage ditch that held no water but was nonetheless muddy as the devil. Carrying its driver and one passenger, the Cherokee negotiated the crossing without difficulty, in spite of the bikers' profane predictions to the contrary. . . .

"A week later we had the questionable pleasure of a 13-hour drive from Snover, Michigan, to New York City. Between Syracuse and Liberty, New York, we encountered a ferocious snowstorm that laid three inches of new powder on the road in about two hours. Once again the Cherokee flatly refused to do anything wrong. We broke trail for dozens of lesser machines, taking curves and passing trucks at 65 mph with gay abandon, and not once did we so much as get the tail end loose. It works."

Car and Driver concluded, "It's the most useable, most comfortable, most driveable four-wheel drive conveyance we've ever messed with, and it has become a serious contender for purchase as *C/D*'s next workhorse staff vehicle. . . . Like we said, strangely lovable."

The CJs again received a major working over with the addition of air-conditioning and power front disc brakes. Stronger front axles and a fully boxed frame led the list of technical revisions, and an interesting option package was offered.

The Golden Eagle option was priced $200 more than a comparably equipped Renegade, or roughly $6800. Only available in a thrush brown with a black, gold, and white eagle decal on the hood, the package included larger tires, rear mounted spare, Levi's soft top, wheel lip extensions, spare tire lock, Convenience group, Decor group, tachometer, clock, and carpeting.

The Honcho package (right, top) returned on the pickups for 1978 and was joined by a new trim option—the 10-4. Consisting mostly of color choices and detailing, the 10-4 package also offered an optional, factory-installed CB radio. The exteriors of the Wagoneers and Cherokees (right, bottom left and middle) were little changed for 1978, but the interiors were given a minor reworking. Changes included new color-keyed seatbelts, a new horn bar, "Soft-Feel" vinyl seat trim, new armrest bases, and a revised fuel filler location. The CJ models received a new heater and defroster, and the Golden Eagle (right, bottom right) option package was again offered in 1978.

'75 Jeep CJ-5 Cherokee Pickup Wagoneer

Basically every convenience option available. There was an initial build of 2000, but later another 200 were produced.

A similar high-styled "Golden Eagle" package became available for the short-wheelbase trucks in 1978. Priced at $999, it included off-road driving lights mounted atop a roll bar. There were Golden Eagle decals on the hood and lower door panels. A chromed front bumper, rear step bumper, gold eight-inch smoked wheels with black accents, wide all-terrain tires, Levi-covered bucket seats, engine-turned instrument panel, bright window frames, tan carpeting, sport steering wheel, and gold/green/orange striping on the doors, cab, and upper box sides completed the layout.

The Wagoneer Limited was introduced during the 1978 model year; and according to the 1979 *New Car Yearbook* it sold out immediately. In addition to the two-barrel 360-cid engine, Quadra-Trac, automatic transmission, power steering, disc brakes, carpeting, and full instrumentation, all of which were standard issue by that time for every Wagoneer, the Limited listed air-conditioning, tinted glass, power tailgate window, AM/FM/CB radio, roof rack, forged aluminum wheels, and a number of other goodies among its enticements. A four-barrel 401-cid V-8 was optional.

It was now quite clear that AMC was positioning the Jeep line upscale of the competitors from Ford and Chevy. Sales of AMC automobiles were up, and the company reported a record profit of $83,944,000. The number of Jeep units produced was up again to 180,514.

Working capital for the company was $235 million. Things seemed to be going very well, but things would change soon.

Changes for the 1979 model year were few, but they centered on meeting the ever-tightening government safety and emissions requirements. The Wagoneer received a new vertical-bar grille with single rectangular headlights. The only engine available on the Wagoneer was the 360-cid V-8, though you could still get the inline six on the Cherokee. An Extra-Quiet Insulation package was a new option, as was a smooth-ride suspension.

The suspension was also available on all models of the Cherokee except the wide track. The smooth-ride package consisted of special front and rear springs plus a front stabilizer bar. However, due to its on-road turning it was not recommended for off-road use.

The Jeep trucks carried most of the changes offered on the Cherokee models, including the new front grille. Also new was a one-piece aluminum front bumper with optional black bumper guards. Engine choices were now down to two—258-cid inline six and the 360-cid V-8.

AMC attempted to get the lead out on the CJs by using lighter body panels. This resulted in an 80-pound weight savings. Golden Eagle and Renegade packages returned, and a new 25th Anniversary CJ package was offered. It consisted of silver metallic paint, silver accent striping, black soft top, black bucket seats, and a commemorative dash plaque.

In 1980 the CJ was given a new standard powerplant. Called the "Hurricane," it was, in reality, Pontiac's "Iron Duke" four cylinder. This engine had a 4.00-inch bore and 3.00-inch stroke, operated in an 8.2:1 compression ratio, and offered up 82 ponies at 4000 rpm. It was an obvious reaction to the latest fuel crisis. Otherwise manually-operating, freewheeling hubs were made standard across the board.

The big news for the SJs and J Series in 1980 was the fact that, for the first time in

The Jeep lineup wasn't particularly diverse, although it did offer four distinct models in 1975 (and would add one more in 1976). Most of the Jeep ads, however, still pictured the vehicles in rural settings.

The entire CJ lineup was revised with the addition of catalytic converters and the use of lighter body panels. Weight was down 80 pounds, and no-lead fuel was now required. The Golden Eagle (right, top) and Renegade (right, bottom) packages were revised for 1979. The Eagle offered an exclusive injection-molded hardtop with tinted rear glass. The hardtop could also be fitted with a pop-up sunroof. Renegade had new exterior designs and spoke steel wheels. Jeep also offered a limited edition Silver Anniversary CJ-5 commemorating its 25th birthday. It featured a silver metallic finish and a commemorative dash plaque.

Not a bird. Not a plane. But a new thrill under the sun—4-wheel drive fun-mobiling.
At first glance, that same familiar profile, but underneath that super-stripe stands a baby brute with the guts to go where others fear to tread.
Super Jeep® is *all* guts from the brawny suspension to the heavy-duty axle—an open-end design that can turn in just 32.9 ft. And while you're checking out the special color treatment on

the front and rear seats, the roll bar's saying "go!" and the 258 six answers "r-r-i-i-ght!"
Oversize L78 x 15 Polyglas® white wall tires are included along with those black rubber lip extensions on the fenders.
Plus chrome front bumper and a safety rail for your more easily flustered passengers. She's available in all kinds of color combinations and lots of extra goodies.
So don't just sit there, hit the trail in a gen-u-ine Super Jeep.

Jeep

Toughest 4-letter word on wheels.

'eep Corporation proudly presents

'76 Jeep

CJ-5 • Cherokee • Wagoneer • Pickup •
and introducing the new more versatile CJ-7 • • •

CJ-5
Cherokee
Wagoneer
Pickup

CHAPTER EIGHT

seven years, they were offered with either full- or part-time four-wheel drive. This was facilitated by an all-new, all-synchro-mesh 4-speed Tremec model transmission and a New Process 208 part-time transfer case. In addition, the transfer case could be used on the new Chrysler TorqueFlite transmission. Also, the Quadra-Trac system was improved by the substitution of viscous drive for the previous cone clutch.

Car and Driver, examining a 1980 Wagoneer Limited, observed, "The Wagoneer's great strength is that it's been around for a long time, long enough for the engineers and manufacturing people to get everything right. It is solid and reliable, and everything seems to be where it is for a reason. . . ."

And then the editors went on to say, "It's unfortunate that a car as good as this one is so close to the end of the trail. It's too big and too thirsty to last much long-er. . . ." However anachronistic *Car and Driver* made the Wagoneer seem, it would carry on for more than 10 additional years.

The trucks also gained a new/old body style. The stepside was offered for the first time since 1973. It was available only on the Sportside model and included bright finish moldings, engine turned instrument cluster trim, and other niceties. However, horsepower was down to 129 on the 360-cid V-8. Meanwhile, trim packages prolifer-ated. Choices for 1980 ranged from "Cus-tom" trim, priced at $149, to the Laredo package costing a stiff $1600.

Nineteen-eighty was a terrible year for AMC as a whole. It reported a loss that was almost beyond belief—$155,672,000. For the calendar year the loss was an even greater $197 million. The recession had knocked the U.S. economy for a loop, and AMC's small size would not allow the company to sustain such losses for an ex-tended period.

AMC had been selling Renault cars through its dealerships for several years at this point, and it was hoped that this diverse model lineup would carry them

For 1976 AMC reintroduced the "Super Jeep" (left, top). This special CJ-5 featured a roll bar, special striping on the hood and seats, the OHV inline six, and Polyglas tires. Jeep focused their sales literature on the new CJ-7 (left, bottom). One easy way to distinguish the Seven from the Five is that the Seven has squared-off door openings while the Five's are rounded at the rear.

The differences between the 1979 (right, top right) Honcho and the 1981 model (right, top left) are quite obvious. The roof lip over the windshield was finally removed, the bodyside striping was altered, a stepside body was offered, the grille was different, and the roll bar was altered. The Cherokee Chief and Wagoneer (right, middle and bottom) received new chromed grilles, and over 90 pounds were shaved from the curb weight of each model.

168

through. This was not to be. AMC was forced to sell 20 million shares of stock to Renault for $122.5 million. This would give Renault 46.4-percent control of AMC, which did not make AMC dealers happy. (However, the only other option was bankruptcy.) The Jeep division was now a part of AMC, who was a part of Renault, who was owned by the French government. Quite an ironic twist for the all-American wonder.

The next year saw the introduction of the Scrambler or CJ-8. It was the first new model Jeep had released since the CJ-7. The CJ-based creation was officially put on sale on March 25, 1981. It was basically a stretched CJ-7 with a five-foot pickup box. In fact, from the cowl forward it was identical to the CJ model. The Scrambler was also identical to the Seven in its essential mechanical components. It offered an optional hardtop, steel doors, and a fold-down rear liftgate.

Jeep offered two appearance packages that could be had in addition to the base model—the SR and SL Sport. The SR consisted of high back bucket seats, the Convenience group, the Decor group, white steel wheels, and Scrambler hood lettering. The SL package included bucket seats, leather-wrapped steering wheel and passenger assist bar, console, clock, and tachometer. Scramblers could even be outfitted with wood side rails. It was an interesting variant on the CJ platform, but sales never amounted to much, peaking at 8355 units in its first year.

The mainline CJs received a reworked and lighter six-cylinder engine that improved both economy and drivability. Also Chrysler's TorqueFlite transmission and locking torque converter were used with the six. Minor adjustments were made to the sidestep and body graphics.

The Wagoneer line expanded to three models for 1981. There was the Custom, Brougham, and the Limited. A front air dam was added that reduced wind resistance, and drag-free front brake calipers were installed.

Though the optional engine on the Wagoneer was still the 360-cid V-8, the standard engine was now the 258-cid in-line six. The reason for this was that it received a significant makeover from AMC. Thirty pounds was shaved from the block, and the redesigned cylinder head was 12 pounds lighter. Aluminum replaced cast iron in the intake manifold and rocker arm covers. Idle speed was lowered with a new cam profile, and a new emissions control system was added. Though rated horsepower dropped to 110 from 1980's 118, drivability and economy were increased, and overall weight was down some 90 pounds.

The J Series received the same improvements as the Wagoneer and Cherokee and also finally lost their front roof lip. Because of this, a new windshield, end caps, and drip moldings were added. Extensive use of one-side galvanized steel was made throughout the body panels with hot wax being applied to the other side of the panels. Pickups were lowered by an inch and a quarter, thanks to redesigned front and rear springs. That same year, power steering was included as standard equipment.

There were more mechanical refinements for 1982. Due to its standard automatic transmission the Wagoneer was left out of the biggest improvement of the year. The Cherokee and the J Series trucks received a Warner Gear T5 5-speed manual transmission. The fifth gear was an overdrive offering either a 0.76:1 or 0.86:1,

For 1977 Jeep sales literature turned nostalgic, echoing Jeep's past. There could be no doubt of the tremendous heritage of the Jeep, but there was also rising opposition to the CJ-5's propensity to roll over.

The 1981 Cherokee Chief (right, top) could also be had with a blacked-out grille and the smaller wheel openings. An unusual factory option for the 1981 Pickup with the Honcho package was the bed cap (right, bottom right). It fitted real wood side rails and a cab header board to the pickup box. This was available on the stepside body style only. For 1980, Jeep introduced the Laredo package on its CJs as the top-of-the-line trim package (right, bottom left). This package cost $1950 and included just about every comfort and convenience option on the docket. It also included a special Laredo dash plaque.

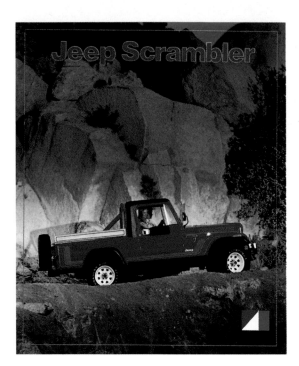

depending on engine and final drive. There were also numerous packages. The Chief and Laredo on the Cherokee; Brougham and Limited on the Wagoneer.

Debuting on the truck side was the Pioneer package. It consisted of everything in the Custom package plus bodyside molding, tailgate stripes, Pioneer decals, dark grille, carpeted cab floor, Western Weave cloth and vinyl bench seat, wood-grain accents on the dash, sport steering wheel, painted step bumper, front bumper guards, extra-quiet insulation, full wheel covers (J-10 only), and Light Group. The Honcho package was continued; however, it was only available with the Sportside.

All of the news for 1982 surrounding the CJs centered around new option packages. The grandest being called the Limited. This package was available in one of five exterior colors on the CJ-7. It included almost every conceivable option on the CJ list, including some added for 1982. This was the ultimate on-road CJ and was the final step in citifying the Jeep. Now, completely across the Jeep lineup one could ride in a vehicle very similar to any other non-four-wheel-drive vehicle.

That year was also the 30th anniversary of the Jeepers Jamboree, and AMC did not let it go unnoticed. They rolled out an exclusive 30th Anniversary Commemorative Edition. Only 2500 were to be built, and standard features included: Jamboree hood lettering decals, black spare tire cover with Jamboree logo, chrome wheels, bumper, and bumperettes, black vinyl top, and Decor Group. In addition the Commemorative Edition had a numbered instrument panel plaque, and each owner received a signed, framed certificate of authenticity.

The Scrambler returned unchanged, although several options were added. A 20-gallon fuel tank and 5-speed overdrive transmission were offered. Sales of the Scrambler were just under 8000 for the year, and it was clear that it was becoming a nitch vehicle and not the mainline small

After several years of trim and option packages, Jeep copywriters finally had a new model to hype. It was the 1981 Scrambler pickup (left).

The Scrambler was a mechanical twin to the CJ-7 that differed in body style by offering a five-foot pickup bed. The factory's MSRP started at $7288 for the soft top and rose to $7922 for the hardtop (right, top). You could also get a soft top with steel doors. For 1982 there were virtually no exterior or interior changes for the Wagoneer (right, middle left) or the Cherokee (right, middle right). The only mechanical changes of note were the use of halogen headlights and the availability of an electronically tuned AM/FM cassette radio. The Renegade (right, bottom right) and Laredo (right, bottom left) packages continued into 1982 with very few changes. However, the price of the Limited package was up to $2895.

1982
Jeep

CJ-5/CJ-7 • Scrambler
Pickup • Cherokee
Wagoneer

pickup truck AMC had hoped it would become—similar to the Chevy Luv.

AMC was coming under more and more control by Renault. W. Paul Tippett, Jr., was elected chairman of AMC, and José J. Dedeurwaerder was elected chief executive officer. Roy Chapin—AMC's previous head—had been elected (demoted) by the board of directors to head a new executive committee, and *Automotive News* stated in a 1982 article, "While AMC officially proclaimed the alliance was a marriage, there was little doubt that Renault was the head of the household."

This undoubtably led to the sale of AM General to LTV corporation for $170 million. AM General, at this point, had won the government contract for the Jeep replacement, the Hummer. Since Renault was owned by the French government, it would not look very good if one of their divisions was producing vehicles for the

U.S. military. Also, Renault was unhappy with the low levels of AMC sales and was looking to rid itself of unnecessary divisions.

Standard on Wagoneers and optional on Cherokees with the automatic was a new Selec-Trac two- or four-wheel-drive system. With Selec-Trac, the front drivetrain was released from the freely-turning front wheels by a vacuum-activated clutch. The transfer from two-wheel drive to four-wheel drive could only be accomplished by bringing the vehicle to a stop and the driver then moving the dash-mounted lever into four-wheel drive. To prevent accidental shifting, a safety had to be released before the lever could be moved. Otherwise trim packages for the SJs were unchanged, though this was the last year for the full-size Cherokee.

J-Series models with automatics could also be fitted with Selec-Trac. In addition the six-cylinder engine was again revised with a higher compression ratio.

The CJ's 258-cid six was given the same improvements as the larger Jeep models, but other than that, 1983 modifications were limited to changes in option packages. Scramblers were slightly more modified. The standard mounting place for the spare tire was moved to the roll bar, and graphics packages for the SR and SL packages were slightly altered.

Jeep sales were up again to 93,169 from 67,646 in 1982, and AMC sales, as a whole, were up to 265,999. All together the corporation produced 97,000 more units in 1983 than in 1982. AMC even showed a slight profit of $7.4 million in the fourth quarter, but the company lost 146 million over the entire year.

Despite the trememdous losses, things were pointing up at AMC. The Renault Alliance was a top seller, and the country, as a whole, was pulling out of the recession and starting to buy cars again. Yet the big news was just under the next rock; Jeep was readying its downsized utility vehicle, the XJ Cherokee.

By 1982, Jeep production (left) had fallen to 75,000. That was less than half of the number produced just four years earlier. However, things were soon to change with the introduction of the new Cherokee and Wagoneer models.

Jeep introduced the Scrambler in two trim levels, the SR and the SL. The SR (right, top and bottom right) had bucket seats, the Convenience group, the decor group, steel wheels, wheel lip extensions, and exterior graphics. The package was priced at $775. To go along with the Renegade and the Laredo, Jeep offered the Limited package (right, bottom left) for the CJ. It was the most extensive options package yet for any CJ product and offered a leather-wrapped steering wheel, convenience dome lights, and floor mats.

Driving the CJ

With the possible exception of the Volkswagen Beetle, the Jeep CJ has the most recognized shape in the automotive world. The new ones, of course, are bigger, taller, and more rounded than the '46 original, but they're obviously part of the same family, separated by a seemingly short 40 years much like a grandfather from grandson.

It's funny how similar these Jeep generations are from behind the wheel. With less weight, smaller size, and a lower center of gravity, the '46 feels like it'll scamper anywhere, and its flathead four certainly seems to have the gumption. The gearbox feels right, and time has changed the rudimentary suspension but little. It's starkly Spartan, of course, but what military vehicle isn't?

Hopping into the CJ-7 is like entering a time warp. You know this is a newly built rig from its seatbelts, "unleaded fuel only" warning, and the contemporary instruments, steering wheel, and bucket seats, yet it's anything but modern. There are more gauges now than there were in the Forties, but most are still low down in the center of the dash. The accessory soft top flaps noisily above 40 mph, and the stiff suspension, with its big radial tires, delivers a bump-and-grind ride even on roads that look smooth.

I wince thinking about that on starting a three-hour drive to the desert, the Jeep packed full of camping gear, wife, and 100-pound German shepherd. The dog solves his comfort problem by riding on my lap. "That strong six has plenty of torque. Just leave it in fifth," he seems to say. But I remember that the '46 got by just fine with only three gears and four cylinders. Through the mountains, I shift between tail wags.

Once in the Anza-Borrego Desert, I realize why the CJ has hung on so long. With the greatest of ease, we charge down trails that don't stand a chance of being paved, and driving through a stream bed is a nice way to cool off. Climbing up from the desert over a boulder-strewn path requires concentration. But had I been there in your average 4x4, I would have taken the long way home. For the more treacherous parts, the dog has to ride in back. Thanks to its amazing ground clearance, the CJ hurtles obstacles so matter-of-factly that you wonder why we ever bothered with roads. This form of travel may take more time, but it's sure a lot more fun.

Sadly, the CJ isn't nearly as much fun around town or on freeway expansion joints. The ride is unnervingly pitchy, top-up vision is mediocre despite the high seating position, and the power steering is overassisted yet slow. A short wheelbase and tall build make hard cornering tippy, and rough surfaces tell you the body structure isn't nearly as stiff as the suspension. As they say, "Only in a Jeep."

So despite air-conditioning, stereo sound, and full carpeting, the last of the CJs is not the best way to reach your cabin in the woods, though it may be the only one of today's off-roaders you'd want to keep there. Yet on the trail to Anza, I know that if I had CJ, I'd never give it up. And that's right. After all, isn't *fighting* what got the Jeep started in the first place?

Sales of the big pickup had been holding steady for years, but in 1980 they dropped from 18,000 to just under 7000. Despite the flair of the Honcho (right, top), the sales would never again pass 10,000 for the J-10. In 1983, the Cherokee was in its final year as a large wagon, but, along with the Wagoneer (right, middle), it introduced an important four-wheel-drive innovation. Called Selec-Trac, the new system could be driven in either two- or four-wheel-drive mode and was much more efficient than Command-Trac.

CHAPTER NINE

Moving to the Head of the Class: 1984-86

merican automakers responded to the oil embargo of 1973 by downsizing—sort of. The Chevrolet Chevette was rushed to market by 1975, but it wasn't until 1977 that General Motors introduced smaller versions of standbys such as the Oldsmobile Delta 88. It took until 1978 for Ford to show it was serious about downsizing with the Fairmont. These cars used less gas than preceding models but were still hefty, old-think designs, with body-on-frame construction and rear-wheel drive.

In the truck field, the Big Three reacted to the fuel crisis by slapping domestic nameplates on small, "captive-import" Japanese pickups. Full-size pickups and vans were unaffected. The sport-utility field remained dominated by the big 4x4s: the Ford Bronco, Chevrolet Blazer and GMC Jimmy, Dodge Ramcharger, and the Jeep Wagoneer.

Then, in 1979, a second energy crisis hit. Gas lines returned. Fuel costs skyrocketed. A chill of uncertainty about future energy supplies raced through America. Now the domestic automakers responded more surely, with modern, front-wheel-drive cars, such as the Chevrolet Citation and Ford Escort. These new models suffered some flaws and lacked refinement, but they sold well in a climate of diminishing expectations.

It was in this atmosphere that AMC set about designing a new sport-utility vehicle. The Wagoneer—designated SJ under AMC's internal codes—would be 20 years old in 1983, and the initial plan was to replace it with a body-on-frame 4x4 wagon

of roughly the same size and powertrain but with updates in appearance and amenities. The fuel crisis changed all that. Suddenly, gas mileage seemed of paramount importance, and European design was exerting a strong, new influence. It became clear that the next Jeep sport-utility vehicle would require some fresh thinking.

AMC coded the new Jeep the XJ and started with a clean sheet of paper. The first big decision was to reject contemporary sport-utility thinking and specify a unibody design. Up to this time, most 4x4 wagons were essentially short-wheelbase pickup trucks fitted with enclosed passenger compartments. Their body-on-frame design was not only a bow to production efficiencies but to a dictum that the ideal off-road vehicle needed a flexible chassis to better accommodate variations in the terrain.

To AMC, however, a vehicle in which the frame and body were a single unit promised weight-saving advantages essential in a future that might include outright fuel rationing. Such a structure also would have greater resistance to twisting and flexing, to the benefit of on-road ride and handling. Maintaining Jeep's traditional off-road prowess would require a suspension tuned to exploit this stiff new structure.

A unibody design would not be enough, however. The overall size had to be reduced. The Wagoneer tipped the scales at nearly 4000 pounds—with the V-8 it was heavier still. To meet a target curb weight of around 2900 pounds, the XJ would have to be significantly smaller. This caused immediate friction in surveys of Wagoneer owners, who were highly protective of the big Jeep's brawny presence. Maintaining

More than any other automaker, independent AMC had been hurt by the fuel crises of 1973 and 1979. They downsized their lineup to compete with the first energy crisis and then brought in a partner, Renault, to battle the second. Their struggle left the company with very little capital. Despite all this, an effort was underway to develop a replacement for the aging, but steady, Wagoneer. The new model would be smaller, more fuel efficient, and offer all of the off-road ability Jeeps were famous for. Early sketches (right, top and bottom) show the variations the designers explored to create a clay (right, middle) that was very close to the final model. However, the clay shows much more aggressive fender flares than the final model would have. It is very interesting to note that two-door sport utilities dominated the market at this time, and the four-door design, found only on the sketches, was very forward-looking. There is no doubt that the body design shows European, particularly Renault, influence, but AMC, and later Chrysler, insisted that the styling was created in-house.

the Jeep character on a downsized 4x4 wagon would be essential to the project.

Work on the XJ began in late 1978 with the expectation that the vehicle would rely primarily on a new four-cylinder engine AMC was then developing. It was the company's first homegrown four and displaced 2.5 liters. It would be augmented by a six-cylinder engine. AMC's 232- and 258-cubic-inch inline-sixes were deemed too inefficient for the XJ application, however. Plus, the trend in six-cylinder engines was toward a V configuration, and AMC had no V-6 in its inventory. So the XJ also was designed specifically to accept the General Motors 2.8-liter V-6, which met the packaging parameters and was available for purchase.

As development progressed, though, the fuel picture began to brighten. Gas prices were nowhere near the three-dollars per gallon that some had forecast. Supplies had stabilized, and Americans were again hungry for larger cars with more power. In response, AMC undertook development of a new six-cylinder engine, a 4.0 liter that compensated for its "old-fashioned" in-line configuration with modern design and excellent power characteristics. The new 4.0-liter six would not be ready until the 1987 model year, but it was designed from the start to fit into the XJ.

There was no turning back on the original unibody design or compact dimensions. The XJ's unitized body structure would be combined with a full-length, boxed steel frame welded around the perimeter of the floor pan. It was lightweight, efficient, and strong.

Then there was the matter of the suspension. On the one hand the need for off-road durability appeared—in the light of Jeep's experience with the earliest Wagoneers—to call for a solid axle. Yet Roy Lunn, AMC's vice president for engineering, was determined to provide the XJ with superior ride and handling, qualities not usually associated with a live front axle.

The solution was to retain a solid axle in front, but to locate it by means of four trailing links and a Panhard rod. Coil springs were employed in lieu of the semi-elliptic leaf springs usually associated with this type of layout. Engineers dubbed the assembly Quadra-Link and completed it with low-pressure gas shocks and an anti-sway bar. Leaf springs were used at the rear, partly because coils would have intruded into the passenger compartment.

Helping to develop the suspension was Francois J. Castaing, who had served as chief engineer of the Formula 1 racing team operated by Renault. The French automaker had begun purchasing AMC stock in 1979. It was seeking a North American channel for its cars and was hungry for a supply of four-wheel-drive vehicles that could be sold in Europe. Renault would eventually increase its share of AMC stock to 46 percent and exercise a good deal of control over the American company's product. But Renault's influence at AMC during the XJ's formative period was focused more on development of what would become the 1983 Renault-badged Alliance sedan.

Thus, while the French company is sometimes credited with the XJ's superbly proportioned shape, the styling was in fact the work of AMC's internal staff. That's not to say the XJ didn't draw inspiration from a variety of sources, including the wedge-shape then so strong in European design. However, the key was in how it blended diverse influences.

For example, the chiseled features that gave the XJ so much character were a union of styling cues popularized by the Volkswagen Rabbit—at the time the best-selling import nameplate in the United States—and the masculine theme demanded by the Jeep heritage. Similarly, the way the XJ pushed the wheels out near the corners of the vehicle reflected both the efficiency of European design philosophy and the reality of minimizing body overhang for off-road maneuverability.

Command of off-road terrain was cer-

Though Jeep still sold the Wagoneer (now called the Grand Wagoneer), they introduced for 1984 a new downsized sport utility. Called the Cherokee and Wagoneer, the XJ had a wheelbase of 101.4 inches and came in two- or four-door versions. Engine choices comprised either a newly designed 150-cid four or GM's 2.8-liter V-6. Several trim levels were available for the new XJs. The Wagoneer had the Brougham and Limited packages (right, top, foreground), and the Cherokee was offered in the Pioneer and Chief (right, bottom right) models. With the continuation of the Grand Wagoneer, it's not surprising that the J Series trucks (right, bottom left) returned, but by this time the Gladiator name was long gone.

tainly part of the Jeep heritage, and here the XJ would seek out its own direction. Though the SJ had used a permanently engaged four-wheel-drive system in the mid-1970s, this Quadra-Trac setup had come to be considered inefficient in terms of fuel economy. By 1980, the big Wagoneer was offered with a Selec-Trac four-wheel-drive system that allowed for more economical two-wheel-drive running.

A similar strategy was followed for the XJ. Standard equipment would be a part-time four-wheel-drive system called Command-Trac. It incorporated full "shift-on-the-fly" capability and automatic-locking front hubs. A vacuum-actuated front axle engagement made it possible to switch from two- to four-wheel drive at any speed simply by pulling a handle mounted on the center console. Command-Trac was not for use on dry pavement, however.

For that, the XJ adopted Selec-Trac as its optional four-wheel-drive setup. Selec-Trac initially did not feature shift-on-the-fly; the vehicle had to be stopped to engage four-wheel drive via a dashboard toggle switch. Once done, the XJ could remain in four-wheel-drive high mode indefinitely, regardless of road surface, with no loss of fuel economy and without causing excessive wear on the drivetrain components. No other compact sport-utility vehicle offered such a system.

AMC didn't break any ground in naming its new vehicle, however. The new Jeep would square off against downsized sport-utility vehicles from Ford and GM, which shamelessly leaned on established full-size 4x4s for their names. The Chevrolet S10 Blazer and GMC S15 Jimmy had bowed for the 1983 model year, and the Ford Bronco II hit showrooms in mid-March 1983, as a 1984 model.

AMC followed suit by building on established Jeep names. It borrowed the name of the base SJ model and tagged the entry-level XJ the Cherokee. For the plusher, up-level XJ model, Jeep simply stole the big 4x4's name entirely and called it the Wag-

oneer. Meanwhile, the full-size SJ was re-christened the Grand Wagoneer. Cherokee and Wagoneer were introduced in the fall of 1983 as '84 models—the first all-new Jeeps in 20 years.

Here's how they stacked up against the Grand Wagoneer and the sales-leading S10 Blazer:

	Cherokee	Grand Wagoneer	S10 Blazer
Wheelbase (in.)	101.4	108.7	100.5
Length (in.)	165.3	186.4	170.4
Height (in.)	63.0	65.9	65.0
Width (in.)	65.9	75.6	64.7
Weight (lbs)	2886	4025	3150
Cargo volume (cu ft)	71.2	74.5	62.7

Jeep had done a laudable bit of packaging. Cherokee was 21 inches shorter overall than the SJ, 9.7 inches narrower, and three inches lower. Yet it retained 90 percent of the big wagon's interior space—and offered as much usable cargo room. Just as significant, the XJ distinguished itself visually from the Grand Wagoneer while maintaining a strong Jeep identity. Gone was the exaggerated protrusion of the SJ's grille. In its place was a more aerodynamic, but no less evocative, arrangement of bold vertical bars. The tailgate was a one-piece fiberglass unit. Front-disc/rear-drum brakes were standard.

Inside, the new instrument panel included provisions for factory air conditioning. Borrowed from the Alliance were front bucket seats mounted on pedestals that provided extra rear foot room. Locating Cherokee's rear bench seat ahead of the rear wheelhousings made it wide enough to accommodate three-across seating, so the Jeep could carry five passengers, not just four like its Ford and Chevy rivals.

Dimensional differences were slight among the Jeep, Ford, and Chevy—and the Isuzu Trooper II, Mitsubishi Montero, Toyota 4Runner, and Nissan Pathfinder that would soon round out the burgeoning compact-sport-utility field.

However, there was one dramatic variation that would prove invaluable to Jeep in the coming years: Cherokee and Wagoneer

CJ-5 production ceased in 1983, ending a run that began on October 11, 1954. However, the CJ-7 and the Scrambler carried on the Jeep tradition. For 1984, the CJ-7 (right, top) received only modest changes, the biggest being a new standard engine. The same powerplant that was offered as standard in the Cherokee, this 2.5-liter four cylinder offered 105 horsepower at 5000 rpm and 132 pounds-feet of torque at 2800 rpm. A six-cylinder engine was still available as an option. The Scrambler (right, bottom) was given the same changes as the CJ-7. The SL and SR Sport Packages returned for their final year.

were offered with four side doors. All competitors had just two. Though the five-door body style was part of the XJ planning from the start, AMC had given it secondary importance and forecast that the three-door would account for the lion's share of sales. But the marketplace was poised for a major shift. Sport-utility 4x4s were evolving from off-road specialty items to mainstream family wagons. Having the only five-door body style in the field sustained the Cherokee and Wagoneer as a major sales force. It would take the competition until the 1990 model year to offer the body style. By then, the five-door accounted for 85 percent of Cherokee sales.

Cherokee debuted in Pioneer and Cherokee Chief trim. With its mud-resistant vinyl upholstery and rugged demeanor, Cherokee was aimed at young, active buyers. Prices for the base three-door started at $9995 and for the base five-door at $10,295. Wagoneer bowed as a five-door only in Brougham and Limited guise, the latter with woodgrain bodyside appliqués. Wagoneer started at $12,444 and ranged to $17,381 for the Limited, not including options. It targeted an upscale audience and came standard with such amenities as whitewall tires and cloth interior trim; the Limited's cabin added leather appointments and fake wood inserts. An interesting styling footnote is that early plans called for the three-door XJ to have expressive fender flares, while five-door models would retain the modest wheel lips. This would have echoed the styling differentiation found in the SJ line, where the three-door was available as a flare-fender "wide-wheel" model. Yet the plan was dropped about one year before the XJ's introduction. Studies concluded that the appearance differences didn't justify the production complications.

The base engine for all variations of the Cherokee and Wagoneer was the new 2.5-liter four cylinder. It was of straight-forward iron-block-and-head construction with overhead valves. It used a one-barrel carburetor and had a compression ratio of 9.2:1. Though AMC did not release horsepower ratings at the time, the four made 105 at 5000 rpm and had 132 pounds-feet of torque at 2800. The torque curve was notably flat. Optional was the 2.8-liter GM V-6. It had a two-barrel carb and was rated at 115 horsepower at 4800 rpm and 145 pounds-feet at 2400. With either engine, a four-speed manual transmission was standard. Optional was a five-speed manual or a Chrysler three-speed automatic.

Though they were conceived to hit a target that had moved during their development, the Cherokee and Wagoneer nonetheless seemed just right for their times. Critics and customers raved.

Right out of the box, a V-6 Cherokee outpointed the S-10 Blazer, Bronco II, and Mitsubishi Montero in a *Motor Trend* comparison test. "It out-performed all comers in instrumented testing," the magazine reported; "it gave the nicest ride on all kinds of surfaces; it kept the best in sight through the nastiest, steepest, axle-bustingest terrain we threw at it; it offered the greatest cargo capacity (by both volume and weight); and when the occupant count rose above two, it was clearly the most accommodating. . . .

"If we had to play the odds, and pick as our recommendation the family four-wheeler most likely to satisfy the broadest range of requirements, we'd bet on the Jeep Cherokee's far-ranging talents."

The styling also won praise. "We like its crisp, sharp styling and were almost unanimous in agreeing that it's the best looking of the new generation of sports/utility vehicles," said *Road & Track*.

Reviewers were surprised by the suspension work. The reaction of *Car and Driver*'s Don Sherman was typical: "I'm most impressed by what the engineers have accomplished with two rigid axles," he wrote. "These went out with coal carts, you know, but the system does work here. Cornering on smooth pavement is in the

Advertising for the 1984 Jeep (right, top) again had that rustic feel. Sales, however, more than doubled from their 1983 level, no doubt helped by the introduction of the XJ. Production spurted to 176,276—the highest level since 1978—and even that number was low compared to what was to come. The Grand Wagoneer was given a new grille in 1983, and for 1985 a coach builder converted the utility wagon into a go-anywhere luxury limo (right, bottom). A wheelbase stretch provided ample seating for five passengers in the rear, with room for a bar and entertainment center.

Two Approaches to Four-Wheel Drive

From the start, Jeep's Cherokee was ahead of the competition by offering two sophisticated four-wheel-drive systems, part-time Command-Trac and full-time Selec-Trac.

Both have shift-on-the-fly capability, so the vehicle can be shifted between two-wheel-drive and four-wheel-drive without having to come to a stop. And both provide a reduced gear ratio of 2.72:1, for use when extra pulling power is required. But they are distinguished by the way in which the wheels on each axle are allowed to rotate during driving maneuvers.

Command-Trac is a reliable and highly capable basic setup. However, the problem with Command-Trac, or any part-time four-wheel-drive system, is that in order to avoid excessive wear, it has to be used only in low-traction situations. Extensive use of the Command-Trac's four-wheel drive on dry pavement causes premature wear of tires and driveline components, as well as exacting a penalty in fuel economy.

When Command-Trac's part-time four-wheel drive system is engaged, both front and rear propeller shafts are locked by a chain and gear set and always turn at the same speed, forming a single driving unit. This rigid connection does not allow for any differential action between front and rear axles. Normal front-to-rear differences in the turning radii of the wheels (e.g., when cornering) is compensated for only through wheel slippage over adverse driving surfaces.

By contrast, Selec-Trac uses a planetary open-center differential. The differential allows the driving wheels of the front and rear axles to rotate at different speeds when turning corners on high-traction surfaces. Moreover, torque is automatically distributed to the axle with the most traction, helping the rear wheels push and the front wheels pull the vehicle through demanding traction situations.

Only in a Jeep®
CJ · Scrambler · Pickup

car range of performance, the ride is decent, and most of the old rigid-front-axle steering problems (wheel shimmy, to name one) are gone."

Michael Jordan, of the same publication, described a 200-mile run over paved mountain switchbacks and wide-open desert highways. At the wheel of the Cherokee was Francois Castaing, who by this time was serving as American Motors' Director of Vehicle Development. Jordan thought the live axles might be rather low-tech for the job at hand.

"As it turned out," he wrote, "there was no cause for alarm. You can fling the Cherokee at switchbacks and keep all four tires on the ground. It's tight and responsive, and it cuts smartly for the apexes; it's flawed only by slow and extraordinarily numb steering. On the Interstate, the Cherokee feels more stable than a Blazer or a Bronco, and the driver is effectively insulated from the small road imperfections that most four wheel-drive vehicles communicate directly to your fillings. On a flat-out run through the desert, the Cherokee bobbed along happily, the suspension was both resilient and able to soak up 80 mph charges through the vados (fords, to us Gringos) of the Anza-Borrego."

Motor Trend was equally flattering. "The Cherokee handles with much greater agility and stability than you expect from a four-wheel-drive truck, and it rides with astonishing smoothness for what is a relatively lightweight vehicle."

Not that the Cherokee was accused of providing a "limousine" ride. But at least it was more comfortable than the Bronco II or S10 Blazer. Not surprisingly, the ride was best on smooth pavement. On a stretch of bad road it tended to develop a side-to-side rocking motion. But off-road, as *Car and Driver* observed, the ride and handling were "absolutely first class.... [It] has better ground clearance, a better ride, and more wheel travel than its most obvious competitors, and it's a genuine delight in heavy going, truly a low-buck Range Rover."

The Cherokee scored an unprecedented sweep of 4x4 of the year awards from all three of the leading off-road magazines in 1984. Similarly, Consumer Guide® named the Cherokee and Wagoneer as "Best Buys" in their class. The editors were among those who criticized the feel of Cherokee's power-assisted Saginaw recirculating ball steering, and they found the steering column itself too long.

There was little debate over the engines: The AMC four cylinder felt just as strong as the GM V-6. And reviewers appear to have been almost unanimous in recommending the five-speed manual as the best transmission choice.

Steve Potter, writing in *Road & Track*, observed that "the four is only five horsepower shy of the Chevy V-6, and the AMC engine actually makes more torque down low." Which, of course, is where a four-wheel-drive vehicle needs it most. At $305 extra, the V-6 was not much of a bargain. Peter Sessler, in his *Jeep Buyer's Guide*, went even further: Having taken note of the Chevy engine's "lackluster reliability," he bluntly recommended, "*Avoid* the V-6—it lacks power for even normal acceleration. If you floor it, all you get is lots of thrashing and noise and very little forward movement."

Frankly, however, none of the reviewers found power to be anything more than adequate. "The AMC four feels bloody wonderful," said *Car and Driver*, at the same time acknowledging what even Jeep realized. "What struck the *C/D* test team most about the Cherokee was its sluggishness. The most frequent complaint in our log book was that the Chief had no beans—especially on the highway. Fifth gear was useless for anything but holding a constant speed on dead-level terrain. Any hill or passing maneuver required a bothersome downshift—or two."

Buyers snapped up 8729 Cherokees and 4842 Wagoneers before 1983 was out. As 1984 unfolded, the new sport-utility wagons zoomed past the CJ-7 to become the

For 1985 Jeep dropped the 118.7-inch wheelbase pickup truck. You could still order the J-10 and J-20 (right, top) but only in the 131-inch wheelbase with the eight-foot bed and Townside styling. There were two trim levels, the base and the Pioneer. The Scrambler (right, bottom left) sauntered into its final year with only minor changes, such as a chrome nameplate at the rear, and two new trim packages. The SR and SL were dropped in favor of the Renegade and Laredo, respectively. Production for the last model year was only 2143. Although the trustworthy old Wagoneer was already over 20 years old by 1985, sales were still strong. A new handling package offered a more comfortable ride and Selec-Trac with shift-on-the-fly capability.

best-selling Jeeps. Sales for calendar '84 were 69,054 Cherokees and 19,889 Wagoneers. The combined total was less than half the number of S10 Blazers that Chevy sold. But it was just 9106 behind the number of Bronco IIs sold by Ford dealers, which vastly outnumbered Jeep outlets.

Despite the newcomer's popularity, the big SJ was not by any means retired. The old soldier lost its three-door body style, and the Cherokee name along with it. But the surviving five-door got a new lease on life as, in AMC parlance, the "Grand Daddy in four-wheel drive." It wore new Grand Wagoneer badges but was mechanically unaltered. So strong was loyalty for the big Jeep that sales were unaffected by the presence of the Cherokee and Wagoneer. AMC sold 19,081 Grand Wagoneers in '84, virtually equal to the number of equivalent models it sold in 1983.

AMC also did some important pruning of the CJ line: It killed the CJ-5. The moved ended a production run that began on October 11, 1954. An astounding 603,303 CJ-5s were built over the period. The CJ-5 had been passed in sales by the CJ-7 in 1978. Thereafter, production of the CJ-5 dwindled steadily; just 6080 were built for 1982 and about half that number for '83. AMC itself had de-emphasized the CJ-5, but the four-wheel-drive market also had begun to favor civilized longer-wheelbase vehicles, and buyers were demanding automatic transmission, which the CJ-5 didn't have at the end. Also, AMC needed to free-up production capacity to satisfy demand for vastly more popular—and profitable—Cherokee and Wagoneer.

The surviving CJ-7 gained the new 2.5-liter four-cylinder as its base engine. The AMC four had 23 more horsepower and seven more pounds-feet of torque than the General Motors "Iron Duke" 2.5-liter four that it replaced. The 4.2-liter inline six, which had been standard in the last CJ-5, remained optional in the CJ-7. With either engine, a four-speed manual transmission was standard and a five-speed manual was optional; a three-speed automatic was optional only with the six cylinder. Also discontinued for '84 was the Limited Package; Renegade and Laredo trim options remained.

The Scrambler also got the new 2.5 liter as its base engine but was otherwise untouched. Jeep carried over its pickup trucks without change.

The addition of the Cherokee and Wagoneer clearly breathed new life into AMC. Ignited by the new models, Jeep sales rocketed 87 percent in calendar 1984, to 153,807 units. AMC reversed its losses and reported a 1983 fourth-quarter profit of $7.4 million.

For 1985, Jeep fine-tuned its award-winning compact sport-utility wagons. The Cherokee gained a new top-line Limited trim level, and the optional Select-Trac four-wheel-drive system gained shift-on-the-fly capability, so the vehicle no longer had to be stopped to changed between two- and four-wheel drive. During the model year, a three-door Cherokee was introduced with two-wheel drive.

Inside, new standard features for most models included front seat headrests and a rocker/recliner capability for the bucket seats. Wagoneer's Limited had standard power seats. The swing-away outside spare-tire option previously restricted to three-door models was extended to five-door models. And Renault's Keyless Entry System joined the list of extra-cost items.

Underhood, a Renault-built 2.1-liter turbocharged diesel four-cylinder engine was newly optional. It was rated at 85 horsepower at 3250 rpm and 132 pounds-feet of torque at 3000. The 2.5-liter four-cylinder continued as standard on all models, with the 4.2-liter inline-six again optional. Transmission choices once more included four- and five-speed manuals and the three-speed automatic.

Sales climbed again, to a combined 112,976 for the two XJ models. With prices that started at $10,405, the Cher-

Jeep gave the CJ-7 (right, top) a mild makeover for 1985. In the rear, there were new fold-and-tumble seats, and in the front, high-back buckets were standard. Option packages remained the Renegade and Laredo. The award-winning Cherokee/Wagoneer returned with only minor changes, though there was a new option package for the Cherokee—the now familiar Laredo (right, bottom right). It was basically a luxury group on top of the Chief package. Another infamous option was the 2.1-liter Renault turbo-diesel engine (right, bottom left). It was available only on the Wagoneer or Cherokee and produced 82 horsepower at 3250 rpm and 132 pounds-feet of torque at 3000 rpm.

okee continued to outsell the Wagoneer more than 7-1. The base Wagoneer stickered for $13,255, and at $17,953, the Wagoneer Limited was among the most-expensive 4x4s on the market. By comparison, most versions of the top-selling S-10 Blazer went out the door loaded for around $14,000. Still, no rival could boast being chosen by the readers of *Off-Road* magazine as the top four-wheel-drive compact utility vehicle of 1985.

Grand Wagoneer was again marketed as a fully equipped luxury wagon. It continued its gentrification by gaining a "Handling Package" that constituted a softer-riding suspension courtesy of lower-friction leaf springs, gas-filled shock absorbers, and new bushings. The standard Selec-Trac four-wheel drive received shift-on-the-fly. Inside, the center armrest on the front seat could be folded up, and a center seatbelt was added, increasing front-seat capacity from two passengers to three. Outside, new gold hub-cover inserts were added to the standard 15-inch alloy wheels.

In its 1985 report, Consumer Guide® said the Grand Wagoneer was "big and clumsy next to the new Jeeps . . . and a crotchety old geezer by comparison." The public evidently didn't see it that way and sales of the Grand Wagoneer, which started at a hefty $20,462, continued strong at more than 17,200 units for calendar '85.

CJ-7s gained a new fold-and-tumble rear seat, and the Renegade and Laredo packages got new interior decor and fresh exterior touches highlighted by revised tape stripe patterns. The offshoot Scrambler pickup also was embellished. Chrome Scrambler lettering on the rear fender supplanted the previous hood identification. The Renegade package replaced the SR Sport package and the Laredo replaced the SL Sport on Scrambler.

Jeep's big J Series pickup truck lost its 118.7-inch wheelbase model, so all now came with the 131-inch wheelbase and eight-foot cargo bed. Again, the J-10 version carried the 115-horsepower 4.2-liter

inline-six-cylinder engine, and the J-20 used the 150-horsepower 5.9-liter V-8.

Despite a decline of eight percent in CJ sales and a drop of 42 percent in sales of pickup trucks, Jeep sales increased a healthy 18 percent overall in calendar 1985.

AMC opened the 1986 model year with some changes. Gone after six years was the Scrambler. During its five-year production run, 27,792 of the unique pickups had been built. Prompting its retirement was the introduction of a new entry with a more-traditional pickup-truck configuration. Just as the big Wagoneer had spawned the Gladiator—later J-Series—pickups back in 1963, so the downsized Cherokee now provided the basis for the handsome new Comanche.

The new pickup rode an XJ platform stretched to provide a 119.6-inch wheelbase. It shared Cherokee's Quadra-Link front suspension, and sheetmetal was Cherokee from the front doors forward. Behind the cab was a 7.5-foot-long cargo bed. The new pickup used Cherokee's four- and six-cylinder engines and transmissions. The two-wheel-drive model was the first Jeep pickup with two-wheel drive. That was good news, because two-wheel-drive models accounted for about 75 percent of sales in the compact pickup field.

Jeep billed Comanche as a compact pickup, but it really belonged to a rare breed, the mid-size pickup.

It was larger overall than any domestic or Japanese-built compact pickup. And at 43.8 inches between wheelhouses, its cargo bed was wider than any compact pickup's; it was equaled in length only by the Chevy S10 pickup. And its 2205-pound maximum payload was higher than either the Ford or Chevy entry.

But Comanche was smaller overall than the full-size domestic pickups. It didn't offer a V-8, and though its cab had three seatbelts, it wasn't really wide enough to hold a trio of adults without squeezing. Finally, it was unique among all pickup

In November of 1985, AMC's executive vice-president of operations, Joseph Cappy, announced that CJ production would end early in 1986. This aroused an uproar of protest from CJ loyalists. Still, four trim levels were available for the 1986 model year. At the bottom of the line was the base at $7500 (right, top right); the Renegade came in at an additional $1253, and the Laredo at $2787. At the top of the line was the Limited (right, bottom).

trucks in having unibody construction.

Regardless of its size category, Comanche would go on to garner "Four Wheeler of the Year" honors from *Four Wheeler* magazine. It also would prove an able replacement for the aged J-Series pickups, themselves entering their last model year. (A new instrument panel and steering-column mounted transmission controls marked the lame-duck J-10 and J-20.)

Changes to Cherokee and Wagoneer were also notable. The 2.5-liter four-cylinder engine exchanged its two-barrel carburetor for throttle-body fuel injection. Horsepower increased from 105 to 117 at the same 5000 rpm, while torque went from 132 pounds-feet at 2800 rpm to 135 at 3500. The AMC four now had two more horsepower than the 2.8-liter GM V-6 that remained optional, and the V-6 had just 15 pounds-feet more torque.

The plush Wagoneer got a new grille. It relinquished the vertical-bar styling for its own horizontal-themed two-tier grille set off by stacked rectangular headlamps. Cherokee, meanwhile, gained exclusive rights to a new off-road package. The option included high-pressure gas shock absorbers painted yellow, 225/75R15 tires mounted on seven-inch-wide spoked white wheels, a skid plate, front and rear tow hooks, and higher ground clearance. Jeep's Trac-Lok limited slip rear differential was made available on either model with the optional Selec-Trac full-time four-wheel-drive system.

Trophies continued to come Cherokee's way. *Popular Mechanics* named the four-wheel-drive Cherokee "One of the 10 Best Cars of 1986." It was the only sport-utility vehicle on the list, which included the likes of the Mercedes-Benz 190 and the Porsche 944 Turbo. In Europe, the Cherokee was named "Four Wheeler of the Year" by the French magazine *4x4*. AMC's Renault connection had opened the European market to Jeep, particularly the diesel-powered Cherokee. Renault would go on to sell about 10,000 Jeeps annually in Europe,

about 50 percent of them in France.

Grand Wagoneer looked different for '86, thanks to a new grille and a new stand-up Jeep hood ornament. Inside, a redesigned instrument panel featured new gauges and fake wood trim. From the revamped steering column sprouted stalks for lights and wiper/washer controls. And the heat/vent controls now were integrated with the air-conditioning controls.

These and other changes were introduced with the debut of the '86 models, in the fall of 1985. At the same time, AMC made an announcement that, while not unexpected in motoring circles, was treated like sacrilege by non-automotive commentators. On November 27, 1985, Joseph E. Cappy, group vice president-sales and marketing, let it be known that in early 1986, AMC would halt production of the CJ-7.

To judge from the reaction of some journalists and many Jeep die-hards, it was as if AMC had eradicated apple pie, John Wayne, or baseball. Here was Jeep rubbing out a hallowed link to America's glorious past, a noble steed that had helped win several wars. Newspaper editorial writers were up in arms.

As it turned out, the CJ's replacement would prove these fears unfounded. If not as outright paramilitary as the beloved CJ, it was nonetheless quite faithful to the CJ ethic and even looked much the same. Given the inevitability of the CJ's demise, this was a better outcome than might have occurred under corporate decision-makers less committed to the Jeep creed.

The real end of the CJ may actually have begun on the evening of December 21, 1980. That's when CBS television's *60 Minutes*, the most-watched news program in history, aired a devastating report on the CJ-5. It alleged that because of the vehicle's high, narrow design, the Jeep was much more prone to tip over in certain conditions than similar four-wheel drives. They also related that this design flaw had already caused several injuries and deaths. CBS's report was based partly on studies

While 1986 may have marked the end of the CJ, Jeep pulled an old trick from CJ's past when they cut and chopped a Cherokee to create the Comanche. The new mid-size pickup had a stretched 119.9-inch wheelbase and a bed that was 88.5 inches by 60 inches. Payload capacity was 2205 pounds, and both Command-Trac and Selec-Trac four-wheel-drive systems were available. The Comanche came in three trim levels: base, X, and XLS (right, top). José J. Dedeurwaerder (bottom) was installed as president and chief executive officer at AMC during the time the Comanche was released—a period when Renault held all of the cards at AMC.

by an insurance-industry lobbying group, the Insurance Institute for Highway Safety. It included interviews with victims or their families, as well as a film purportedly made by AMC that demonstrated the Jeep's relative lack of stability.

The *60 Minutes* story rightly pointed out that any vehicle with a high center of gravity is more likely to tip over on a steep incline than one with a lower center of gravity. And in the vehicle's defense, *Four Wheeler* magazine pointed out that the CJ-5s shown tipping over were "driven" by servos that generated lateral forces no human could duplicate.

However, the damage was done. The TV report stirred additional lawsuits that alleged rollovers. Eventually, several consumer watchdog groups, including Public Citizen and the Center for Auto Safety, formally petitioned the federal government's National Highway Traffic Safety Administration (NHTSA) to undertake a defect investigation of CJ-5s and CJ-7s built by AMC. The controversy unleashed a torrent of adverse publicity that hurt CJ sales. While trying to settle quietly, AMC attempted to shore up demand with rebates, low-rate financing, even price cuts. And it accelerated work on the CJ's replacement.

NHTSA eventually denied the petitions involving the Jeeps. According to its final report: "After an extensive inquiry—involving the expenditure of far more agency resources and effort than in most formal investigations—the agency has concluded that . . . there was no evidence of a safety defect in the vehicles that would cause them to roll over."

The inquiry did highlight some indisputable 4x4 facts of life. Basically, NHTSA's study found that small 4x4s indeed have higher rollover rates than standard vehicles. And it pointed out that while the rollover rate for CJs was "at the high end of the range, they do not stand out significantly when compared to many other similar vehicles."

The episode did prompt Jeep to tone down its advertising, and it did move NHTSA to require that all sport-utility vehicles carry warnings inside the cabin and in the owner's manual. Stickers pasted to the inside of a soft-top Jeep were typical. One read: "This is an open-body utility vehicle. It handles and maneuvers differently from many passenger cars both on road and off. You must drive it safely. As with other utility vehicles, if you make sudden sharp turns or abrupt maneuvers, you may cause this vehicle to go out of control and roll over or crash—you or your passengers may be seriously injured."

The controversy also revealed how the world of small 4x4s had changed. The CJ's rugged demeanor encouraged its use off-road. Consequently it attracted buyers who understood the compromises required for it to perform its mission. But by the early 1980s, the open-top Jeeps were attracting a different audience. Buyers now treated them as fashionable runabouts and showed little understanding of the functional design philosophy behind their "cute" styling.

"The profile of our small sport utility vehicle buyer has changed dramatically in recent years," pointed out AMC's Francois Castaing as the CJ's replacement was being readied. "Ninety-five percent now use their vehicles for everyday transportation, compared to only 17 percent in 1978. Frequent off-roading is common with only 7 percent of our owners today, compared with 37 percent back then."

Jeep also was facing pressure in the marketplace from a slew of four-wheel compact pickup trucks, a breed that didn't exist in the mid-1970s. These trucks offered greater comfort and similar go-anywhere ability for the same or less money than a CJ. Then there was competition from the impending flood of well-made, low-cost Japanese 4x4s. Could the CJ's successor successfully incorporate this new demand for civility, yet still perform off-road like a genuine Jeep?

Jeep fans shouted bloody murder when they heard that the CJ line was going to end in 1986. These fears proved unfounded as details and spy photos of the CJ's replacement were released. The Wrangler (right) most certainly looked like a Jeep, and people would soon learn that it would perform every bit as well as a Jeep—in some cases, better. One likely reason for the demise of the CJ was the frequency of rollover accidents; the designers of the new Wrangler made increased stability one of their priorities as they developed the new model.

The world got its answer on May 13, 1986, when AMC unveiled its new 4x4. Except for rectangular headlamps in place of round ones, it had a comfortingly familiar look to CJ fans. And to those who may have taken part in the Comanche clinics, its name was familiar, as well: Wrangler.

AMC was forthright in acknowledging that its new 4x4 aimed to satisfy a broader set of expectations. "A key design objective for the Jeep Wrangler was to provide on-highway ride comfort primarily associated with larger vehicles," it said in a news release introducing the newcomer.

Code-named the YJ, the Wrangler was the first modern Jeep to be built not in AMC's Toledo, Ohio, plant, but at its new factory in Brampton, Ontario, Canada. The product of a five-year, 600,000-mile development program, it retained the beloved CJ character but was somewhat heavier, lower, wider, and—significantly—had a broader track. Wrangler bowed as a 1987 model. Here's how it stacked up against the 1986 CJ-7 and the first of the Japanese mini-4x4s to hit the United States, the Suzuki Samurai:

	Wrangler	CJ-7	Samurai
Wheelbase (in.)	93.4	93.4	79.9
Length (in.)	152.0	153.2	135.0
Height (in.)	68.6	69.1	65.6
Width (in.)	66.0	65.3	60.2
Front track (in.)	58.0	55.8	51.2
Rear track (in.)	58.0	55.1	51.6
Weight (lbs)	2868	2596	2094

Wrangler retained body-on-frame construction, per CJ tradition, but its chassis was a new perimeter design with four crossmembers and rectangular-section tubular siderails. To achieve on-road ride and handling objectives, designers borrowed major chassis components from the XJ-series Cherokee, including the front and rear axles (supplied by Dana), recirculating-ball steering (from GM's Saginaw Division), the front-disc/rear-drum brakes (with standard vacuum assist), the five-speed manual transmission, and the part-time Command-Trac four-wheel drive with shift-on-the-fly (from New Process Gear). The wheels were adopted from those of the Cherokee, but the XJ's Quadra-Link front suspension was not carried over. Instead, Wrangler used longitudinal semi-elliptic leaf springs all-round, with traction bars at each end, and a front stabilizer bar.

Wrangler's body used two-sided galvanized steel panels with full anti-corrosion underbody spray added as an additional rust fighter. Flexible flares outlined the wheel openings.

Base, Sports Decor, and Laredo models were available. Base and Sports Decor came with a removable soft top and half metal doors. A hard top that used full metal doors was optional. The top-line Laredo came only as a hard top. Instead of the CJ's snap fasteners, Wrangler's soft top used a new tongue-and-groove system that sealed better and resisted rusting. A roll bar was again standard, but it was now padded and differed from the CJ's by adding lateral beams that extended from the main horizontal bar to the outboard corners of the windshield frame. A swing-out tailgate and rear-mounted spare tire were retained, and a fuel-tank skid plate was standard.

The rectangular theme was repeated inside. Gone were the CJ's trademark round gauges in favor of instruments set in squared-off plastic surrounds. A tachometer was standard, and controls for the washer/wiper, high-beam lights, and optional cruise control were mounted on the steering column. A passenger-assist handle was molded into the dashboard, and slide-levers for the heat and ventilation system replaced knob controls. High-back front bucket seats and a fold-and-tumble rear bench were part of the base equipment. Standard wheel size stayed at 15 inches, and power steering was again an option.

Standard power was provided by AMC's 2.5-liter four-cylinder with throttle-body fuel injection and the same horsepower and torque ratings as in the Cherokee. A six-cylinder engine was optional, but it was AMC's 4.2-liter inline unit with two-barrel carburetor. It was rated at 112 horsepower at 3000 rpm and 210 pounds-feet of torque at 3000. Replacing a four-speed manual as the standard transmission was a five-speed unit. When mated to the four-cylinder, the manual gearbox was one manufactured by Aisin of Japan. When used with the six, it was from Peugeot of France. Chrysler's three-speed TorqueFlite automatic was optional with the six only.

All Wranglers came with four-wheel-drive, but unlike the CJ-7's permanently engaged system, Wrangler adopted the XJ's Command-Trac. This allowed two-wheel-drive running for better fuel economy but enabled the driver to shift into four-wheel-drive High while on the move simply by working a transfer-case lever mounted on the floor next to the gear shift. Command-Trac was not intended for use on dry pavement, but no other vehicle in Wrangler's class offered full shift-on-the-fly four-wheel-drive capability. The transfer case could be shifted into low-range, and for serious off-pavement duty, Wrangler's options list included a Trac-Lok rear differential and an Off-Road Package with 225mm tires and gas-filled heavy-duty shocks. Wrangler hit showrooms with a starting price of just under $10,000 for the base model and around $12,000 for the Laredo.

From even the earliest reviews, it was clear that Wrangler retained the no-nonsense aura that had endeared the CJ to generations of Americans. Jeep fans celebrated, yet ironically it was precisely the inheritance of the CJ's personality that caused critics to moan. If Wrangler was going to compete for the dollars of customers who would use it as nothing more than a sporty car, then reviewers were quite willing to judge it as an automobile.

"For an all-new design, the Wrangler came out of the box looking much like the old CJ-7, and with several of the same drawbacks," said Consumer Guide®.

AMC had indeed succeeded in softening the ride, but backwoods maneuverability required that the wheelbase remain short and that the suspension remain taut. So reviewers still complained about bouncing and pitching over bumps. The ride height was dictated by ground clearance requirements, and the body had to be narrow enough to thread rocky crevasses. So automotive writers were still sensitive to any feeling of tippiness in quick changes of direction. Steering, geared to absorb the shock of impacts with boulders and tree stumps, felt numb and imprecise to reviewers trundling along the boulevard.

Journalists bemoaned high levels of wind and road noise at any speed over 30 mph. The tall step up over the door sills was "inconvenient," the rear seat was "cramped," and the gauges "were mounted too low to be easily read." Acceleration with the four-cylinder was only adequate. Even with the 4.2-liter six, 0-60-mph times were a mediocre 14 seconds. Though no worse than the CJ-7's, fuel economy was nothing special, either, with most drivers averaging around 17 mpg with the four-cylinder and 14-15 with the six.

But those who strayed from the pavement found the very traits that were Wrangler's liabilities on-road turned out to be its assets off-road.

"With a ground clearance of 8.1 inches and a relatively short wheelbase, the Jeep feels unstoppable," said *Car and Driver*. "Even the Wrangler's sloppy steering—its two or three inches of play are a constant nuisance on the highway—works to your advantage off-road, where kickback is virtually nonexistent."

The CJ-7 went down fighting, with sales for 1986 estimated at around 26,000, while Wrangler ramped up with a first-season total of around 10,000. It would eventually surpass even the CJ's best years. The American icon was alive and well, a point even automotive critics had to concede.

Concluded *Car and Driver* in its Wrangler write-up: "... it is only in a Jeep that you can stand in the driver's seat and, peering at distant sand dunes, shout, 'Rommel, you magnificent bastard! I read your book!'"

CHAPTER TEN
Chrysler at the Helm: 1987-94

ometimes you have to take the good with the bad. Then, through time, you take the bad and make it good and take the good and make it great. American Motors had both the good and the bad.

So it was in the last months of 1986 that Chrysler Corporation maneuvered to acquire American Motors. Chrysler made no secret that its goal was to own Jeep. If that meant it had to buy all of the corporation, so be it.

AMC was ripe for the picking. It was long past its peak market share of 7.5 percent. That was in 1960, when the Rambler compact accounted for two-thirds of the company's 460,000 sales. By 1986, AMC clung to just 1 percent of the U.S. market. Jeep was AMC's only consistently profitable line, generating two-thirds of the company's revenue and three-quarters of its sales. In 1986, for example, Jeeps accounted for 77 percent of the 234,028 vehicles AMC sold in the United States and 78 percent of the 53,706 it sold overseas.

However, Jeeps weren't enough, and AMC lost $91.3 million in 1986. Chrysler, meantime, was earning $1.4 billion. It had paid off its government-backed loans three years earlier and, spurred by its popular minivans, was enjoying its best sales year to date.

Unlike Ford and Chevrolet, Chrysler had no high-volume sport-utility vehicle—a costly shortcoming. Profit potential on these vehicles was high. Some analysts said AMC cleared $3000 on the sale of each Jeep.

For Chrysler to develop its own sport-utility vehicle and set up an assembly plant to build it would take three years and $1.2 billion. And it still wouldn't be able to claim the coveted Jeep brand name.

Chrysler already had its foot in AMC's door. Its three-speed automatic transmission was used in Jeeps. And in February 1987, Chrysler began building its rear-drive sedans at AMC's Kenosha, Wisconsin, plant. Rumors of a bigger deal circulated. Then, on March 10, 1987, the number three automaker announced it had agreed to purchase American Motors Corporation for about $1.5 billion.

Under the plan, Chrysler would buy Renault's 46-percent stake in AMC and acquire from shareholders the balance of AMC's stock. This was no small undertaking. Despite its financial troubles, AMC was still a multibillion-dollar enterprise with 19,300 employees, 1450 dealers, 111,000 public stockholders, and millions of dollars in debts, subsidiary holdings, and legal contingencies.

Complications were inevitable. The original April 9 sale deadline was pushed back to April 23, rescheduled for May 5, then delayed again. Even as negotiations continued, Chrysler Chairman Lee A. Iacocca told *Automotive News* that his company was already looking for "worldwide opportunities to exploit the Jeep name."

The sale was finally completed on August 6, 1987. It was the first acquisition involving a pair of domestic automakers since 1954, when—ironically—Nash-Kelvinator and Hudson had linked to form AMC.

With Chrysler assuming $855 million in AMC debt, plus $350 million in pension liabilities, the actual sale price was estimat-

Despite Renault's influence, AMC was unable to emerge from the doldrums caused by a recession and two energy crises. So, by 1986 the last of the independents was on the block. Chrysler, who like AMC more than 15 years earlier, wanted to fill out its lineup, stepped in and purchased AMC and its Jeep subsidiary for a cool $2 billion. Chrysler quickly reorganized and formed the Jeep-Eagle division to sell Jeep products and the Eagle Premier. Another important acquisition in Chrysler's takeover of AMC was the transfer of Francois J. Castaing to Chrysler/Dodge engineering. Castaing would play a large role in the development of the Grand Cherokee and the Dodge Viper.

199

ed at an eventual $2 billion. In return, Chrysler received the Jeep franchise, which alone was worth an estimated $850 million, plus AMC's modern assembly plant in Brampton, Ontario, worth as much as $650 million.

Chrysler moved quickly to reshape its new holdings. It promptly killed some slow-selling AMC cars, including the Eagle four-wheel-drive wagon. It prepared to replace the antiquated Jeep plant in Toledo, Ohio. And to market the Renault-designed Premier sedan and its newly acquired sport-utility vehicles, Chrysler created a new division, Jeep-Eagle. The 1400 former AMC/Jeep/Renault dealerships would be its sales arm. Joseph E. Cappy, who had been AMC's chief executive officer, would head Jeep-Eagle.

Brought over to direct engineering for Jeeps and Dodge trucks was Francois J. Castaing, who had served as chief engineer of Renault's Formula 1 racing team and then as an AMC group vice president.

Production of the slow-selling Jeep J-10 and J-20 full-size pickups was halted one month after Chrysler assumed control. (Chrysler's Dodge division already had its own line of light pickup trucks.) But the new owners didn't fiddle with changes already on line for the other Jeeps.

Most significant of the alterations for 1987 were powertrain upgrades for the Cherokee and its Wagoneer-trim cousin.

Dropped was Chevrolet's lackluster 2.8-liter V-6. The replacement was an AMC-designed inline-6 of 4.0 liters (242 cubic inches), which became known as the Power Tech six. Like the 2.5-liter AMC four cylinder that remained standard, this new engine was derived from the company's aging 258-cubic inch six. And unlike the carbureted 258, which continued as a popular Wrangler option, the Power Tech was fed by multiport electronic fuel injection.

The 4.0 shared with the 2.5 a number of components, including combustion chambers, main bearings, connecting rods and bearings, oil pump, pistons, rocker arms,

and lifters. Both had a 3.88-inch bore, but the six used a 3.44-inch stroke, compared to the four's 3.18.

Rated at 173 horsepower, the 4.0 had 58 more horsepower than the 2.8-liter V-6 it replaced. And it had 220 pounds-feet of torque, 75 more than the 2.8. Available as an option on all Cherokee and Wagoneer models, it increased towing capacity to 5000 pounds from 4200. And it transformed the Cherokee from among the slowest vehicles in its class to the fastest.

Car and Driver correctly pegged the Power Tech as "the most potent powerplant available in a vehicle of this type." The magazine clocked an 1987 Wagoneer Limited, the heaviest model in the lineup, at 9.1 seconds 0-60 mph. Models with the 2.8 typically had taken around 15 seconds. *Car and Driver*'s plush 4x4 ran the quarter-mile in 17 seconds at 79 mph and topped out at 110 mph.

Buyers who wanted something more sedate for 1987 could again go with the 2.5-liter four. It retained single-point injection but gained four horsepower, to 121. The Renault-built 85-horsepower turbodiesel 2.1-liter four-cylinder remained available outside California.

Also bowing for '87 was a new four-speed automatic transmission to replace the Chrysler three-speed automatic. Jointly developed by Aisin Seiki of Japan and Warner Gear in the United States, the new gearbox had electronic shift controls and a 0.71:1 overdrive top gear. A switch on the instrument panel permitted the driver to select either "comfort" or "power" modes. In the latter, the transmission upshifted at higher rpm, downshifted more quickly, and had greater sensitivity to throttle position. The "comfort" setting used more conventional shift points for smoother operation and better fuel economy.

The four speed was standard on Wagoneer models and optional on Cherokees. A five-speed manual remained standard on Cherokee and was available on base Wagoneers as a credit option.

The Jeep Wrangler (right, top) debuted on May 13, 1986. From the cowl back, the vehicle used the CJ's sheetmetal but was considerably different under the skin. All body panels were galvanized, and steel half doors came standard on the soft top. The hardtop was given full-steel doors. For its first year there were four trim levels. Base and Laredo were originally available, then, later in the year, Jeep added the S and the upscale Sahara. AMC had begun work on a 4.0-liter inline six when they introduced the Wagoneer (right, middle), and Chrysler finally brought the motor out in 1987. This engine gave the XJs a 0-60 time of less than 10 seconds and increased towing capacity to an even 5000 pounds. Horsepower was 174 at 4500 rpm, and torque was 220 pounds-feet at 2500 rpm. For the 1987 auto show circuit, Chrysler unveiled the Thunderchief (right, bottom). Based on the Comanche, it featured aggressive fender flares and a grille that was very similar to the one that would appear on the Grand Cherokee several years later.

Finally, when the optional Selec-Trac full-time four-wheel-drive system was ordered, buyers got a new transfer case that mounted all controls on a single shift lever, eliminating the separate dashboard switch for two-wheel drive/four-wheel drive.

Praise for the improvements was universal. Said Consumer Guide®: "With the six and the new four-speed overdrive automatic transmission, a loaded Cherokee charged up steep mountain grades readily, didn't run out of breath at high altitude, and cruised quietly in overdrive."

Elsewhere in the 1987 Jeep line, the Comanche pickup gained a short-bed version with a 113-inch wheelbase and six-foot cargo box. The Power Tech was Comanche's new optional six, and the new four-speed automatic was made available. Selec-Trac was dropped as an option, however, so four-wheel-drive Comanches now came only with the simpler Command-Trac, which did not permit the use of four-wheel drive on dry pavement.

Grand Wagoneer lost its 4.2-liter inline-six, so now standard was the previously optional AMC-designed 5.9-liter V-8. It had 144 horsepower and a two-barrel carburetor. This 4600-pound wagon shuddered over bumpy roads but was tough off-road. And with 280 pounds-feet of torque at a low 1500 rpm, the 5.9 had enough muscle to muster 0-60 mph times of 13 seconds.

This also was the year Jeep got back in racing—thanks to an injection of financing from Chrysler marketing. Six fully sponsored vehicles competed in three series. The Archer Brothers in Jeep Comanches won the Manufacturer's Championship in the SCCA Racetruck Challenge, while Mike Lesle added a second Comanche championship in the HDRA/Score Desert Racing Series.

In a year when passenger-car sales slumped nearly 11 percent, the truck market grew 1.4 percent over '86. Jeep sales for 1987 edged upward less than 1 percent, but they would have declined if not for the Cherokee/Wagoneer and Comanche. While sales of Wrangler and Grand Wagoneer fell, Cherokee and Wagoneer found 124,184 buyers, a 3-percent increase over '86. Comanche sales, meanwhile, hit an all-time high of 38,094.

Chrysler had arrived just as the market for compact sport-utility vehicles was defining itself. Chevrolet's S10 Blazer was still the top seller, at 153,000 units, but Cherokee/Wagoneer—with the only five-door body style in the segment—was poised to overtake Ford's Bronco II for the No. 2 slot.

Americans had begun to view these vehicles as replacements for the family automobile and, more significantly, as companions for the BMW or Jaguar in their driveway. Window stickers reflected this new image. Base price of the Wagoneer Limited, for example, was now $20,400, up from $18,600 in 1986. Going with the upscale trend, Chrysler, during the model year, added a loaded Limited model as the new top-line Cherokee.

Fine-tuning was the theme for 1988. The 4.0-liter six was increased to 177 horsepower—tops in the class. It was made standard on the Wagoneer Limited and Cherokee Limited. And all Limited models now came with the four-speed automatic and Selec-Trac four-wheel drive.

Introduced in the spring of 1988 was the three-door Cherokee Sport, which featured the 4.0, unique exterior graphics, and new alloy wheels shod with 225/70HR15 tires. At $12,679 for the two-wheel-drive version and $14,141 for the four-wheel drive, the Sport took aim at younger buyers.

The Power Tech six remained optional on other Cherokees and was now the only alternative to the 2.5-liter four. Gone was the unpopular Renault turbo-diesel four. The least-expensive Cherokee, the two-wheel-drive four-cylinder three-door, began the model year with a base price of $11,063, while the Cherokee Limited was the costliest model, at $23,253.

Despite its growing role as a prestige

For 1988 the Comanche and Cherokee received a new eight-slot grille. The Chief (right, top) and Laredo packages returned only on the short (113-inch) wheelbase pickups. Chrysler began offering "special value" option packages this year, which made purchasing a group of options cheaper than buying them separately. In addition to the base, S, Laredo, and Sahara, the Wrangler was also available in Islander trim (right, bottom). The main visual differences between the Islander and other Wranglers were sunset-orange graphics on the hood, doors, and spare tire cover. There were also four unique colors to choose from and additional comfort and convenience equipment.

family wagon, Cherokee continued to earn respect from the hard-core off-road crowd. It was selected "4x4 of the Year" for a second time by the editors of *4 Wheel & Off Road* magazine and was named best sport-utility vehicle by *Four Wheeler* magazine.

Taking its cue from the Cherokee Sport, Comanche got a new Eliminator performance model for 1988. Based on the two-wheel-drive short-bed, the Eliminator came standard with the Power Tech six, plus tape graphics, color-keyed grill, fender flares, front air dam, and new 10-hole alloy wheels with 215/64HR14 tires. Inside were a tachometer, bucket seats, a sport steering wheel, and upgraded trim. With less curb weight than the Cherokee, a 4.0-liter Eliminator could easily smoke its rear tires on acceleration.

A newly optional power sunroof, some new exterior colors, and an upgraded audio system made news for Grand Wagoneer, which soldiered on with the 5.9-liter V-8 and Selec-Trac as standard. The 1988 Wrangler could be dressed to go on safari as the new Sahara model. It came in either khaki metallic or coffee exterior colors with khaki-colored spoked wheels, and khaki soft top (a tan hard top was optional). Inside was new water-resistant "Trailcloth" fabric, also in Khaki with tan accents. Other standard features on the $11,995 Sahara were fog lamps, gas shock absorbers, wheel flares, and integrated body-side steps. Dealer-installed accessories included a brush/grille guard, soft-top boot, and a bug-screen kit.

Wrangler also came in $10,595 base and $13,385 Laredo models, the latter with a standard hardtop. As before, the standard engine was the 2.5-liter four-cylinder, here rated at 117 horsepower; the old 112-horsepower 4.2-liter inline-6 was optional. A five-speed manual was standard, and an optional three-speed automatic could be ordered with the six.

With sales of minivans and sport-utility vehicles leading the way, Americans purchased a record 4.8-million light trucks in

Not only was the original CJ discontinued, but now its replacement, Wrangler, was being built in Canada. Actually, the Brampton, Ontario, plant was as modern as they come, and Chrysler built 69,565 Wranglers in 1989—20,000 more than the peak CJ-7 number. The Sahara model (right top and bottom left) *was available in two colors, khaki metallic or coffee. It also featured fender-mounted fog lights and color-keyed wheel flares. The interior* (right, bottom middle), *though still not car-like, was quite a bit more civilized and comfortable. Round gauges had been replaced by square ones when the Wrangler replaced the CJ. The Laredo* (right, bottom right) *was the top-of-the-line trim package for the Wrangler; almost every Wrangler option was fitted as standard equipment.*

1988. And Jeep's overall gain of 21 percent in calendar 1988 was the largest of any high-volume competitor. Though Wagoneer-version sales actually declined 25 percent, to 9138, Cherokee sales soared 34 percent, to 149,566 units. And Wrangler sales jumped 37 percent, to 42,076. Chrysler had gotten what it came for.

Cherokee/Wagoneer was already lauded as the most car-like compact sport-utility, and Chrysler enhanced that status for 1989 by making it the first light truck available with four-wheel anti-lock brakes (ABS). Other light-truck ABS systems worked only on the rear wheels. Another advantage to the Jeep system was that it worked in both two- and four-wheel drive; most ABS systems on 4x4s worked only in two-wheel drive. Jeep's ABS system was designed by Bendix and retained the front-disc/rear-drum setup. It was optional on models with the 6-cylinder engine, automatic transmission, and Selec-Trac.

Comanche did not get the optional ABS system and returned unchanged. Grand Wagoneer, now in its 27th model year, added an overhead console, a remote-control entry system, and a rear wiper/washer as standard.

Wrangler was mechanically unaltered but gained a new entry-level S model, as well as the tropical-theme Islander version.

The new S model was in response to an influx of Japanese mini-4x4s. The least-expensive 1988 Wrangler had a $10,595 base price. However, Suzuki was selling lots of $8500 Samurais, and for 1989, it had introduced the new Sidekick with a $8998 base price. The Wrangler S answered with a list price of $8995—made possible by doing without such items as the folding rear seat, radio, and right outside mirror.

The Islander was essentially a graphics package featuring such exterior colors as "Malibu yellow" and "Pacific blue" offset by a large sunset-orange globe decal. Base, Sahara, and Laredo trim levels rounded out the Wrangler line.

Increases in sales of Cherokees and Wranglers again offset declines in other Jeep models. For calendar 1989, Cherokee sales were up 4 percent, to 156,118 units, and Wrangler gained 20 percent, to 50,726. Wagoneer versions of the Cherokee continued to lose popularity and were now outsold more than 20-1 by the broader Cherokee line.

Wrangler was by far the best-selling mini 4x4. But Chevy's S10 Blazer clung to the No. 1 slot in the profitable compact sport-utility segment. Thanks in large measure to greater production capacity and more dealer outlets, it again ran some 30,000 units ahead of Cherokee for the model year.

Things were different in 1990, when the sport-utility market came of age. No longer would the Cherokee/Wagoneer be the only compact sport-utility with a five-door body style.

Ford's Explorer charged onto the scene in April as a 1991 model and began a sales climb that would soon make it the most popular 4x4 in history. Explorer allowed Ford to quickly displace Cherokee as runner-up in the compact-sport-utility sales race. Chevy retained the top spot on the strength of renewed interest in its S10 Blazer, which finally came in a five-door model. The body style was shared by the GMC S15 Jimmy and used for Oldsmobile's first entry in the segment, the upscale Bravada. Adding to the competition were the Japanese giants, who waded in with the first five-door versions of the Nissan Pathfinder and Toyota 4Runner.

Under the onslaught, Jeep sales fell 21 percent for calendar 1990, with Cherokee and Wrangler showing their first decline in years. One bright spot was the announcement that on March 22, the one-millionth Jeep Cherokee/Wagoneer was driven off the Toledo Jeep assembly line. It was a five-door model, like 85 percent of the XJ models produced in the previous six-and-a-half years. And tellingly, it was a Cherokee Limited shipped to the affluent California coast—continually one of Jeep's

With the addition of the 4.0-liter engine, the XJ (Cherokee-Wagoneer) project had finally reached fruition. Jeep now offered the most powerful engine and most comprehensive four-wheel-drive drivetrain in its class (right, top). *The four-door Limited* (right, middle left) *continued to be the most expensive Cherokee at $24,958, even more expensive than the Wagoneer. Lesser trim packages like the Laredo* (right, middle right) *and the Pioneer* (right, bottom right) *were still available.*

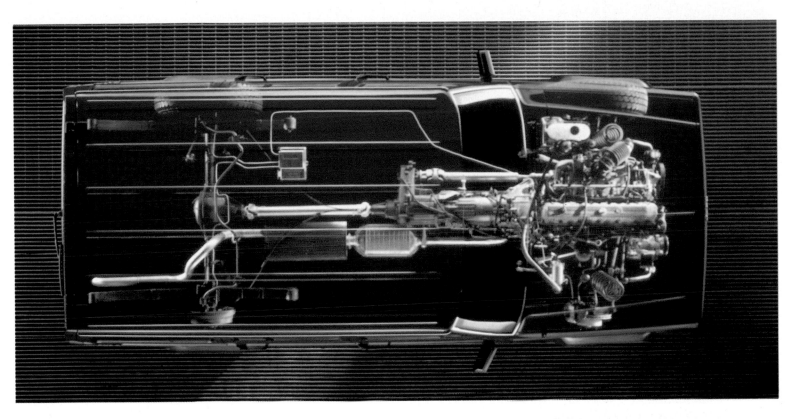

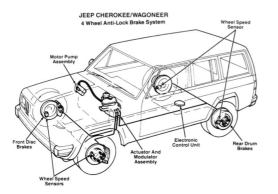

JEEP CHEROKEE/WAGONEER
4 Wheel Anti-Lock Brake System

Wheel Speed Sensor

Motor Pump Assembly

Front Disc Brakes

Electronic Control Unit

Rear Drum Brakes

Actuator And Modulator Assembly

Wheel Speed Sensors

strongest markets. Behind the scenes, Jeep engineers working feverishly on Cherokee's successor chaffed at Explorer's success. But frankly, little was new to spur interest in America's premier sport-utility vehicles for 1990.

Cherokee/Wagoneer added a standard AM/FM radio and rear shoulder belts. And standard on Limited models and optional on Laredo was a new overhead console with a compass, outside temperature readout, map lights, and compartments for a garage-door opener and sunglasses.

Despite the tough new competition, Consumer Guide® cautioned against underestimating the Cherokee. Testing a Cherokee Limited, the editors praised the 4x4's on-road manners and off-road prowess, as well as its engine, low-step-in height, and the comfort of its leather-upholstered seats. Steering feel was too vague, however, and there was criticism for poorly marked climate controls. Driven 1500 miles, the Limited returned 19.6 mpg on highway and around 13 in city, for an overall average of 15.2. With the optional ABS and metallic paint, the list price was a hefty $27,300.

Car and Driver pitted a Cherokee Laredo against six other 4x4 wagons: an Explorer Eddie Bauer, an S15 Jimmy SLX, an Isuzu Trooper LS, a Mitsubishi Montero LS, a Pathfinder SE V6, and a 4Runner SR5 V6.

With the most-powerful engine and the lightest curb weight (3652 pounds), the Jeep Cherokee was the quickest 4x4 tested, clocking 0-60 mph in 10.5 seconds and the quarter mile in 17.7 at 76 mph, and registering a 107-mph top speed. It also placed a solid second on the skidpad with a 0.70g reading.

But *Car and Driver* disliked the overassisted steering and found the front seats uncomfortable and the rear seat cramped. It said assembly quality was suspect and noted that at $25,615, the Laredo was the second-most expensive vehicle tested. It

During 1989 there were two major developments at Jeep that, for the most part, went unnoticed. First, Jeep offered a fully-operational (two- or four-wheel drive) anti-lock braking system on its XJ models. The option was available only on Selec-Trac equipped models, but it would be years before competitors could come up with even two-wheel-drive anti-lock systems. Also, Jeep introduced the Concept (left, bottom) 1 at the Detroit Auto Show. As we now know, this was the precursor to the current Grand Wagoneer model that made its debut in 1993.

As the most expensive model in the Jeep lineup at $26,395, the Grand Wagoneer carried on without much change for the 1989 model year. One of Chrysler's first acts after taking control of Jeep was to axe the full-size pickups (they competed directly with the Dodge trucks). Then, in 1989, Laredo and Chief models were cut from the Comanche lineup. The 1987 introduction of the Dodge Dakota had spelled the end of the Comanche (right, bottom left), and it was only a matter of time before the Cherokee-based pickup would be killed. The only significant change for the 1990 Wranglers was the addition of a standard rear window wiper/washer system (right, bottom right) for models equipped with the hard top.

finished fourth in the test, behind the Nissan, Ford, and Toyota.

"It seems proper that the venerable Cherokee finished dead center in our ratings," the magazine concluded. "From there, it anchors the field, pulling the stragglers along as it keeps the leaders in sight."

Jeep's other 1990 models could also be described as "venerable." There were few changes anywhere in the line. The Comanche Eliminator was made available with four-wheel drive. The Grand Wagoneer gained a one-piece steering knuckle intended to simplify assembly and to reduce weight, and modified brake rotors and calipers to reduce weight and help fuel economy.

Wrangler got a host of minor alterations, foremost among them, door locks for soft-top models. All models got new high-back bucket seats that featured revised backrest wings for improved lateral support. A removable folding two-place rear seat was made available on the S model, which now accounted for about 40 percent of Wrangler sales. A rear wiper/washer was added to the hard top. A 20-gallon fuel tank, previously an option in place of a 15-gallon unit, was made standard on Sahara and Laredo models. And the off-road package now included 225/75R15 tires, up from 215s.

For 1991, Jeep responded to the competition by juggling its Cherokee roster and pouring on the power. The popular Sport model was now available in the hot-selling five-door body style. Retailing for under $20,000 with ABS, the new five-door Sport was the best value in the Cherokee line. At the upper end of the roster, the new Cherokee Briarwood replaced the Wagoneer. It inherited the Wagoneer's woodgrain bodyside graphics and full complement of luxury features but used the standard Cherokee dual-headlamp grille in place of the Wagoneer's quad-lamp setup.

Underhood, revisions to intake and exhaust systems boosted the 4.0-liter six to 190 horsepower, making it again the most muscular engine in the class.

Demand for the 4.0 was so strong that it now was standard on all Cherokee models except the entry-level two-wheel drive versions, which used the 2.5-liter four. For '91, the four gained nine horsepower, to 130, thanks to a switch from single-point fuel injection to a system similar to the six-cylinder's sequential multi-point system.

Pulling out all the stops, Jeep actually lowered Cherokee prices. The company said decreases averaged 3.2 percent compared to similarly equipped '90 models. But a Limited or Briarwood with ABS still listed for around $26,000.

Power increases in the four- and six-cylinder engines were carried over to the Comanche line, while the Grand Wagoneer got only some new colors to mark 1991.

Changes were more significant for the 1991 Wrangler. The 4.0-liter, here rated at 180 horsepower, replaced the antiquated 112-horsepower 4.2-liter as the optional six-cylinder engine. And the base 2.5-liter four-cylinder gained multi-point fuel injection that boosted the horsepower rating by six, to 123.

Bumping Laredo as the top Wrangler trim level was a new Renegade Decor Package. It cost a hefty $4266 and included sculpted, wrap-around plastic fenders with integral running boards and fog lamps. A decorative front stone shield was provided, as well.

Also new were redesigned front buckets for all but the S model. They were the first on Wrangler to offer reclining backrests and also allowed Jeep to fit a larger center console with exposed cup holders. A new option for all but the S model was the "sound bar," a speaker enclosure that mounted to the horizontal section of the roll bar. Finally, the hard top was now a stand-alone option after being part of the Laredo package. It cost $755 with "regular" tinted glass and $923 with "deep" tinted glass.

Climbing behind the wheel of a new 4.0-liter Wrangler, the seat-of-the-pants

The base, Sahara, Islander (right), and Laredo models all returned to the Wrangler lineup for 1990. However, only minor jiggling was done to the package options. In 1989 Dodge introduced the Dakota Convertible, and Jeep followed suit with the 1990 concept vehicle called the Freedom (far right, top). It featured a power-actuated top plus a "sport bar" behind the front seats. Jeep also fitted a decklid to the portion of the pickup bed not used by the convertible top. While the Cherokee Laredo (far right, bottom) returned for 1990, two new models were available. One was the Comanche Eliminator (far right, top middle), which had previously been available only on the two-wheel-drive model. The second, the Cherokee Sport (far right, bottom middle), was introduced as a mid-year model.

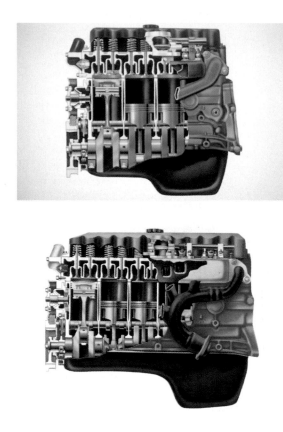

impression was that it didn't seem to have much more snap off the line than it did with the previous 6-cylinder engine. Horsepower was up dramatically, but the Power Tech six required twice as much rpm to produce roughly the same amount of torque as the old 4.2. Once underway, however, the new engine showed its stuff. Standing-start acceleration to 60 mph took about 10 seconds with automatic transmission, down from about 14 seconds with the 4.2. Fuel injection not only made the 4.0 a much smoother runner, but serious off-roaders were happy to find that it solved the fuel-starvation problems that sometimes afflicted the carbureted 4.2 when the Wrangler found itself tilted at a sharp angle.

Despite the improvements, Jeep's 1991 calendar-year sales fell another 10 percent. One problem was that competition was stronger than ever, particularly from the Explorer, which had become one of the nation's best-selling vehicles—car or truck. The other problem was that Jeep's lineup seemed stale. That was about to change.

In the winter of 1989, auto-show audiences had been shown a Jeep design study called the Concept 1. It was a five-door wagon, bigger than Cherokee, with bold body-side cladding and wind-swept lines. Concept 1 was, in fact, a thinly disguised Grand Cherokee.

American Motors had been working on a successor to the XJ as far back as 1983. That work generated the ZJ concept in September 1984, and by July 1986 was on course to produce a new 4x4 wagon for the 1990 model year.

Chrysler's takeover in August 1987 altered those plans. AMC's new owner recognized that the ZJ was superior to the 4x4 concept it was considering, a five-door sport-utility derivative of the mid-size Dodge Dakota pickup truck for introduction as a 1990 or 1991 model. Nonetheless, Chrysler ordered that work on the ZJ be dramatically slowed. The parent company decided instead to concentrate on

Except for the V-8 in the Grand Wagoneer, the only engines available in Jeep products were the 2.5-liter four (left, top) and 4.0-liter six (left, bottom). The old 4.2-liter six that had been available on the Wrangler was dropped and replaced by the 4.0 during the 1991 model year. The 2.5 was fitted with sequential multiport fuel-injection and pumped out 130 horsepower and 149 pounds-feet of torque in 1991. The 4.0 cranked out a class-leading 190 horsepower and 225 pounds-feet of torque.

Wrangler's front seats were new for 1991 and included driver and passenger recliners and incorporated wider cushion and backrest pads for better support and increased comfort. The addition of the 4.0-liter engine and the updating of the 2.5-liter four led to a single-board engine control computer to monitor underhood functions. An optional sound board with two Jensen speakers could be incorporated into the Sport Bar on all models except the S. The Comanche Eliminator (far right, bottom) continued into 1991 with only minor modifications.

a 1991 update of its minivans.

To Chrysler's credit, it had brought AMC's ZJ staff over as a team. Now that team had an extra 18 months, and it had access to Chrysler's test labs, engineering facilities, and computerized design systems. The timing also allowed Chrysler to build the new 1.7-million square-foot Jefferson North Assembly Plant in Detroit, where the ZJ would benefit from improved assembly processes.

The main parameters of the vehicle had been locked in while the ZJ was still in AMC's hands. These included its unibody construction, and its wheelbase, and overall length and width. A five-door body was specified, and its sheetmetal was too far along for major revisions, so the general shape would have to carry the European aero influence brought in by Renault.

However, a combination of the timing delay and Chrysler's presence did alter some design and engineering elements.

For example, the styling was made less car-like by enlarging the wheel openings and fitting more aggressive wheel flares and bumper fascias. A V-8 engine was not originally part of the ZJ program, but Chrysler wanted one, so structural improvements were made to the engine-cradle area. Work on a new permanently engaged four-wheel-drive system had begun with AMC but gained momentum under the new parent company.

The ZJ group had not penciled in a driver-side air bag. But Chrysler mandated one, so the team had to both redesign the steering-column structure and pioneer the testing of an air bag in rugged off-road conditions. The team needed to be certain that the bag would deploy only in a legitimate collision and not as the vehicle slammed through backwoods obstacles. More than 50 Cherokee "mules" and ZJ prototypes were sacrificed in controlled crash tests of the air-bag system. Anti-lock brakes also were added during this period.

Superb off-road capability was a Jeep creed with which Chrysler wisely did not tamper. To achieve greater ground clearance than allowed by independent suspension designs, the ZJ was developed using Cherokee's basic solid-axle, leaf-spring suspension. And though solid axles traditionally furnished a cruder ride than independent suspensions, the trade-off was a better grip on off-road ruts. However, Chrysler had specified that the new 4x4 should have European-sedan-style on-road ride and handling properties. To meet these two seemingly opposed requirements, there would obviously need to be some innovations.

Solid axles were retained. The ZJ team did refine the Cherokee's front coil-spring setup with a system of four locating arms and coil springs, which it dubbed Quadra-Coil. But the big advance came at the rear, where Quadra-Coil was adapted to replace the XJ's leaf springs. The arrangement gave 1.5 inches more suspension rebound than Cherokee for great off-road traction. It reduced road noise and provided better overall control of the axle, so there was less side-to-side rocking motion and dramatically less juddering of the tail over washboard surfaces.

To achieve the smooth ride, the ZJ crew exploited the strong unibody, which was 20 percent more rigid than Cherokee's and fit relatively soft springs. Suspension damping was further improved because the Quadra-Coil solution allowed the rear gas-charged shock absorbers to be mounted at less of an angle than would have been required with leaf springs.

One final issue was the emotional subject of a name. AMC had planned to retire the XJ Cherokee upon introduction of the ZJ; it simply did not have the resources or production capability to build both simultaneously. So the ZJ probably would have worn the proud Cherokee name.

Yet, Chrysler had the ability to keep producing the Cherokee along with its "successor," so a new moniker would be needed. The ZJ team pushed for a new name that would distinguish its new creation.

The Cherokee models received the updated 2.5- and 4.0-liter powerplants in 1991. The 4.0 was standard on all models except the base Cherokee. The Limited (right, top) remained at the top of the line, but the new Briarwood cost only $500 less. The Briarwood (right, bottom left) replaced the Wagoneer Limited and offered new wheels and teak woodgrain exterior accents. The 1991 model year also brought a four-door Cherokee Sport (right, bottom right).

Laramie topped the list. Chrysler, however, wanted to capitalize on the strong name recognition of the word Cherokee. The final decision fell to Iacocca himself, who simply slapped on a "Grand" prefix and sent the ZJ out into the world as the Grand Cherokee. It made the auto-show circuit in January and was released for sale in April.

It was an immediate hit. Dealers quickly collected a backlog of orders, and automotive magazines put it on a wide range of Best Buy and 10-best lists.

Grand Cherokee owed its success to a variety of factors. It was a friendly size. Exterior dimensions placed it squarely between Cherokee and the five-door Explorer. At 105.9 inches, the wheelbase was 4.5 inches longer than Cherokee, six inches shorter than Explorer. At 176.5 inches, the body was eight inches longer than Cherokee, eight inches shorter than Explorer. Base curb weight was 3633 pounds, 600 more than the comparable Cherokee and about 400 less than the Ford.

Standard safety features also were a lure. It boasted the first air bag in the sport-utility field and backed that up with standard four-wheel anti-lock brakes that worked in both two-wheel drive and four-wheel drive. It had a center high-mounted stop lamp, and the window in the one-piece rear liftgate contained a standard wiper/washer.

Powerful engines were a big plus. Grand Cherokee debuted in base, Laredo, and Limited trim levels, all with the 190-horsepower Power Tech six. A top-of-the-line Grand Wagoneer model joined them in the fall and introduced Chrysler's 5.2-liter (318 cubic inches) V-8 to the line. It was rated at 220 horsepower and 285 pounds-feet of torque. The V-8 was then made optional on the other models. As for transmissions, the six-cylinder engine could be mated to a five-speed manual; a four-speed overdrive automatic was optional with the six and mandatory with the V-8.

No other sport-utility wagon offered as wide a choice of four-wheel-drive systems.

(continued on page 220)

Due to the tremendous success of the Concept 1 on the auto-show circuit, Jeep decided to pursue the design further. Several full-size studies were done, one looking like the Voyager/Caravan (left, top), and the other closer to the finished Grand Cherokee (left, bottom). Chrysler had intended for the new model to replace both the Cherokee and the Grand Wagoneer, but because Cherokee sales remained strong and because Chrysler had the ability to build both at the same time, the model was continued.

By 1991 the Grand Wagoneer (right, top) had been around, in basically the same body, for almost 30 years. The base price was $29,189, and fitting it with options easily put the retail tag over $30,000. Changes for this model were limited to new color offerings. In 1992, the Cherokee Limited (right, bottom left) added two new color options, midnight blue and hunter green. The Sport Laredo, Limited, and Briarwood trim levels all returned, but the Wagoneer name was dropped. Jeep also freshened the Sahara model for 1992. There were new low-gloss sage and sand exterior paints, and new full-face steel wheels. Across the Wrangler line was a gauge package and a new radio with a clock function.

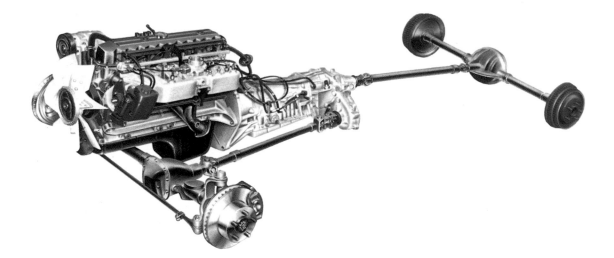

The One and Only

"After reading your story, I wanted to call your attention to your obviously unintentional but nevertheless incorrect use of the word Jeep," read the letter from the Chrysler Corporation public relations official. It went on to explain that the word Jeep is not a generic term, but a worldwide registered trademark. As such, it can be used to identify only a genuine Jeep vehicle.

Chrysler sends dozens of such letters annually in an aggressive campaign to protect the Jeep name. Manufacturers in other fields have similar problems. Kleenex, for example, is not an umbrella term for facial tissue, but the trademark of a specific brand; Styrofoam doesn't describe just any plastic foam, but a particular company's version. But no other automaker is so actively on guard.

Chrysler regularly sends the media "informational" letters in an effort to head off misuse of the Jeep name *before* it happens. It even buys advertising space to make its trademark pitch. Says one ad: "In a world of fakes and forgeries, there's one original no one has been able to copy—Jeep."

The thrust of the campaign is that "Jeep" identifies a brand of vehicle, not a type of vehicle. The J should always be capitalized. The word should not be hyphenated (Jeep-like or Jeep-type), and Chrysler even discourages its use as a verb (Jeeping).

"So the next time you see our name, remember this:" says one ad, "There may be a lot of sport utility vehicles on the road today, but there's only one Jeep. . . ."

When a newspaper reporter wrote an article that casually described a variety of small, off-road vehicles as jeeps, little did he realize that the trademark guardians were about to spring into action.

Chrysler carried over Jeep's 4.0-liter six and four-wheel-drive systems (left) to the Grand Cherokee. However, there were fundamental changes in the suspension setup, and later in the 1993 model year Jeep would again offer a V-8 in their largest of sport utilities.

Jeep engineers replaced the Grand Wagoneer's old-think body-on-frame construction with a more modern unibody construction for the Grand Cherokee. Wheelbase was now 105.9 inches, and length was 179.0, both down from the Grand Wagoneer of a year before; interior volume was almost the same. Two of the most impressive features of the new Grand Cherokee were the front and rear suspension systems. At the front (right, bottom right), engineers adapted the Cherokee's solid axle with coil springs. In the rear was an all-new system dubbed "Quadra-Coil" (right, bottom left). This system took a solid axle and adapted coil springs (instead of leaf springs), shock absorbers, and pivot arms to create a highly durable setup in a tight package. The new setup allowed for greater wheel travel and increased on-road stability.

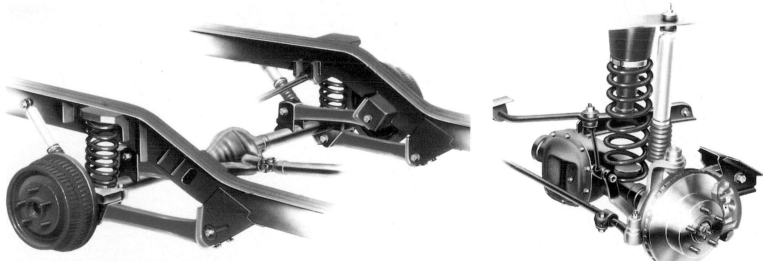

Standard on base and Laredo was Jeep's Command-Trac part-time setup, which had shift-on-the-fly but was not for use on dry pavement. Optional was Selec-Trac full-time, four-wheel drive, which could be used on dry pavement.

Standard on the Limited and V-8 models and optional on the others was Jeep's new Quadra-Trac permanently engaged four-wheel drive. This system distributed power equally between the front and rear axles until it detected wheel slip. Once detected, Quadra-Trac reapportioned power as needed to regain traction without requiring any action from the driver.

Unlike the permanently engaged four-wheel-drive systems on Chrysler's own minivans and on the rival Oldsmobile Bravada, Quadra-Trac was suitable for serious off-road use. A viscous center differential would lock automatically when extra traction was demanded. It also had driver-selected low-range gearing.

Aimed at an upscale audience, Grand Cherokee's interior featured front bucket seats and a 60/40 split folding rear bench—Jeep's first—standard on all models.

Grand Cherokee was a formidable contender right out of the box, and comparisons with the best-selling Explorer were inevitable.

The Ford had 30 fewer horsepower and weighed more than the Jeep, but its 4.0-liter V-6/automatic powertrain matched Grand Cherokee's torque, and did so at 2400 rpm, 1600 rpm sooner than the Jeep. In everyday driving, then, Explorer's acceleration felt equally as smooth and very nearly as strong as the six-cylinder Grand Cherokee's. With Ford's towing capacity 5400 pounds, 400 pounds more than the Jeep's. By the stopwatch, however, the Power Tech's advantage was evident, as the Grand Cherokee ran 0-60 mph in 9.4 seconds, to Explorer's 10.5. The EPA rated both at 15 mpg city and 21 highway with automatic transmission.

The Explorer could not match the Grand's V-8 engine, however. Though it was louder than the six, Jeep's V-8 felt stronger than the Power Tech in all circumstances and had a 0-60 mph time of around 8.0 seconds—better than some sports sedans. It also increased Grand Cherokee's towing capacity to 6500 pounds, most in the compact sport-utility class.

Explorer's ride was supple for a 4x4, but no sport-utility provided a more car-like suspension feel than the Grand Cherokee. It was firm but absorbent on all surfaces.

"We were amazed at what we could hit at 50 mph—like half-buried boulders the size of 50-pound bags of dog chow and railroad crossings with rails protruding four inches high," marveled *Car and Driver*.

The optional "Up Country" suspension raised the Grand Cherokee one inch on larger tires. It enhanced off-road control but made the on-road ride stiff and jittery.

Grand Cherokee was larger inside than Cherokee, the biggest gain coming in a back seat that was wider by several inches because the rear wheel wells were aft of the rear seatbacks. Head room was generous all around, but leg room was no improvement over Cherokee.

Compared to its Ford rival, Grand Cherokee had 8.0 inches of ground clearance, the Explorer 6.3. Yet, the Jeep's unibody construction gave it a roughly one-inch lower sill than the body-on-frame Ford, so getting in and out wasn't much different than with an automobile. The lip of the cargo floor was lower, too, and while Grand Cherokee's liftgate had a handy molded-in grab handle for easy closing, it lacked the separate-opening window of most competitors. With the seatbacks up, there wasn't much more luggage room than in a mid-size car—unless the load was allowed to eat into rear visibility. Here, Explorer, with its spare tire stowed below the body, had an advantage over the Jeep and its mandatory inside tire mount.

Buyers stepping up from the Cherokee found the new Jeep's light, slightly vague steering familiar, but import-car owners likely wished for a sharper, meatier feel.

The exterior styling of the Grand Cherokee had been locked up from the time of Concept 1 back in 1989. However, designers did slight reworks of greenhouse, trim, and hood details. Jeep offered four distinctly different packages on the Grand: base, Laredo, Limited, and Grand Wagoneer. The Laredo (right, bottom) added tilt wheel, cruise, power mirrors, leather-wrapped steering wheel, center console, lighted mirrors, extra sound insulation, cargo cover, roof rack, and floor mats. The Limited (right, top) added to the four-speed automatic power leather seats, air-conditioning, power windows and locks, anti-theft alarm, overhead console, trip computer, rear defogger, heated mirrors, fog lamps, and other convenience options.

With ABS that worked on all four wheels, even in four-wheel drive, Grand Cherokee enjoyed predictable stopping power on all surfaces and had a significant leg up on most other sport-utilities, including Explorer, where ABS worked only on the rear wheels and only in two-wheel drive.

Similarly, Quadra-Trac added a new dimension to Jeep's versatile four-wheel-drive systems, and even Selec-Trac allowed running four-wheel drive on dry pavement. Explorer's part-time four-wheel drive could not be used on dry pavement, and unlike any of Jeep's systems, it required that the vehicle be stopped and backed up to fully disengage.

At highway speeds, Grand Cherokee's rounded corners and semi-flush side glass kept wind rush relatively low, and tire noise was not intrusive.

Clear analog gauges and a simple control layout lent the dashboard a sport-sedan ambience, and the silken movement of the various switches and dials signaled a new standard for Chrysler. Also noteworthy was the Limited's automatic climate system, which allowed several combinations of manual and automatic settings.

The steering wheel had an available tilt feature but was still too close to the driver's chest for some tastes. Yet, while the new seats were wider than Cherokee's, the fronts lacked lumbar adjustments. Some drivers found them too softly padded for long-distance comfort. Jeep shortened the rear seat cushion to facilitate entry and exit, sacrificing some thigh support.

Overall, its air bag, sophisticated ABS, superior four-wheel-drive systems, and excellent suspension gave Grand Cherokee an unprecedented array of features in this class. Initial base prices for 6-cylinder models ranged from $18,980 for the entry-level Grand Cherokee to $27,433 for the top-of-the-line Limited.

Introduction of the Grand Cherokee signaled the demise of the elder statesmen of 4x4s, the Grand Wagoneer. When it bowed in 1963 as the Wagoneer, the big wagon

For the 1993 auto-show circuit Jeep came up with the Ecco (left). It was considered as a far-flung replacement for the Wrangler and rode on a 100.3-inch wheelbase. Power came from a two-stroke three-cylinder engine. Designer Tervor Creed said, "it looks like a turtle—it's smooth underneath and it's got the rounded upper rollcage and the wheels stick out sort of like legs."

During the 1993 model year Jeep offered a Wrangler Sport (right, top), designed to combat lower priced imports. It had a lower price than other Wranglers and a fixed number of available options. The Grand Wagoneer (right, bottom left) came standard with a 220-horsepower 5.2-liter engine. This powerplant was taken from the Dodge line of trucks and pumped out 285 pounds-feet of torque at a low 3600 rpm. The Grand package also included woodgrain bodyside appliqués and front-door courtesy lights. Many people thought that the Cherokee might disappear with the introduction of the Grand, but that was not the case. Sales remained strong, and a new Country trim level (right, bottom right) was added. The Country replaced the Limited at the top of the line; the Laredo and Briarwood were also killed.

had America's four-wheel-drive market virtually to itself. It built a cult following. But by 1992, the segment contained no less than 27 entries, not counting 4x4 pickups or minivans, and there was little room for a throwback to an earlier age.

Chrysler was preparing to reposition the Cherokee toward the lower end of the sport-utility spectrum so as not to encroach on the Grand Cherokee. But for 1992, the top-line Cherokee Limited and Briarwood were still in the $25,000 range, clearly in Grand Cherokee territory. New options for 1992 included a sunroof for Sport models and leather upholstery for Laredos.

Despite dismal sales, Comanche carried on with a new Sport option group and some minor interior trim alterations. Jeep would sell only 3181 Comanches for calendar 1992, however. That placed it last in a field of 11 compact pickups, and it would not be back for the 1993 model year.

Though it was on sale for only eight months in 1992, the Grand Cherokee found 86,859 buyers. That placed it fourth in calendar-year sales among compact sport-utility vehicles behind Explorer (306,681 units), S10 Blazer (147,742), and the Cherokee (128,960). With Cherokee and Wrangler sales on the rise, Jeep sold 268,724 vehicles for calendar 1992, a robust 41.3-percent increase over the previous year.

Grand Cherokee continued into 1993 as the only entry in its segment with an air bag. Two-wheel-drive models debuted in base and Laredo trim, and the four-speed automatic transmission gained electronic shift controls.

As promised, Cherokee dropped a clear tier below the Grand Cherokee but was functionally unchanged. Repackaged to appeal to a younger buyer, the lineup was trimmed to base, Sport, and the new Country models. Base price of the most expensive four-wheel-drive Cherokee was now around $19,500, some $200 below the least-expensive four-wheel-drive Grand Cherokee. The best deal was again the five-door four-wheel-drive Cherokee Sport, which started at about $16,800, roughly $1900 less than a similar 1992 Sport.

Wrangler for 1993 became the first mini-4x4 to offer anti-lock brakes. The system was a $599 option, and was only available with the six-cylinder engine. It worked in both two- and four-wheel drive.

Helped by the available V-8 engine, Grand Cherokee sales soared to 217,232 for calendar 1993, surpassing the S10 Blazer and trailing only the Explorer, which had sales of 302,200. Wrangler jumped 25 percent for the period, to an all-time high of 65,648. Overall, Jeep sales leaped 51.9 percent. On top of the 1992 increase, Jeep sales had more than doubled in two years.

For 1994, Grand Cherokee Limited gained rear disc brakes, and all models got side door guard beams. The base model was renamed SE, Laredo continued as the most popular model, and the Limited was back. The Grand Wagoneer model, with its imitation bodyside wood paneling, was discontinued.

Cherokee returned for its 11th season with side door guard beams and a center high-mounted stop lamp—both of which were now federally required on truck-based vehicles. Also an automatic transmission was offered for the first time with the four-cylinder engine.

Wrangler was back with an automatic transmission available for the four-cylinder engine. All models got a center high-mounted stop lamp affixed to a gooseneck bracket on the tailgate. And available for the first time was a new folding soft top with hardtop-style full metal doors instead of half-doors. The entry-level Wrangler retained the S designation, but an SE took the place of the former "base" model. A new "junior Renegade" Sport option included body-colored fender flares and bodyside steps among its features.

Continued strong sales were evidence of the success of the Chrysler-Jeep linkup. Wrangler was more popular than ever. And the Cherokee had found a second life as a

For 1994 the Wrangler was available as either the S or SE. From that, option and trim packages could be added. The Sahara (right, top left) was again available and added a 20-gallon fuel tank, power steering, gas shocks, full-face steel wheels, exterior graphics, and other interior convenience options. The Wrangler S (right, bottom) was the base model and retailed for $11,390 in 1994. That compared very favorably to the Geo Tracker at $11,015 and the Suzuki Sidekick at $11,449. Jeep also continued the Cherokee Sport (right, top right) as the 4.0-liter standard mid-line model for 1994. The sport came equipped with improved gauges, intermittent wipers, Sport Decor Group, spare tire cover, and cargo tie-down hooks.

On pavement, "It outperformed every other vehicle in the group by a comfortable margin." And off-road, Quadra-Trac's ability to keep the Jeep going was limited only by traction shortcomings of the Grand's all-season highway tires. "This sort of versatility is unexpected in a vehicle marketed as a kind of high performance station wagon," said the editors.

Here's how the field ranked in standing-start acceleration:

	0-60 mph (seconds)	Quarter-mile (seconds @ mph)
Jeep:	8.0	16.3 @ 84
Mitsubishi:	9.7	17.5 @ 87
Range Rover:	10.4	17.9 @ 77
Toyota:	10.7	17.9 @ 76
Isuzu:	10.0	18.1 @ 75
Ford:	11.0	18.3 @ 75

"classic" sport-utility wagon. But it was the Grand Cherokee—the vehicle most affected by the Chrysler-Jeep marriage—that now accounted for fully half of all Jeeps sold. Its blend of safety and power, refinement and ruggedness, continued to earn accolades from the public and press.

For its March 1994 issue, *Car and Driver* put six top compact sport-utility vehicles to the test on highways and the drag strip, in mud bogs and deep snow, and on rock-strewn trails.

A Grand Cherokee Limited with the V-8 engine emerged on top. Reflecting the "gentrified" nature of the contemporary 4x4 wagon, the field had an average sticker price of $36,320. Finishing in order behind the Jeep ($31,332 as tested) were the Toyota Land Cruiser ($41,631), Ranger Rover County ($47,525), Mitsubishi Montero SR ($34,756), Isuzu Trooper LS ($32,580), and Ford Explorer Limited ($30,100).

Despite intrusive noise from the engine and "occasionally wandery steering," the magazine said the Grand Cherokee "continues to be the only sport-ute that makes us forget we're driving a truck."

In braking, the Grand Cherokee's four-wheel ABS hauled it down from 70 mph in 180 feet—shorter than all but the Land Cruiser's 178 feet. On the skidpad, the Grand Cherokee hung on to register a lateral force of 0.75g, the best in a field that averaged 0.70g. The Grand Cherokee was also the quickest through *Car and Driver*'s "emergency lane-change maneuver," whipping through the cones at 58.7 mph, against a test average of 53 mph.

Meanwhile, engineers that created the Grand Cherokee are hard at work on the next Jeep update, that of the Wrangler. Early reports described a slightly retro look for the new vehicle—highlighted by a return to round headlamps. Overall size is likely to be unchanged, and the shape, though not as square, will still be bold and unmistakably Jeep. Live axles probably will be retained, but the suspension is likely to be new, possibly with a version of the Grand Cherokee's Quadra Coil setup. The interior will feature dual air bags.

Introduction is targeted for January 1996, as a 1997 model. But as early as 1992, the first prototypes were hammering away off-road. To ensure that the next Wrangler is pure Jeep, the testing ground was none other than the Rubicon Trail.

The interior of the Grand Cherokee (left) was a revolution in Jeep products. Ergonomically correct and pleasant to look at, the dash and instrumentation exhibited the positive influence Chrysler was having at Jeep. Another Chrysler influence was the driver-side air bag, which forced a slight redesign of the steering column and many miles of off-road testing to prevent false expansions. Critics complained that the exterior surfaces of the dash, while pleasant to look at, had a cheap feel.

Three versions of the Grand Cherokee were offered for 1994, the SE, Laredo (right, top), and the Limited (right, bottom left). The SE and Laredo could be had with either two- or four-wheel drive (Selec-Trac or Quadra-Trac), and the Limited came standard with Quadra-Trac. The big 5.2-liter V-8 was no longer standard at the top of the line but still had to be mated to the four-speed automatic. Jeep design and engineering have already begun work on a replacement for the Wrangler (right, bottom right). Tentatively scheduled for a 1997 release, the new vehicle will have more curves and a retro-look grille. Powertrains are expected to be very similar to those available today.

CHAPTER ELEVEN
Off-Road and Into Adventure

ne of motoring's ironies is that only 5 percent of sport-utility vehicles are taken off-road. To many owners these all-terrain conveyances are nothing more than trendy lifestyle accessories.

Jeeps venture from the pavement at about twice the rate of all sport-utilities. But even at 10 percent, they're underused. That's a pity, for even the plushest Grand Cherokee is highly capable in the harshest terrain. In fact, Chrysler President Robert Lutz has decreed that every Jeep vehicle must be able to run the torturous Rubicon Trail.

Lutz could hardly pick a tougher proving ground. Traversing 70 miles of scenic vistas, boulder-strewn gullies, and semi-suicidal descents, the trek through California's Sierra Nevada Mountains is a mecca for serious off-roading. It's the site of the original Jeepers Jamboree and the model for a cavalcade of off-road Jeep trips nationwide.

These events attract thousands, from trail-hardened veterans in jacked-up CJs to families in shiny Cherokees getting their first taste of off-road driving. They demonstrate not only the go-anywhere tenacity of a Jeep but the camaraderie this special vehicle can inspire.

Jeep, of course, was born to the backwoods. Its original military parameters were for a light troop transport that could defeat the most inhospitable geography. Even before World War II had ended, its peacetime commercial and recreational possibilities were being plotted.

In 1944, Willys-Overland built several prototypes of civilian Jeeps, and by August 1945, the first CJs were proving their mettle all over the United States. They were used for everything from farm vehicles to personnel carriers. They transported sportsmen into the field and even performed public services.

As early as 1946, a group of jeep owners in remote Bountiful, Utah, had turned Sunday excursions up and down the winding mountain roads of the Wasatch Range into a valuable community resource.

Given certain limited powers of policing, the group became known as the "Official Bountiful City Jeep Posse." Consisting of 27 jeeps and 54 men, the posse evacuated the injured from a mountainside plane crash, organized search parties for missing persons, and served as mounted game wardens. Its most important function was to rush in firefighters during the first critical hours of a forest fire.

The February 1948 issue of *Popular Mechanics* described the posse's attempt to cut a road up a mountain, providing a vivid account of the little 4x4's stoutness:

"The lead jeep started up the steep incline and at one of the dangerous spots it got out of control. The driver leaped to safety, but the car rolled down the slope like an awkward snowball. It turned over 20 times by actual count before landing upside down, suspended in some trees. It took ten men to get it back up the cliff.

"Once back on its four wheels the rugged jeep went back to town under its own power! To be sure, it needed a new windshield, some new headlights and a few dents had to be pounded out of the body, but it was ready for the next attempt the following Sunday."

It's too bad that so few people have a chance to experience the thrill of taking a Jeep off-road. Only about 10 percent of Jeep owners ever experience real off-road use—and that is twice the national average. Many owners have formed clubs that do just that—they take their Jeeps on deep excursions into places four-wheeled vehicles were never meant to go. Jeeps have a long heritage in civilian off-road situations dating back to the days right after World War II. In 1946 Jeeps were already being used to patrol the wilderness of Utah. Today they are respected around the world for their boulder-topping ability and are used for both work and play.

Similar excursions were being played out anywhere the road ended and adventure began.

The original Rubicon trek was in 1952. Mark Smith, Ken Collins, and a group of their friends—most of them members of the Georgetown Divide Rotary Club—organized it to bring outside dollars into the region's depressed economy. The route was based on a path blazed by Native Americans and later used by stagecoaches.

A test run by four Jeep Universals and 12 men was followed in August 1953 by the first Jeepers Jamboree. It attracted 150 participants in 55 jeeps. They skirted the shores of picture-postcard Lake Chiquita, scraped their way down the "Big Sluice," camped overnight at lush Rubicon Springs, then bounced on to magnificent Lake Tahoe.

Even from the beginning, men and women of all ages took part. There was Dan Bassi, who had been a stage driver along the Rubicon Trail back in 1904, and Beatrice Luce, of Georgetown, who admitted to being "past seventy." Some of the machines were old-timers, too. Several Jeeps were of World War II vintage, and one was a Model MA—one of the original 1940 Willys pilot vehicles. That MA is today the centerpiece of the Jeepers Jamboree Museum in Georgetown.

The annual four-day Rubicon trip was an instant success. By 1974, organizers were forced to set a limit of 400 vehicles and 1500 people. Demand sparked a second Rubicon trip (for up to 200 vehicles), and the two events are now held each year in July and August. Participants come from all over the world.

The Rubicon Trail itself crosses private land held by 20 separate property owners. Rubicon Springs in fact has been purchased by Smith and some of his associates to be maintained in its natural state. The route is open to any 4WD vehicle—weather permitting—and the Jeep Division of Chrysler makes regular use of it as a testing ground. The original Jeepers Jamboree is now an independent corporation with exclusive rights to the "Jeepers Jamboree" name. It opens its runs to Jeeps and to the older, smaller Toyota Land Cruisers and British Land Rovers that were Jeep's only contemporaries in the early days of the Rubicon.

In the late 1980s, the Jeepers Jamboree concept was applied to events in other states under a separate entity called Jeep Jamboree USA. (Jeep Jamboree USA is a division of Mark A. Smith Off-Roading Inc. and is underwritten by the Jeep Division of Chrysler Corporation.)

Today, 25 of these three-day Jeep Jamboree USA events are held in 21 states. They take place from February through October and are strictly limited to Jeep vehicles. Events on the 1994 calendar included the Red River Jamboree in New Mexico, the Mohawk Trail Jamboree in Massachusetts, and the Ghost Town Jamboree in Nevada. Each attracts an average of 100 Jeeps and roughly 500 participants, half of whom are first-timers. Both the Jeepers Jamboree and the Jeep Jamboree USA events charge fees, which include meals but not lodging. The full four-day Rubicon trip, for example, costs $235 per person, while the shorter Jeep Jamboree USA events cost $160 per adult, less for children.

Some Jeepers, particularly those with easy access to off-road running, avoid these mass excursions. Their main objection is that moving large numbers of Jeeps through the wilderness dictates too many compromises, including some bumper-to-bumper running—an incongruous sight when you're miles from civilization.

Granted, a lone Jeep pounding through the brush, as if in some TV commercial, is a uniquely satisfying image. And officials in selected areas, such as the region around Telluride, Colorado, actively promote unorganized four-wheeling on mountain trails. But with ever-tighter controls on public and private lands, Jamborees are the only way many Jeep owners get to experience their vehicles off-road. Indeed, as the *San Jose Mercury News*' Bob Scheid reported from the Rubicon Trail, "The ability of these vehicles to proceed where common sense shouts 'impassable!' is astounding to the city-bred driver."

Jamboree officials grade off-road trails by degree of difficulty on an ascending scale from one to 10. Most trails fall in the four to eight range. Some Jeep Jamboree USA routes earn a nine. But the Rubicon Trail proudly lays claim to the only 10 rating.

Standard practice on Jeep Jamboree USA trips is to make available several trails of varying difficulty. The assemblage is divided into caravans of 50 or so Jeeps. Progress along the route is usually steady until the group comes upon an obstacle: Say it must descend a gully, ford a creek, then scramble up the adjoining slope. Jeepers queue up, take on the challenge one by one, then stop again to wait for the rest of the group. There can be lots of waiting. But that's time to talk Jeep or to wander over and offer encouragement as each member of the caravan tackles the obstacle.

Regardless of how free-form or how structured the off-road experience, there are rules and tricks that apply equally.

Some are simple, such as anticipating a four-wheel-drive situation and engaging four-wheel drive *before* you get stuck. Others are not as obvious. For instance, drivers should grip the steering wheel with thumbs outside the rim. Do otherwise and the steering wheel's spokes could do some painful damage as the wheel reacts to the impact of hitting a log or rock.

Even mildly undulating terrain provides an education in the value of ground clearance and suspension travel. Cherokees and Grand Cherokees get along surprisingly well just as they come from the factory, though lowering tire pressure to 22 psi helps the tread to flex and grip outcroppings.

By comparison, Wranglers and CJs, with their shorter wheelbases, more-modest ground clearance, and relatively limited suspension travel, can benefit from larger non-stock tires and suspension lifts. One

Originally there was only one Jeepers Jamboree (right, top), and riders traveled on the notorious Rubicon Trail. Today, there are over 25 three-day Jamboree events in 21 states. One of the most difficult parts of four-wheeling is traveling over rocks (right, middle and bottom). Common sense would dictate that the safest route would be to drive between or around rocks. However, Jeepers have learned that it is best to keep the tires of the vehicle directly on top of the rocks, to avoid catching the frame or becoming squeezed into a tight situation. Oftentimes caravans of Jeeps will travel single file down a stretch of particularly tough trail. They travel so slowly that spotters will often guide drivers over the toughest parts (right, bottom right).

trick is to disconnect the Wrangler's front roll bar, which frees the suspension to accommodate widely different side-to-side elevations. Aftermarket locking differentials and winches are useful, and tow hooks are required on all trails with a rating of four or higher.

Engine modifications are rare. Most off-roading is done at a strolling pace, and even Jeeps with four-cylinder engines have enough torque to ascend most any slope. The keys are traction and gearing—and not just for going uphill. Few automotive sensations rival shifting a Jeep into first gear, setting the transfer case in low range, and trusting against all instinct as the machine noses easily down a grade too steep to walk. Experienced Jeepers know to stay off the brakes in such situations—and to rarely use the clutch.

"Jeeping well is a fine art," Pete Lyons wrote in *Car and Driver* after his first Rubicon. "First of all, speed has no place on this sort of trail. You must maintain what I've started calling the Jeepers Creep. You just chug-chug along in the lowest gear available, usually keeping your foot completely off the gas. . . . You open the throttle for quick little bursts of torque to surmount a boulder. If you're driving a manual transmission, you are not supposed to use the clutch—too much risk of burning it out. Even if the engine dies, you're supposed to restart in gear, without declutching. It's hard to remember that in a crisis."

Helping Jamboree participants remember such dictums is the job of official volunteers familiar with each trail. Their on-sight advice about gear selection or exactly where to place the tires to avoid hanging up on that boulder is priceless data to neophytes and veterans alike.

AutoWeek's Wes Raynal, poised to drive a Wrangler through a New York stream on the Adirondack jamboree, got this counsel from a trail volunteer: "Just take it slow, try not to let the water hit the base of the windshield. And don't worry about those scraping noises."

"Yeah, right," thought Raynal. "As it turned out," he said, "we made it across the pond with no problems."

There is satisfaction to be found in more sedate off-roading exercises, as well, and Jeepers appreciate gliding gently down a forest path beneath a canopy of leaves—especially in an open CJ or Wrangler.

If there is one spot that embodies the challenge, exhilaration, and spectacle of true Jeeping, it is a section of the Rubicon known as the "Big Sluice."

The Sluice is actually a dried waterfall, a chute-like descent amid pitiless granite boulders—with a dangerous 45-degree turn thrown in for good measure. It is only 30 to 40 yards long, but it can seem to stretch for miles. One driver negotiating it paused to glance at his inclinometers. His Wrangler was tilted left 35 degrees and tipped forward 55 degrees.

"Those who've driven the Sluice insist it's the worst single trail open to vehicles they've ever seen," declared Mark Williams in *Four Wheeler* magazine. "The margin for error is very small, and for those who don't give the terrain the respect it demands, the winch cable waits. . . .

"On a hillside next to the run," Williams wrote, "where the granite provides bare spots in between the scrub, people sit [after already having done their time on the rocks] and prepare to watch the next victim. . . . [They're] calling, pointing, cheering, supporting . . . all watching the vehicle directly below negotiate the tricky boulders and sharp drops. The towering trees provide shade and cool breezes, but it seems that every driver who passes through breaks a sweat in the first few moments."

"The ideal Jeep would have a hinge in the middle for this section," observed *Car and Driver*'s Pete Lyons.

The Sluice is the exclamation point to a 7.5-mile leg of the Rubicon that can take up to 14 hours to traverse. Veterans say the average speed is minus two mph. But the Sluice also is the last hurdle before en-

campment at Rubicon Springs, which represents another powerful symbol of Jeeping: The party.

Hoedowns here are legendary, and set a standard other Jamborees have yet to match. They've been that way from the start.

Before the very first Rubicon trip, organizers got hold of an old World War II weapons carrier and hauled in enough pine decking to build a 16x32-foot dance pavilion, complete with a shiny linoleum floor. In the second year, a piano was brought in. Lashed to the back of a Jeep truck, the instrument was rather dreadfully out of tune by the time it arrived at Rubicon Springs. "But it didn't seem to matter," organizer Collins recalled, "because no one else was in tune, anyway!"

Rubicon Jeepers expect unexpected entertainment. Some years there are bluegrass musicians. Serenading the encampment on one occasion were the Twelve Singing Nuns of St. Celeia's Chorale. Another year, a Scottish bagpipe band came marching out of the brush. And to replace the out-of-tune spinet, a Hughes 500D helicopter has lately set down a shiny black concert grand, complete with classical pianist. (The chopper always is on standby in case of medical emergency.) In 1974 two participants—Charles Donahue and Susann Marie Bernard—were married in a ceremony held at Rubicon Springs.

Great food is another Rubicon tradition. Steaks, chicken, and fish are helicoptered in and grilled over coals. The typical trip's menu includes 2.6 tons of meat, 1094 dozen eggs, 500 pounds of pancake mix with 60 gallons of syrup, 1500 ears of corn, 35,000 slices of bread, 255 pounds of butter, and 150 pounds of coffee. Included among the supplies, by official calculation, is 9.4 miles of toilet paper.

Food and festivities offer a respite from the rigors of the Rubicon. Some Jeep adventures offer no such reprieve.

In 1978, Smith, Collins, and some of their colleagues undertook what Smith

Some of the worst enemies of the off-road driver are small streams or fords (right, middle and bottom left). Often, by the time you have found out how deep they are, you've already gone too far to go back. This is when the power winch comes in very handy. Jeeps are such stellar off-road performers that very few owner modifications need be made. One that is almost always made, however, is the switch to all-terrain tires. Also, most off-roaders will add skid plates to the underside and beef-up the roll bar on top (right, top and middle). Often, one or more of the wheels of a CJ will be off the ground when traveling over uneven terrain. This is a common feature of the solid axle suspension and allows the body to remain fairly level. It's interesting to note that while all Jeeps are great off-road performers, some are better in certain situations than others. The CJs and Wrangler, because of their narrow width, can turn around and get into places a larger four-wheeler would never dream of. The Cherokee and Grand Cherokee, on the other hand, have a longer wheelbase, which allows them to span a broader area of ground in search of traction for at least one wheel. No matter what vehicle you are driving, one of the best parts of any jamboree event is the sundown cookout (right, bottom right).

232

brands the ultimate Jeep trip, a 21,000-mile odyssey from Tierra del Fuego, at the southern tip of South America, to Prudhoe Bay, Alaska.

Two years of intense planning preceded the *Expedicion de las Americas*. Five new CJ-7s were battle tested on the Rubicon Trail, then shipped south to begin the ordeal.

The journey consumed four months. While eking out a trail through dense South American forests, the Jeepers lived off the land, eating alligator, Iguana, Scarlet McCaws, and whatever else could be shot, trapped, or hooked.

Between Panama and Colombia they encountered a nearly impenetrable 250-mile expanse of jungle and swamp. "It was 10 times longer and 10 times rougher than the Rubicon," Smith said. "On an average day we would make two to three miles. One day we worked for nine hours and only moved 500 feet."

Within this leg was the 110-mile Darien Gap. It had been crossed only once before by vehicles, when a 1972 British Army expedition did it with 250 men. It took the British 100 days, and eight Colombian Marines were lost. The Jeepers' crossing was made by 14 North Americans, three Colombians, and 25 Indians. It took 30 days. There were no casualties.

The only modifications to the CJ-7s on the *Expedicion de las Americas* CJs were the addition of winches, extra lighting, brush guards, and carriages to carry provisions and cans of extra fuel. Even the tires were close to stock size, at a modest 31x11.5 R15, and were fitted without suspension modifications.

Adventures like this seem at odds with the notion that relatively few Jeeps venture off-road. Those that do, however, seem to wear their mud and dents like badges of honor. And their drivers tend to sport a certain smile and walk. Some lifestyle. Some accessory.

Specifications and Production

Production of jeeps: 1940-45[1]

American Bantam Car Company

Model	Production:
Prototype(Sept. 23, 1940)	1
MK II	69
40BRC (March 31, 1941)	1175
40BRC (2nd order)	1430
Total	**2675**

Willys-Overland Motors, Inc.

Model		Production:
Quad	(Nov. 11, 1940)	2
MA	(June 7, 1941)	1500
MB (slat grill)		25,808
MB		335,531
Total		**362,841**

Ford Motor Company

Model		Production:
Pigmy	(Nov. 23, 1940)	2
GP	(Feb. 8, 1941)	3550
GPW		277,896
Total		**281,448**
Total		**646,964**

[1]It is doubtful that these numbers will ever be established as fact, because the government bought many parts and subassemblies, such as chassis for experimental bodies.

Jeep Corporation[2]

	Production:
1945:	1824
1946:	78,808
1947:	97,581
1948:	159,002
1949:	86,151
1950:	90,424
1951:	119,200
1952:	57,879
1953:	75,759
1954:	46,002
1955:	64,166
1956:	64,267
1957:	64,639
1958:	43,303
1959:	52,483
1960:	67,842
1961:	49,073
1962:	85,457
1963:	110,549
1964:	120,868
1965:	108,574
1966:	99,623
1967:	116,744
1968:	117,573
1969:	93,160
1970:	86,254
1971:	53,051
1972:	71,205
1973:	94,035
1974:	93,317
1975:	108,612

Jeep Corp. (cont.)

1976:	126,125
1977:	139,140
1978:	180,514
1979:	134,624
1980:	62,841
1981:	92,248
1982:	75,269
1983:	75,534
1984:	176,276
1985:	225,914
1986:	207,514
1987:	248,930
1988:	308,564
1989:	319,149
1990:	229,327
1991:	226,209
1992:	323,233
1993:	464,020
Total:	**6,192,856**

[2]Due to the various ownership changes at Jeep, production numbers are, at best, an accurate guess. These numbers do not include military or government production. Total production of the Dispatcher (DJ-3A, DJ-5A, and DJ-6A) was 22,264.

Jeep Universal, Model CJ-2A 1945-49

	Production:
1945:	1824
1946:	71,455
1947:	77,958
1948:	62,861
1949:	104
Total:	**214,202**

Jeep Station Wagon/Sedan Delivery 1946-65

	Production:
1946:	6534
1947:	27,515
1948:	44,381
1949:	37,547
1950:	39,911
1951:	36,995
1952:	12,069
1953:	18,811
1954:	7116
1955:	21,875
1956:	14,970
1957:	13,493
1958:	9248
1959:	14,340
1960:	16,440
1961:	11,429
1962-65:	N/A
Total:	**N/A[3]**

Jeep Pickup Truck 1947-65

	Production:
1947:	4988
1948:	30,173
1949:	15,712
1950:	18,634
1951:	38,047
1952:	16,155
1953:	16,498
1954:	4477
1955:	13,856
1956:	16,654
1957:	9594
1958:	8445
1959:	11,742
1960:	14,636
1961:	3546
1962-65:	N/A
Total:	**N/A[3]**

Jeep Jeepster 1948-50

	Production:
1948:	10,326
1949:	2961
1950:	5845
Total:	**19,132**

Jeep Universal, Model CJ-3A 1948-53

	Production:
1948:	309
1949:	31,491
1950:	24,060
1951:	40,121
1952:	34,654
1953:	1208
Total:	**131,843**

Jeep Universal, Model CJ-3B 1952-68

	Production:
1952:	2360
1953:	33,047
1954:	35,972
1955:	12,567
1956:	10,145
1957:	5756
1958:	6178
1959:	5420
1960:	6139
1961:	1147
1962:	9416

CJ-3B (cont.)

1963:	9801
1964:	5271
1965:	2847
1966:	5459
1967:	2523
1968:	1446
Total:	**155,494**

Jeep Universal, Model CJ-5 1954-83

	Production:
1954:	3883
1955:	23,595
1956:	18,441
1957:	20,819
1958:	12,401
1959:	17,488
1960:	19,753
1961:	2064
1962:	14,072
1963:	12,499
1964:	16,029
1965:	21,014
1966:	17,974
1967:	18,186
1968:	19,683
1969:	20,262
1970:	13,518
1971:	12,559
1972:	22,601
1973:	30,449
1974:	43,087
1975:	32,486
1976:	31,116
1977:	32,996
1978:	37,611
1979:	41,501
1980:	24,574
1981:	13,477
1982:	6080
1983:	3085
Total:	**603,303**

Jeep Universal, Model CJ-5A 1964-67

	Production:
1964:	4128
1965:	1987
1966:	1190
1967:	89
Total:	**7394**

Jeep Universal, Model CJ-6 1955-81

	Production:
1955:	581
1956:	2523
1957:	1236
1958:	1387
1959:	1947
1960:	2201
1961:	244
1962:	2502
1963:	1534
1964:	1702
1965:	2062
1966:	3521
1967:	2295
1968:	2395
1969:	2433
1970:	2234
1971:	1806
1972:	1175
1973:	1720
1974:	2826
1975:	2935
1976:	2431
1977:	2754
1978:	743
1979:	992
1980:	1633
1981:	360
Total:	**50,172**

Jeep Universal, Model CJ-6A 1964-67

	Production:
1964:	164
1965:	115
1966:	160
1967:	20
Total:	**459**

Jeep Forward Control Truck 1957-65

	Production:
1957:	9738
1958:	3594
1959:	1546
1960:	4925
1961:	3671
1962-65:	N/A
Total:	**N/A[3]**

[3]Individual production numbers not available during early Kaiser Jeep years.

Jeep Gladiator/ J-Series Pickup Truck 1963-87

	Production:
1963-73:	N/A[1]
1974:	15,524
1975:	13,958
1976:	16,188
1977:	17,252
1978:	20,495
1979:	18,966
1980:	6839
1981:	8048
1982:	6113
1983:	4705
1984:	3082
1985:	1953
1986:	1515
1987:	1153

Jeep Wagoneer 1963-92

	Production:
1963-73	N/A[1]
1974:	13,746
1975:	16,708
1976:	21,912
1977:	20,298
1978:	28,871
1979:	27,437
1980:	10,481
1981:	13,741
1982:	18,709
1983:	18,478
1984:	20,019
1985:	17,814
1986:	17,254
1987:	14,265
1988:	14,117
1989:	10,159
1990:	6449
1991:	1560
1992:	330

[1]Individual numbers not available for the first 10 years of production.

Jeep Jeepster/ Commando 1966-73

	Production:
1966:	2345
1967:	12,621
1968:	13,924
1969:	11,289
1970:	9268
1971:	7903
1972:	10,685
1973:	9538
Total:	77,573

Jeep Cherokee 1974-83

	Production:
1974:	14,082
1975:	16,294
1976:	26,365
1977:	33,684
1978:	40,698
1979:	39,183
1980:	7614
1981:	6321
1982:	6911
1983:	6186
Total:	197,338

Jeep Universal, Model CJ-7 1976-86

	Production:
1976:	21,061
1977:	25,414
1978:	38,274
1979:	55,264
1980:	38,183
1981:	27,767
1982:	23,820
1983:	37,673
1984:	42,644
1985:	43,315
1986:	25,939
Total:	379,354

Jeep Universal, Model CJ-8 (Scrambler) 1981-86

	Production:
1981:	8355
1982:	7759
1983:	5405
1984:	4130
1985:	2015
1986:	128
Total:	27,792

Jeep Wagoneer 1984-90

	Production:
1984:	11,944
1985:	10,021
1986:	12,800
1987:	15,033
1988:	10,092
1989:	6898
1990:	3888
Total:	70,676

Jeep Cherokee 1984-93

	Production:
1984:	93,326
1985:	120,328
1986:	107,225
1987:	139,295
1988:	187,136
1989:	207,216
1990:	151,230
1991:	151,578
1992:	137,826
1993:	144,961
Total:	1,410,121

Jeep Comanche 1985-92

	Production:
1985:	29,245
1986:	33,386
1987:	43,070
1988:	43,718
1989:	25,311
1990:	9576
1991:	5188
1992:	952
Total:	190,446

Jeep Wrangler 1986-93

	Production:
1986:	16,853
1987:	36,114
1988:	52,691
1989:	69,565
1990:	58,184
1991:	65,135
1992:	59,690
1993:	72,903
Total:	431,135

Jeep Grand Cherokee 1992-93

	Production:
1992:	121,333
1993:	246,156
Total:	367,489

1955 Jeep Station Wagon

1963 Jeep CJ-5

1993 Jeep Cherokee

1993 Jeep Grand Cherokee Wagoneer

U.S. Military Jeep, Model MB 1940:

Engine: 4-cylinder, iron block
Bore x stroke (in.): 3⅛ x 4⅜
Displacement (cu in.): 134.2
Compression ratio: 6.48:1
Horsepower (gross): 60 @ 4000 rpm
Torque (gross): 105 16-ft @ 2000 rpm
Main bearings: 3
Valve configuration: L-head
Carburetor: l-bbl downdraft
Transmission: 3-speed
Ratios: 2.665/1.564/1.00
Reverse 3.554
Transfer case: Two-speed with front axle de-clutching
Ratios: Low 1.97:1
High 1.00:1
Steering: Cam and twin pin lever
Minimum turning radius (ft): 18
Brakes: 4-wheel hydraulic
Drum diameter (in.): 9
Effective area (sq in.): 117.8
Suspension: Semi-elliptic springs, front and rear; live axles
Spring length (in.): 36¼ front, 42 rear
Leaf width (in.): 1¾
Leaves: Front, 8 (2-leaf torque reaction spring on left front
Rear, 9
Wheels: 4.00/16 drop-center (combat wheels 4.50/16)
Tires: 6.00/16
Dimensions:
Wheelbase (in.): 80
Overall length (in.): 132.25
Overall width (in.): 62
Overall height (in.): 69.75 top up, 51.25 to top of steering wheel
Tread (in.): 48.25
Curb weight (lbs): 2315

Willys Jeep CJ-2A and CJ-3A Universal 1946:

Engine: 4-cylinder, iron block
Bore x stroke (in.): 3⅛x 4⅜
Displacement (cu in.): 134.2
Compression ratio: 6.48:1
Horsepower (gross): 60 @ 4000 rpm
Torque (gross): 106 lbs-ft @ 2000 rpm
Main bearings: 3
Valve configuration: L-head
Carburetor: 1 single downdraft Carter WO 596S
Transmission: 3-speed, synchronized 2nd and 3rd gears
Ratios: 2.798/1.55/1.00
Reverse 3.798
Steering: Cam and lever
Turning circle (ft): 36
Brakes: 4-wheel hydraulic
Drum diameter (in.): 9
Effective area (sq in.): 117.8
Suspension:
Front (in.): 36¼ x 1¾ semi-elliptic, 10 leaves
Rear (in.): 42 x 1¾ semi-elliptic, 9 leaves standard, 11 leaves heavy duty
Wheels (in.): 4.50E-16 wheels standard,

CJ-2A and CJ-3A (cont.)
4.50E-15 optional
Tires (in.): 6.00/16 4-ply standard, 7.00/15 4-ply optional
Dimensions:
Wheelbase (in.): 80
Overall length (in.): 123⅛
Overall width (in.): 57⅛
Overall height (in.): CJ-2A, 64; CJ-3A, 66⅜
Tread (in.): 48¼
Curb weight (lbs): 2240

Willys Jeep Station Wagon 1949:

Engine: Four-cylinder, L-head
Bore x stroke (in.): 3⅛ x 4⅜
Displacement (cu in.): 134.2
Compression ratio: 6.48:1
Horsepower (gross): 63 @ 4000 rpm
Torque (gross): 105 lbs-ft @ 2000 rpm
Main bearings: 3
Carburetor: single downdraft Carter
Transmission: 3-speed selective, sliding gear, synchronized 2nd and 3rd speeds. Borg-Warner overdrive
Ratios: 2.60
Reverse: 3.53
Steering: Ross cam- and twin-lever
Turning circle (ft): 35
Brakes: Bendix 4-wheel hydraulic drum type
Drum diameter (in.): 9.9
Effective area (sq in.): 133.7
Suspension:
Front: Planadyne, independent upper A-arms, single transverse leaf spring
Rear: Conventional axle, semi-elliptic leaf springs, torsional stabilizer bar
Wheels: Pressed steel, drop-center rims
Tires: 6.00/15 4-ply, tube type
Dimensions:
Wheelbase (in.): 104
Overall length (in.): 174 13/16
Overall width (in.): 68
Overall height (in.): 71
Front tread (in.): 55¼
Rear tread (in.): 57
Curb weight (lbs): 2898

Willys Jeep Jeepster 1949:

Engine: Six-cylinder, L-head
Bore x stroke (in.): 3 x 3½
Displacement (cu in.): 148.4
Compression ratio: 6.42:1
Horsepower (gross): 72 @ 4000 rpm
Torque (gross): 117 lbs @ 1600 rpm
Main bearings: 4
Valve configuration: F-head
Carburetor: 1 bbl. Carter downdraft carburetor, mechanical pump
Transmission: 3-speed selective, sliding gear, synchronized 2nd and 3rd speeds; Borg-Warner overdrive
Ratios: 2.60/1.63/1.00/0.70
Reverse: 3.53
Steering: Ross cam and lever
Turns, lock-to-lock (ft): 4½
Turning circle (ft): 35

Willys Jeep Jeepster (cont.)
Brakes: Bendix 4-wheel hydraulic, drum type
Drum diameter (in.): 9.9
Effective area (sq in.): 133.7
Suspension:
Front: Planadyne, independent upper A-arms, single transverse leaf spring
Rear: Conventional axle, semi-elliptic leaf springs, torsional stabilizer bar
Wheels: Pressed steel, drop-center rims
Tires: 6.70/15 4-ply, tube type
Dimensions:
Wheelbase (in.): 104
Overall length (in.): 174
Overall height (in.): 62
Overall width (in.): 69
Front tread (in.): 55½
Rear tread (in.): 57
Curb weight (lbs): 2890

Jeep Universal, Model CJ-3B 1952:

Engine: 4-cylinder, iron block
Bore x stroke (in.): 3⅛ x 4⅜
Displacement (cu in.): 134.2
Compression ratio: 7.4:1 (6.9:1 optional, used on Military M606)
Horsepower (gross): 75 @ 4000 rpm (72 with 6.9:1 c/r)
Torque (gross): 114 lbs/ft @ 2000 rpm (112 with 6.9:1 c/r)
Main bearings: 3
Valve configuration: F-head
Carburetor: 1-bbl downdraft carburetor, mechanical pump
Transmission: 3-speed selective, synchronized 2nd and 3rd gears
Ratios: 3.339/1.55/1.00
Reverse 3.798
Transfer case ratios:
Normal: 1.00:1
Underdrive: 2.46:1
Steering: Cam and lever
Turning circle (ft): 35.5 left, 33.8 right
Brakes: 4-wheel hydraulic
Drum diameter(in.): 9
Total effective area (sq in.): 117.8
Suspension:
Front (in.): 36¼ x 1¾ semi-elliptic, 10 leaves
Rear (in.): 42 x 1.75 semi-elliptic, 9 leaves
Shock absorbers: Double-acting, hydraulic
Wheels: 4.50/16 disc wheels, 5-stud
Tires: 6.00/16 4-ply standard, other sizes optional
Dimensions:
Wheelbase (in.): 81.0
Overall length (in.): 129.88 (Military 129.91)
Overall width (in.): 68.88
Overall height (in.): 67.75 (Military 68.55)
Tread (in.): 48.44 (Military 49.19)
Minimum ground clearance (in.): 8.8
Curb weight (lbs): 2243 (Military 2418)

Jeep Universal, Model CJ-5 1954:

Engine: 4-cylinder, iron block
Bore x stroke (in.): 3⅛ x 4⅜
Displacement (cu in.): 134.2

CJ-5 (cont.)
Compression ratio: 6.9:1
Horsepower (gross): 75 @ 4000 rpm
Torque (gross): 114 lbs-ft @ 2000 rpm
Main bearings: 3
Valve configuration: F-head
Carburetor: 1-bbl downdraft carburetor, mechanical pump
Transmission: 3-speed selective, synchronized 2nd and 3rd gears
Ratios: 2.798
Reverse: 3.798
Transfer case ratios:
Normal: 1.00:1
Underdrive: 2.46:1
Steering: Cam and lever
Turning circle (ft): 36
Brakes: 4-wheel hydraulic
Drum diameter (in.): 9
Total effective area (sq in.): 117.8
Suspension:
Front (in.): 39⅝ x 1¾ semi-elliptic, 7 leaves
Rear (in.): 46 x 1.75 semi-elliptic, 9 leaves
Shock absorbers: Double-acting, hydraulic
Wheels: 4.50/16 disc wheels, 5-stud
Tires: 6.00/16 4-ply standard, other sizes optional
Dimensions:
Wheelbase (in.): 81
Overall length (in.): 135.5
Overall width (in.): 71.75
Overall height (in.): 69.5
Tread (in.): 48.44
Minimum ground clearance (in.): 8.0
Curb weight (lbs): 2274

Jeep Universal, Model CJ-6 1955:

Engine: 4-cylinder, iron block
Bore x stroke (in.): 3⅛ x 4⅜
Displacement (cu in.): 134.2
Compression ratio: 6.9:1
Horsepower (gross): 72 @ 4000 rpm
Torque (gross): 114 lbs-ft @ 2000 rpm
Main bearings: 3
Valve configuration: F-head
Carburetor: 1-bbl downdraft carburetor, mechanical pump
Transmission: 3-speed selective, synchronized 2nd and 3rd gears
Ratios: 2.798/1.551/1.00
Reverse: 3.798
Transfer case ratios:
Normal: 1.00:1
Underdrive: 2.46:1
Steering: Cam and lever
Turning circle (ft): 39
Brakes: 4-wheel hydraulic
Drum diameter (in.): 9
Total effective area (sq in.): 117.8
Suspension:
Front (in.): 39⅝ x 1¾ semi-elliptic, 7 leaves
Rear (in.): 46 x 1.75 semi-elliptic, 9 leaves
Shock absorbers: Double-acting, hydraulic
Wheels (in.): 4.50/16 disc wheels, 5-stud
Tires (in.): 6.00/16 4-ply standard, other sizes optional
Dimensions:
Wheelbase (in.): 101
Overall length (in.): 155.56
Overall width (in.): 71.75

CJ-6 (cont.)
Overall height (in.): 68.25
Tread (in.): 48.44
Minimum ground clearance (in.): 8.0
Curb weight (lbs): 2413

Jeep Forward Control, Model FC-150 (FC-170) 1957:

Engine: 4-cylinder, iron block (6-cylinder, iron block)
Bore x stroke (in.):3⅛ x 4⅜ (3 5/16 x 4¾)
Displacement (cu in.):134.2 (226)
Compression ratio: 6.9:1 (6.86:1)
Horsepower (gross): 75 @ 4000 rpm (105 @ 3600)
Torque (gross): 114 lbs-ft @ 2000 rpm (190 @1400)
Main bearings: 3 (4)
Valve configuration: F-head (L-head)
Carburetor: 1-bbl downdraft carburetor, mechanical pump
Transmission: 3-speed selective, synchronized 2nd and 3rd gears
Ratios: 2.798/1.441/1.00
Reverse: 3.798
4-speed selective (optional)
Ratios: 6.398/3.092/1.686/1.00
Reverse: 7.820
Transfer case ratios:
Normal: 1.00:1
Underdrive: 2.46:1
Steering: Cam and lever
Turning circle (ft): 36 (43.83)
Brakes: 4-wheel hydraulic
Drum diameter (in.): 11
Total effective area (sq in.): 176.2
Suspension:
Front (in.): 39⅝ x 1¾ semi-elliptic, 7 leaves (46 x 2½ semi-elliptic, 6 leaves
Rear (in.): 52 x 2½ semi-elliptic, 9 leaves (52 x 2½ semi-elliptic, 6 leaves)
Shock absorbers: Direct-acting, hydraulic
Wheels (in.): 6.00/15 disc wheels, 5-stud
Tires (in.): 7.00/15 4-ply standard, other sizes optional
Dimensions:
Wheelbase (in.): 81 (103.5)
Overall length (in.): 147.5 (180.5)
Overall width (in.): 71.375 (76.5)
Overall height (in.): 77.375 (79.375)
Tread (in.): 48.375 (63.5)
Minimum ground clearance (in.): 8.0 (8.25)
Curb weight (lbs): 3020 (3331)

Jeep Pickup Truck 1961:

Engine: 6-cylinder, inline, iron block
Bore x stroke (in.): 3.94 x 4.375
Displacement (cu in.): 226.2
Compression ratio: 6.861:1
Horsepower (net): 105 @ 3600 rpm
Torque @ (net): 190 lbs-ft @ 1400 rpm
Main bearings: 4
Valve configuration: L-head
Carburetor: 1-bbl Carter
Transmission: 3-speed manual
Ratios: 3.44/1.85/1.00
Transfer case ratios:
Normal: 1.00:1
Underdrive: 2.43:1

Pickup Truck (cont.)
Steering: Cam and twin pin lever
Turning circle (ft): 47.25
Brakes: 4-wheel hydraulic
front drum (in.): 11
rear drum (in.): 11
Suspension:
Front: Live axle, semi-elliptic leaf springs
Rear: Live axle, semi-elliptic leaf springs
Shock absorbers: Double acting
Wheels (in.): 5/16 forged aluminum, 5-bolt
Tires (in.): 7.00/16 4-ply standard
Dimensions:
Wheelbase (in.): 118.0
Overall length (in.): 183.75
Overall width (in.): 66.625
Overall height (in.): 74.38
Tread front/rear (in.): 56/63.5
Ground clearance (in.): 8.125
Curb weight (lbs): 3500

Jeep Wagoneer 1963:

Engine: Inline six cylinder, iron block
Bore x stroke (in.): 3.34 x 4.38
Displacement (cu in.): 230
Compression ratio: 8.5:1
Horsepower (net): 140 @ 4000 rpm
Torque (net): 210 lbs-ft @ 1750 rpm
Main bearings: 4
Valve configuration: SOHC
Fuel system: 1-2 bbl downdraft carburetor, mechanical pump
Transmission: 3-speed synchromesh manual, standard
Ratios: 2.798/1.551/1.00
Reverse: 3.798
3-speed automatic planetary with torque converter, optional
Ratios: 2.40/1.467/1.00
Reverse: 2.01
Transfer case ratios:
Normal: 1.00:1 (2.03 automatic)
Underdrive: 2.03:1
Steering: Cam and lever, power assist optional
Turning circle (ft): 38.3
Brakes: 4-wheel hydraulic, cast iron drums, power assist optional
Drum diameter (in.): 11
Effective area (sq in.): 161.16
Suspension:
Front: Solid axle, 4 leaf springs (standard); Independent, single pivot swing axle with torsion bars (optional)
Rear: Solid axle, leaf springs
Shock absorbers: Direct-acting tubular
Wheels (in.): 5.5/15, 5-lug steel disc
Tires (in.): 6.70/15, 4-ply
Dimensions:
Wheelbase (in.): 110
Overall length (in.): 183.7
Overall width (in.): 75.6
Overall height (in.): 64.2
Tread (in.): 57
Minimum ground clearance (in.): 7.75
Curb weight (lbs): 3700

Jeepster Commando 1967:

Engine: V-6, iron block (optional)
Bore x stroke (in.): 3.75 x 3.40

Jeepster Commando (cont.)

Displacement (cu in.): 225.2
Compression ratio: 9.0:1
Horsepower (gross): 160 @ 4200 rpm
Torque (gross): 235 lbs-ft @ 2400 rpm
Main bearings: 4
Valve configuration: OHV
Fuel system: 1-2 bbl Rochester downdraft carburetor, mechanical pump
Transmission: 3-speed manual, synchromesh
Ratios: 3.39/1.85/1.00
Reverse:4.531
Turbo-HydraMatic 3-speed automatic planetary with torque converter (std. automatic)
Ratios: 2.48/1.48/1.00
Reverse: 2.08
Transfer case ratios:
Normal: 1.00:1
Underdrive: 2.03:1
Steering: Cam and roller gear
Turning circle (in.): 43.6
Brakes: 4-wheel hydraulic, drum type
Drum diameter (in.): 10
Swept area (sq in.): 251.4
Suspension:
Front: Longitudinal leaf springs, Panhard rod
Rear: Hotchkiss type, longitudinal leaf spring
Shock absorbers: Telescopic
Wheels (in.): 5.5/15, 5-stud steel
Tires (in.): 8.45/15 Power Cushion
Dimensions:
Wheelbase (in.): 101
Overall length (in.): 175.3
Overall width (in.): 65.2
Overall height (in.): 64.1
Tread (in.): 50
Minimum ground clearance (in.): 7.5
Curb weight (lbs): 3000

Jeep Gladiator 1969:

Engine: V-8, iron block and heads
Bore x stroke (in.): 3.80 x 4.85
Displacement (cu in.): 350
Compression ratio: 9.0:1
Horsepower (net): 230 @ 4400 rpm
Torque (net): 350 lbs-ft @ 2400 rpm
Main bearings: 5
Valve configuration: OHV
Fuel system: 1-2 bbl carburetor
Transmission: 3-speed synchromesh manual, standard
Ratios: 2.997/1.8332/1.00
Reverse: 2.997
4-speed synchromesh manual, optional
Ratios: 4.02/3.092/1.686/1.00
Reverse: 7.439
3-speed automatic planetary with torque converter
Ratios: 2.482/1.482/1.00
Reverse: 2.08
Transfer case ratios:
Normal: 1.00:1 (2.03 automatic)
Underdrive: 2.03:1
Steering: Recirculating ball, power optional
Turning circle (ft): 49.5
Brakes: 4-wheel hydraulic, cast iron drums, power assist optional
Drum diameter (in.): 11
Effective area (sq in.): 161.16
Suspension:
Front: Solid axle, 6 to 8 leaf springs

Gladiator (cont.)

Rear: Solid axle, 7 to 10 leaf springs
Shock absorbers: Direct-acting tubular
Wheels (in.): 5.5/15, full drop center
Tires (in.): 8.15/15, 4-ply
Dimensions:
Wheelbase (in.): 120 (J-2000)-132 (J-3800)
Overall length (in.): 183.8 (J-2000)-205.64 (J-3800)
Overall width (in.): 75.93
Overall height (in.): 71.0
Tread (in.): 63.5 (J-2000)-63.75 (J-3800)
Minimum ground clearance (in.): 8.75
Curb weight (lbs): 3555 (J-2000)-4018 (J-3800)

Jeep Cherokee 1974:

Engine: 6-cylinder, inline, iron block
Bore x stroke (in.): 3.75 x 3.90
Displacement (cu in.): 258
Compression ratio: 8.0:1
Horsepower (net): 120 @ 3400 rpm
Torque @ (net): 200 lbs-ft @ 2000 rpm
Main bearings: 7
Valve configuration: OHV
Carburetor: 1-2 bbl
Transmission: 3-speed manual, synchromesh
Ratios: 3.00/1.03/1.00
Reverse: 2.08
4-speed manual, synchromesh on top three gears
Ratios: 6.32/3.09/1.68/1.00
Reverse: 2.08
3-speed automatic, planetary with torque converter
Ratios: 2.57/1.48/1.00
Reverse: 2.08
Transfer case ratios:
Manual, Normal: 1.00:1
Underdrive: 2.03:1
Quadra-Trac Normal: 1.00:1
Underdrive: 2.57:1
Steering: Recirculating ball, power-assisted
Turning circle (ft): 37.7
Brakes: 4-wheel hydraulic, power-assisted
front disc (in.): 12
rear drum (in.): 11
Swept area (sq in.): 376
Suspension:
Front: Live axle, semi-elliptic leaf springs, anti-sway bar
Rear: Live axle, semi-elliptic leaf springs
Wheels (in.): 6.0/15 forged aluminum, 5-bolt
Tires (in.): H78/15
Dimensions:
Wheelbase (in.): 108.7
Overall length (in.): 183.5
Overall width (in.): 75.6
Overall height (in.): 66.9
Tread front/rear (in.): 59.2/57.7
Ground clearance (in.): 7.7
Curb weight (lbs): 4150

Jeep Universal, Model CJ-8 (Scrambler) 1981:

Engine: Inline 4, iron block (inline 6, iron block)
Bore x stroke (in.): 4.00 x 3.00 (3.75 x 3.40)
Displacement (cu in.): 151 (258)
Compression ratio: 8.2:1 (8.3:1)
Horsepower (gross): 82 @ 4000 (110 @ 3500 rpm)
Torque (gross): 125 lbs-ft @ 2600 rpm (205 lbs-ft @ 1800)

CJ-8 (cont.)

Main bearings: 5 (7)
Valve configuration: OHV
Fuel system: 2-bbl Rochester (2-bbl carburetor)
Transmission: 4-speed manual, synchromesh
Ratios: 4.07/2.39/1.49/1.10
4-speed manual, top three gears synchromesh
Ratios: 3.52/2.27/1.46/1.00
3-speed automatic, planetary with torque converter
Ratios: 2.74/1.55/1.00 (2.45/1.45/1.00 6-cylinder)
Transfer case ratios:
Normal: 1.00:1
Underdrive: 2.62:1
Steering: Recirculating ball (power optional)
Turning circle (ft): 37.6
Brakes: 4-wheel hydraulic, drum type (power optional)
Front disc (in.): 10.4
Rear Drum (in.): 10
Suspension:
Front: 4-leaf semi-elliptic springs, free-running hubs, anti-roll bar
Rear: 4-leaf semi-elliptic springs
Shock absorbers: Tubular
Wheels (in.): 5.5/15, 5-stud steel
Tires (in.): H78 x 15B
Dimensions:
Wheelbase (in.): 103.5
Overall length (in.): 177.3
Overall width (in.): 68.6
Overall height (in.): 67.6 (70.5 hardtop)
Tread front/rear (in.): 51.5/50
Minimum ground clearance (in.): 6.9
Curb weight (lbs): 2759

Jeep Cherokee 1984:

Engine: 4-cylinder, inline, iron block (V-6, iron block)
Bore x stroke (in.): 3.88 x 3.19 (3.50 x 2.99)
Displacement (cu in.): 150.45 (173)
Compression ratio: 9.2:1 (8.5:1)
Horsepower (net): 105 @ 5000 rpm (115 @ 4800)
Torque @ (net): 132 lbs-ft @ 2800 rpm (145 @ 2400)
Main bearings: 5 (4)
Valve configuration: OHV
Carburetor: 1-bbl (1-2 bbl Rochester)
Transmission: 4-speed manual, synchromesh
Ratios: 3.93/2.33/1.45/1.00
Reverse: 3.76
5-speed manual, synchromesh
Ratios: 3.93/2.33/1.45/1.00/0.85
Reverse: 3.76
3-speed automatic
Ratios: 2.74/1.55/1.00
Reverse: 2.20
Transfer case ratios:
Selec-Trac Normal: 1.00:1
Underdrive: 2.61:1
Command-Trac, Normal: 1.00:1
Underdrive: 2.61:1
Steering: Recirculating ball, (power optional)
Turning circle (ft): 36.1
Brakes: 4-wheel hydraulic, power-assisted
front disc (in.): 10.98
rear drum (in.): 10
Suspension:
Front: Coil springs with leading links, track bar stabilizer bar
Rear: Live axle, semi-elliptic leaf springs, stabilizer bar
Wheels (in.): 6.0/15 forged aluminum, 5-bolt
Tires (in.): P195/75R15

Cherokee (cont.)

Dimensions:
- Wheelbase (in.): 101.4
- Overall length (in.): 165.3
- Overall width (in.): 70.5
- Overall height (in.): 64.1
- Tread (in.): 58
- Ground clearance (in.): 8.7

Jeep Universal, Model CJ-7 1986:

Engine: Inline 6, iron block (V-8, iron block)
- Bore x stroke (in.): 3.75 x 3.90 (3 75 x 3.44)
- Displacement (cu in.): 258 (304)
- Compression ratio: 8.0:1 (8.4:1)
- Horsepower (gross): 110 @ 3500 rpm (150 @ 4200)
- Torque (gross): 195 lbs-ft @ 2000 rpm (245 @ 2500)
- Main bearings: 7 (5)
- Valve configuration: OHV
- Fuel system: 1-bbl Carter or Holley carburetor (2-bbl carburetor)

Transmission: 3-speed manual, synchromesh
- Ratios: 3.00/1.83/1.00
- Reverse: 3.10
- 4-speed manual, top three gears synchromesh
- Ratios: 4.02/2.41/1.41/1.00
- Reverse: 4.73
- 3-speed automatic, planetary with torque converter
- Ratios: 2.48/1.415/1.00
- Reverse: 2.08

Transfer case ratios:
- Normal: 1.00:1
- Underdrive: 2.03:1

Steering: Recirculating ball
- Turning circle (ft): 35.75

Brakes: 4-wheel hydraulic, drum type (power)
- Drum diameter (in.): 11
- Swept area (sq in.): 180.8 (276)

Suspension:
- Front: 4-leaf semi-elliptic springs
- Rear: 4-leaf semi-elliptic springs
- Shock absorbers: Double-acting, hydraulic
- Wheels (in.): 6/15, 5-stud steel
- Tires (in.): F78 x 15B

Dimensions:
- Wheelbase (in.): 93.416
- Overall length (in.): 147.75
- Overall width (in.): 68.5 (side-mount spare)
- Overall height (in.): 67.5
- Tread front/rear (in.): 51.5/50
- Minimum ground clearance (in.): 6.75
- Curb weight (lbs): 2650

Jeep Comanche 1986:

Engine: 4 cylinder, inline, iron block (4-cylinder inline, turbo diesel)
- Bore x stroke (in.): 3.88 x 3.19 (3.49 x 3.51)
- Displacement (cu in.): 150.45 (126)
- Compression ratio: 9.2:1 (25.5:1)
- Horsepower (net): 117 @ 3500 rpm (85 @ 3250)
- Torque @ (net): 135 lbs-ft @ 3500 rpm (132 @ 3000)
- Main bearings: 5
- Valve configuration: OHV
- Carburetor: Throttle body injection (Bosch injection)

Transmission: 4-speed manual, synchromesh
- Ratios: 3.93/2.33/1.45/1.00
- Reverse: 4.74
- 5-speed manual, synchromesh

Comanche (cont.)

- Ratios: 3.93/2.33/1.45/1.00/0.85
- Reverse: 4.74
- 3-speed automatic
- Ratios: 2.74/1.55/1.00
- Reverse: 2.20

Transfer case ratios:
- Selec-Trac, Normal: 1.00:1
- Underdrive: 2.61:1
- Command-Trac, Normal: 1.00:1
- Underdrive: 2.61:1

Steering: Recirculating ball, (power optional)
- Turning circle (ft): 36.1

Brakes: 4-wheel hydraulic, power-assisted
- front disc (in.): 10.98
- rear drum (in.): 10

Suspension:
- Front: Coil springs with leading links, track bar stabilizer bar
- Rear: Live axle, semi-elliptic leaf springs, stabilizer bar
- Wheels (in.): 6.0/15 forged aluminum, 5-bolt
- Tires (in.): P195/75R15

Dimensions:
- Wheelbase (in.): 119.9
- Overall length (in.): 195.5
- Overall width (in.): 71.7
- Overall height (in.): 64.7
- Tread (in.): 57
- Ground clearance (in.): 7.5
- Curb weight (lbs): 3200

Jeep Wrangler 1987:

Engine: 4-cylinder, inline, iron block (6-cylinder inline, iron block)
- Bore x stroke (in.): 3.88 x 3.19 (3.75 x 3.90)
- Displacement (cu in.): 150.45 (258)
- Compression ratio: 9.2:1
- Horsepower (net): 117 @ 5000 rpm (112 @ 3200)
- Torque @ (net): 135 lbs-ft @ 3500 rpm (210 @ 2000)
- Main bearings: 5 (7)
- Valve configuration: OHV
- Carburetor: Electronic fuel injection (1-bbl Carter)

Transmission: 4-speed manual, synchromesh
- Ratios: 3.93/2.33/1.45/1.00
- Reverse: 3.76
- 5-speed manual, synchromesh
- Ratios: 4.03/2.39/1.52/1.00/0.72
- Reverse: 3.76
- 3-speed automatic
- Ratios: 2.74/1.55/1.00
- Reverse: 2.20

Transfer case ratios:
- Command-Trac, Normal: 1.00:1
- Underdrive: 2.60:1

Steering: Recirculating ball, (power optional)

Brakes: 4-wheel hydraulic, power-assisted
- front disc (in.): 11.02
- rear drum (in.): 9.84

Suspension:
- Front: Leaf springs, shock absorbers, stabilizer bar
- Rear: Leaf springs, shock absorbers
- Wheels (in.): 7.0/15 forged aluminum, 5-bolt
- Tires (in.): P215/75R15

Dimensions:
- Wheelbase (in.): 93.4
- Overall length (in.): 152.0
- Overall width (in.): 66.0
- Overall height (in.): 68.1 (72.0 soft top)
- Tread (in.): 58

Wrangler (cont.)

- Ground clearance (in.): 8.14
- Curb weight (lbs): 3100

Jeep Grand Cherokee 1993:

Engine: 6-cylinder inline, iron block (V-8, iron block)
- Bore x stroke (in.): 3 13/32 x 3 13/32 (3 7/8 x 3/16)
- Displacement (cu in.): 242.0 (318.0)
- Compression ratio: 8.8:1 (9.2:1)
- Horsepower (gross): 190 @ 4750 rpm (220 @4800)
- Torque (gross): 225 lbs-ft @ 4000 rpm (285 @ 3600)
- Main bearings: 7 (5)
- Valve configuration: OHV
- Carburetor: Sequential, multi-port, electronic

Transmission: 5-speed selective, overdrive
- Ratios: 3.83/2.33/1.44/1.00/0.79
- Axle: 3.55
- 4-speed automatic, overdrive
- Ratios: 2.74 (2.45)/1.54 (1.45)/1.00/0.69
- Axle: 3.55 (3.73)

Transfer case ratios:
- Normal: 1.00:1
- Underdrive: 2.73:1

Steering: Power recirculating ball with damper
- Turning circle (ft): 36.6

Brakes: 4-wheel hydraulic, ABS
- Front disc (in.): 11.0 x 0.94
- Rear drum (in.): 10.0 x 1.75 (11.2 x 1.44)
- Total effective area (sq in.): 315

Suspension:
- Front: Live axle, "Quadra-link" leading arms, track bar coil springs, stabilizer bar, gas charged shock absorbers
- Rear: Live axle, "Quadra-link" trailing arms, track bar, coil springs, stabilizer bar, gas charged shock absorbers
- Wheels (in.): 7.00/15 steel (cast aluminum), 5-stud
- Tires (in.): P215/75 R15 (P225/75 R15)

Dimensions:
- Wheelbase (in.): 105.9
- Overall length (in.): 179.0
- Overall width (in.): 70.9
- Overall height (in.): 64.8
- Tread (in.): 58.0
- Minimum ground clearance (in.): 8.0
- Curb weight (lbs): 3530 (3674)